The Adjmi & Bayar Edition

A Legend of Humility and Leadership

Rabbi Mordechai Eliyahu

Rishon LeZion, Sephardic Chief Rabbi of Israel

Rabbi Shmuel Eliyahu & Yehuda Azoulay

ISRAEL BOOKSHOP
Publications

SLS
sephardic
Legacy series
www.sephardiclegacy.com

The Adjmi & Bayar Edition

A Legend of Humility and Leadership

Rabbi Mordechai Eliyahu
Rishon LeZion, Sephardic Chief Rabbi of Israel

Rabbi Shmuel Eliyahu & Yehuda Azoulay

SLS sephardic
Legacy series
PRESERVING SEPHARDIC HERITAGE
www.sephardiclegacy.com

Book & cover design by:

VIVIDESIGN
SRULY PERL | 845.694.7186
mechelp@gmail.com

Published and distributed by:

Israel Bookshop Publications
501 Prospect Street
Lakewood, NJ 08701
Tel: (732) 901-3009
Fax: (732) 901-4012
www.israelbookshoppublications.com
info@israelbookshoppublications.com

Printed in the USA

Distributed in Israel by:
Tfutza Publications
P.O.B. 50036
Beitar Illit 90500
972-2-650-9400

Distributed in Europe by:
Lehmanns
Unit E Viking Industrial Park
Rolling Mill Road,
Jarrow, Tyne & Wear NE32 3DP
44-191-406-0842

Distributed in Australia by:
Gold's Book and Gift Company
3-13 William Street
Balaclava 3183
613-9527-8775

Distributed in South Africa by:
Kollel Bookshop
Ivy Common
107 William Road, Norwood
Johannesburg 2192
27-11-728-1822

לעילוי נשמת
אליהו בן
הרב שלמה עזוז
שהלך לעולמו
ד׳ שבט תש״נ

January 30, 1990

Your legacy lives on forever

דניאל וברכה בכר

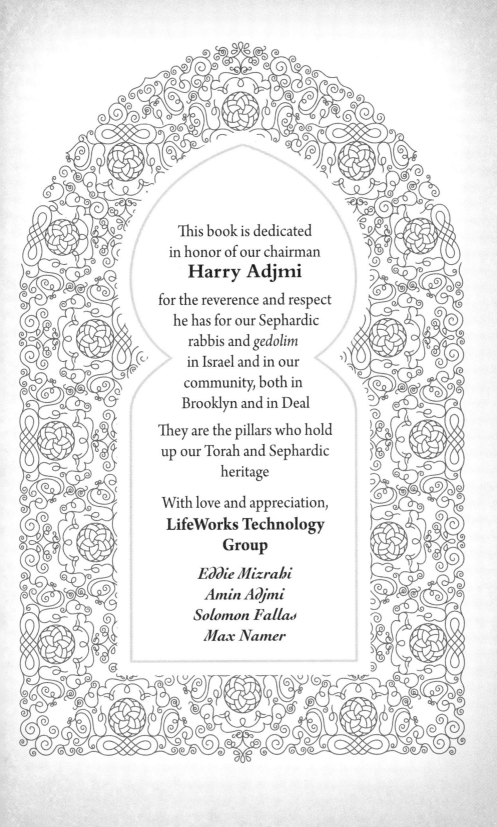

This book is dedicated
in honor of our chairman
Harry Adjmi

for the reverence and respect
he has for our Sephardic
rabbis and *gedolim*
in Israel and in our
community, both in
Brooklyn and in Deal

They are the pillars who hold
up our Torah and Sephardic
heritage

With love and appreciation,
**LifeWorks Technology
Group**

Eddie Mizrahi
Amin Adjmi
Solomon Fallas
Max Namer

Table of Contents

Foreword
By Yehuda Azoulay

The Biographical Narrative of Hacham Mordechai Eliyahu[1]

It was 1951 when Mr. Isaac Shalom, a wealthy community leader from New York, traveled to Israel and approached the *rosh yeshivah* of Porat Yosef,[2] Hacham Ezra Attiya, seeking to bring another rabbi to his community. The *rosh yeshivah* immediately summoned his finest prospect for the position.

When the student arrived, Hacham Ezra turned to the visitor, saying, "This young man is proficient in all areas of the Torah. He will respond on any topic you choose to question him about."

Mr. Shalom looked at the young rabbi — a mere twenty-two years old — and asked, "Is it true?"

"Are you questioning the word of the *rosh yeshivah*?" the *talmid hacham* asked in disbelief.

Impressed with the young scholar's instincts, Mr. Shalom

---

1. "The Biographical Narrative of Hacham Mordechai Eliyahu," by Yehuda Azoulay, is an excerpt from *Community Magazine*, July 2010.

2. A famous Sephardic yeshivah in Jerusalem, originally founded as Yeshivat Ohel Moed by Rabbi Ezra Harari-Raful and Rabbi Refael Shlomo Laniado in 1904. The cornerstone for Yeshivat Porat Yosef was laid in 1914, in Jerusalem's Old City, at the behest of the Ben Ish Hai. The yeshivah's alumni include many of Sephardic Jewry's foremost leaders. There are two branches of the yeshivah today: one in the Old City and one in the Geulah neighborhood.

proceeded to test him and found his knowledge to be both vast and deep. Then Hacham Ezra Attiya turned to his student and said, "This man wants you to serve as a rabbi in New York."

At that time, the young rabbi was teaching for an hour and a half in the mornings in a Talmud Torah before returning to his studies at the yeshivah. After hearing the offer, he said, "Let me remain in Israel for five years so that I can master the entire *Shas*, *Tur*, and *Shulhan Aruch* in preparation for the position. During this time, I will dedicate all my efforts to studying. I only ask for a stipend equal to the salary I will give up from my job at the Talmud Torah. Then, in five years, I will be ready to come."

Because of the urgent nature of the available position, Mr. Shalom could not accommodate the young rabbi's request for a five-year delay. He was determined to persuade the young rabbi to accept the post immediately, and he offered very generous compensation, comfortable living arrangements, and more if this young rabbi would agree to continue his studies in New York.

In spite of his dire poverty and having been orphaned of his father at a young age, the young scholar could not be swayed by the magnanimous material offer. Seeing how strong the young man's desire was to continue growing in Torah, the *rosh yeshivah* relented, finally accepting the young scholar's decision to decline the position.

The wisdom of this decision would become evident to all some three decades later, when, in 1983, this Jewish sage, known to us as Rabbi Mordechai Eliyahu, succeeded Maran Ovadia Yosef and became the chief rabbi of Israel.

A Child Prodigy

Rabbi Mordechai Tzemah Eliyahu *zt"l* was born to Rabbi Salman and Mazal Eliyahu on 21 Adar 5689 (March 12, 1929) in

Jerusalem's Old City. His father was one of the greatest *mekubalim* (kabbalists) in Jerusalem, and his mother was renowned for her charity and kindness, and for helping her husband achieve his lofty spiritual stature.

In spite of their grinding poverty, the Eliyahus' house radiated Torah. Young Mordechai grew up in one small room together with his siblings.[3] Their parents raised them in accordance with the teachings and customs of Rabbenu Yosef Haim ben Eliyahu of Baghdad — the Ben Ish Hai,[4] who was a relative[5] of Rabbanit Mazal. The family's financial hardship and cramped quarters did not deter the young Mordechai from devoting himself to Torah, and he often studied by candlelight beside the family's table — or even underneath it.

Hacham Salman[6] passed away when Mordechai was just eleven years old. Nevertheless, he had already succeeded in instilling in his son some of his extraordinary piety and love of Torah, as well as a special devotion to the hidden areas of Torah. Hacham Mordechai's connection to Kabbalah developed over the years, as reflected in his personal customs as well as in his halachic rulings — and the countless stories about him that surfaced after his death.

After Hacham Salman passed away, Hacham Mordechai's righteous mother decided that her gifted son must continue along the path of Torah that he had been following since he was born, and she ensured that his life would be dedicated to it. With her encouragement, he devoted himself to his studies with remarkable

---

3. His siblings were Rabbi Naim Ben Eliyahu, Rabbi Shimon, Rabbi Efraim, and Rabbanit Rahel.

4. This leading Baghdadi scholar lived from 1835 to 1909, and was a renowned halachic authority and kabbalist.

5. The Ben Ish Hai's sister was Rabbanit Mazal's grandmother.

6. 1872–1940.

diligence. Upon reaching the age of bar mitzvah, he joined the prestigious Yeshivat Porat Yosef, which was near his home. As a student, he displayed exceptional talents and diligence, sitting in the yeshivah from the early morning hours until very late at night. He quickly became a beloved disciple of the *rosh yeshivah*, Hacham Ezra Attiya.

The young Mordechai spent day and night engrossed in Torah and serving the great sages of his time, including Hacham Ezra Attiya[7] and Hacham Tzadkah Hussin.[8] He was also very close to the Hazon Ish, Rabbi Avraham Yeshayah Karelitz,[9] and spent much time serving him and learning from his ways.

Going Out to the People

Hacham Mordechai came of age during the genesis of the State of Israel. He, like many people in that era, felt that the manners and behaviors adopted at that time would set the tone for the future of the country. As a young student, he decided to do his part in injecting spiritual substance into the fledgling state. Along with his learning, he traveled daily to far-flung settlements with his friend, Rabbi Shabtai Yudelevitz,[10] and they would each deliver a lecture.

Hacham Mordechai taught halachah (Jewish law), and Rabbi Shabtai taught *aggadah* (rabbinic homilies). The young scholars also joined forces in the struggle for an alternative to the drafting of

---

7. Rabbi Attiya was the *rosh yeshivah* of Porat Yosef for forty-five years. He lived from 1885 to 1970, and was one of the greatest Sephardic Torah leaders of the twentieth century.

8. Often spelled Sadqa Hussein, Hacham Tzadkah, 1876–1961, was renowned as a leader of Iraqi Jewry, first in Baghdad and later in Israel.

9. One of the leaders of *haredi* Jewry in the land of Israel, the Hazon Ish, 1878–1953, was an internationally recognized authority in matters of Jewish law.

10. 1926–1996. He was a noted speaker and scholar.

girls into the Israeli army, and against the sale of pork in Jewish cities.

When he was twenty-four years old, Hacham Mordechai married Rabbanit Tzviyah Hana, the daughter of Hacham Nissim David Ezran,[11] his teacher in Porat Yosef.

Hacham Mordechai studied in the *bet midrash* (study hall) for rabbis and *dayanim* (rabbinic judges) led by the *Rishon LeZion*, Chief Rabbi Hacham Yitzhak Nissim.[12] He excelled on all his exams, and at the age of twenty-eight, Hacham Mordechai Eliyahu was appointed to be a rabbinical judge. He was the youngest rabbinical judge in Israel at the time.

A Career of Religious Leadership

Hacham Mordechai's career in the Israeli rabbinate began in Be'er Sheva, which at that time was a remote, southern village. His job entailed numerous responsibilities, and yet he extended even beyond his designated role, expanding the work of the *bet din*, specifically concerning abandoned wives (*agunot*) and other complex issues. He was extremely sensitive to the plight of downtrodden Sephardic Jews in those peripheral areas, as they were largely poverty-stricken and neglected by the government. Due to their difficult situation, Rabbi Eliyahu did his utmost to find lenient halachic rulings that would ease their life circumstances.

Several years later, a job became available in the Jerusalem district *bet din*. The rabbis of Jerusalem remembered Hacham Mordechai from his years living there, and invited him to fill the position. He held that job for several years, until he was appointed to the

---

11. 1910–1984. He was the founder and *rosh yeshivah* of Yeshivah Bet Shmuel in Jerusalem.

12. 1896–1981. Rabbi Nissim was born in Baghdad and immigrated to Israel in 1925. He served as the Sephardic chief rabbi of Israel from 1955 to 1972.

bet din hagadol, the high court of Jewish law. During these years, he nurtured a connection with the wider community, who saw in him not only a *posek* (halachic authority), but also someone who could solve any problem, be it halachic, personal, or emotional. Gradually, Hacham Mordechai's relationship with the public grew to include people in even the world's most far-flung places.

There are different types of Torah leaders. Some dedicate their lives to learning Torah and do not interact much with society. Others dedicate their lives to helping the public, leaving them very little time for Torah learning. In Hacham Mordechai, however, these aspects coalesced. He acquired mastery over all areas of Torah — and simultaneously tended to communal matters on a daily basis. For him, Torah learning and public responsibility were one and the same. This rare fusion of first-rate Torah scholarship with tireless public service was an inspiring example of true greatness.

Despite his intensive involvement in public affairs, Rabbi Eliyahu never officially aligned himself with any political party. He did this to ensure that people from all streams would feel comfortable seeking his assistance and guidance. Rabbi Eliyahu was known for emphasizing the importance of encouraging all people to continue the good deeds they performed, rather than criticizing them for their mistakes.

During Rabbi Eliyahu's term as chief rabbi, he focused strongly on providing secular Jews with a basic understanding of Judaism. He would travel to their moshavim (settlements) and kibbutzim (collective communities) to lecture and reach out to them.

Everyman's *Posek*

Rabbi Eliyahu's nonpolitical stance made him an address and resource for people from all backgrounds, as evidenced in the wide array of people who passed through the chief rabbi's office during his tenure, from 1983 to 1993. People from all walks of life and social circles could be seen entering and exiting the rabbinate offices regularly, from *bet din* judges, *roshe yeshivah*, and community rabbis from the Diaspora, to doctors, secular childless couples, and downtrodden individuals — and everyone in between.

His fax machine was constantly buzzing with halachic questions from all over the world, and his telephone rang at all hours of the day and night with more of the same. In dispensing advice and rendering halachic decisions, Hacham Mordechai would combine practical logic and worldly knowledge with his vast Torah wisdom and understanding. By viewing the entire picture, he rendered halachic decisions that would bolster Torah observance — even in light of the unique challenges and needs of the generation.

His decisions in halachah are recorded in many *sefarim* (holy books), including the volumes he personally authored: *Sefer Halachah, Darche Taharah, Sefer Hahagim, Maamar Mordechai, Imre Mordechai, Hilchot Berachot*, and more. Many additional *sefarim*, including his responsa, are still in the publication process. A large portion of his halachic rulings can also be found in the archives of the Israeli rabbinate.

Hacham Mordechai consistently followed the views of the Ben Ish Hai, who advocated combining the rulings of the *Shulhan Aruch* with the practices of the Arizal, the great kabbalist Rabbi Yitzhak Luria,[13] whose customs were accepted and followed by the Jews of Israel. In addressing new questions that arose after the establishment of the State, Hacham Mordechai showed how the rulings of the Ben Ish Hai could be applied to modern-day halachic issues. Thus, the halachic approach forged by the Ben Ish

---

13. Rabbi Luria lived from 1534 to 1572, and was the foremost scholar in Safed at the time.

Hai and the Arizal was perpetuated through Hacham Mordechai's decisions.

Divine Protection from Sin

Hacham Mordechai delivered lectures in halachah and *aggadah* in *kollelim* (institutes for full-time advanced Talmudic study, usually for married men) all over Israel. Once, as he was giving a *shiur* in a certain *kollel* in Jerusalem, he became very enthusiastic and animated, gesturing and waving his arms as he clarified important points. A student prepared a cup of tea for the rabbi and placed it on the table in front of him. The rabbi acknowledged the favor with a nod and continued speaking. As he motioned with his arm, his sleeve knocked over the cup and the tea spilled. Another tea was quickly prepared and placed a bit further away on the table, but again the rabbi knocked it over with his arm.

"It's all right," he announced. "I don't need to drink."

The students nevertheless prepared a third cup, but it met the same fate as its predecessors. This time, the rabbi stopped the *shiur* and said, "If it happened three times, there must be a lesson to be learned."

He turned to the one who had brought the tea and asked how he had prepared it. "In the usual manner," he replied. "I boiled water in the teapot and made tea."

"What is this pot generally used for?" the rabbi inquired.

"The *avrechim* [kollel students] use it only to prepare their tea and coffee."

"Does anyone else use it?"

Suddenly, one of the *avrechim* stood up and called out, "Yes, yes! There is a gentile who cleans up here, a foreign worker from Romania. He occasionally cooks an egg for himself in the pot."

Everything became perfectly clear. The rabbi was very stringent with regard to the law of *bishul akum* (the prohibition against eating food cooked by a non-Jew), and he would not use a utensil with which a gentile had cooked. The three spilled cups of tea were Hashem's Divine providence, protecting the rabbi from violating his ruling.

The Judge's Prayer

In an interview with *Israel National News*,[14] Rabbi Shmuel Zafrani, one of Hacham Mordechai's main assistants, related the story of a major discovery that was made just before the rabbi's burial. As the youngest *dayan* ever elected, he explained, Hacham Mordechai "very strongly felt the heavy responsibility that weighed upon him. He actually composed a prayer that he would recite every day before entering the courtroom. However, we never knew the wording of the prayer — until just two hours before the burial, when I found a note in his wallet with the prayer." (See below for the text of this prayer.)

Rabbi Zafrani then proceeded to describe an amazing "rescue" witnessed by Hacham Mordechai, which the latter attributed to the power of prayer, both his own and that of others.

When Rabbi Eliyahu first became a *dayan* in Be'er Sheva, in 1957, his was the only rabbinical court in the entire Negev region. On his first day on the job, he saw a woman standing outside, praying from a small *sefer Tehillim* (book of Psalms). She remained outside all day. This repeated itself the next day, and then for several days thereafter. Finally, he asked the court secretary to summon the woman. He asked her why she stood outside and prayed all day, and she related, "I moved to Israel from Morocco by myself, and

---

14. The prayer was first shared during the eulogies at Rabbi Eliyahu's funeral. News outlets picked up and publicized the prayer, and the story behind it, on June 8, 2010, the day after Rabbi Eliyahu's passing.

they sent me to Be'er Sheva. I asked where the closest rabbinical court was, and I was told it was here, and so here I am."

"What are you praying for?" the rabbi asked.

"My husband," the woman explained, "was a taxi driver in Morocco. A week after we were married, at the end of the *sheva berachot* [the week of wedding festivities], his taxi was completely destroyed in a terrible accident. He was killed, but his body was not recovered. After a while, I went to the rabbis at the Casablanca rabbinical court to be declared a widow so that I could remarry, but they said that without a body, they could not be certain that he was dead — and so I remained an *agunah* [a 'chained' woman who is unable to remarry according to Jewish law]. But when I came to Israel, I had faith that what the rabbinical courts in Morocco could not accomplish, the courts in Israel would be able to do."

"So why do you remain outside the court?" Rabbi Eliyahu asked. "Why don't you come in to plead your case to the *dayanim*?"

"Plead to the *dayanim*?" the woman asked. "I pray to Hashem, not to *dayanim*!" Rabbi Eliyahu immediately took up her case. He took all her papers and took a taxi to Netivot, to consult the Baba Sali, Rabbi Yisrael Abuhatzera.[15] The Baba Sali told him that his brother, the Baba Haki, Rabbi Yitzhak Abuhatzera,[16] a leading rabbi in the Israeli city of Ramle, knew everyone in Morocco and was surely acquainted with the officials involved in Jewish burials in Morocco.

Rabbi Eliyahu traveled to Ramle to speak with the Baba Haki, who informed him that there were only two Jewish *kavranim* (gravediggers) in Morocco, both of whom had since moved to

---

15. Rabbi Yisrael Abuhatzera, 1889–1984, was a leading Moroccan rabbi and kabbalist renowned for his ability to bring about miracles through his prayers.

16. 1895–1970.

Israel. One lived in the southern town of Dimona, and the other in Kiryat Ata, near the port city of Haifa.

"I live in the south," Hacham Mordechai figured, "so I might as well go to Dimona." He went to the address given to him by the Baba Haki — only to learn that the man's family was sitting *shivah* for him. He had died just a few days prior.

Though disappointed, Rabbi Eliyahu went inside and stayed for Minhah. While they were waiting for Arvit, he shared some words of Torah and solace with the grieving family and friends, explaining why he was there. Immediately, a man jumped up and said, "I am the other *kavran*, and I know the story. I was the one who buried the taxi driver!"

Rabbi Eliyahu asked him to accompany him to visit other rabbis, who questioned him and determined that his testimony was acceptable. Rabbi Eliyahu convened the rabbinical court, and the woman was declared "unchained" and permitted to remarry.

"This is the power of prayer," Rabbi Eliyahu later said, "both hers and mine."

The following is a translation of the prayer composed and recited daily by Rabbi Mordechai Eliyahu before entering the rabbinical courtroom:

> *Master of the Universe, it is revealed and known before You that it was not my idea to stand and serve Your holy nation, to judge and teach. I well know my small worth.*
>
> *I did not seek to do what is beyond me, but my rabbis instructed me to take this path, and this is how You arranged matters... Your wisdom has decreed that I serve the holy nation, teaching and judging... But trembling has overtaken me, fear and shaking have come over me, regarding the terrible danger that faces me and the vast abyss that is open before me...*

I have trust in Your vast mercies...for You are He Who hears prayer. Please G-d, have compassion on all those who sit in justice, and especially upon me, your servant, son of Your handmaid, Mordechai Tzemah ben Mazal. Have mercy on me and give me a heart that hears, as well as knowledge to understand and judge Your people...

Grant us wisdom, and let us not rule "impure" that which is "pure," nor on that which is "permitted" shall we say "forbidden," nor shall we deem guilty he who is innocent — and vice versa. Save us from all errors, and let my heart be strong, and allow me to rebuke those who oppress others; let us not be tempted to ignore injustice, and give us the merit to correct that which needs to be corrected, institute new regulations and directives when necessary, and to teach Torah, so that the Name of Heaven be sanctified by us. Let the people respect and fear us, and let us remain far from arrogance, anger, and pettiness...

Rabbi Mordechai Eliyahu's personal prayer upon becoming a *dayan* (credit: Eliyahu Family)

Divine Insight

On the last Sukkot of his life, when Hacham Mordechai awoke after undergoing surgery, he was unable to speak. He communicated by writing notes. His first note, a request for water, seemed appropriate enough. Then he quickly added, "They've brought here a 'white covering,' a *tallit* cover."

Rabbi Zafrani, who was attending to him, indicated that he did not understand the note. The rabbi underlined the word "here" on the note. Rabbi Zafrani, however, was still confused.

"It has many crosses," Hacham Mordechai added.

Rabbi Zafrani was taken aback and even more baffled.

The sage then added in writing, "Five minutes ago," compounding his disciple's confusion.

Finally, Hacham Mordechai pointed a finger toward the dividing curtain in the recovery area.

Rabbi Zafrani approached a nurse and asked if there was a patient wearing or carrying crosses. She shook her head. Faithful to his rabbi's instincts, he continued to ask who else was in the ward.

"An Arab woman," she said, adding that someone had come to visit her.

"Did she bring crosses with her?" he asked.

"I imagine not."

"But the rabbi knows what he is saying," Rabbi Zafrani insisted, and finally, they went over to the visitor and, after some inquiries, learned that she had several crosses in her handbag. Only then did Rabbi Zafrani understand that "the white *tallit*" referred to that woman, based on kabbalistic terminology.

Rabbi Zafrani politely asked if she could remove the crosses from her handbag. "There is a holy man here who sensed their presence and it disturbs him," he explained. The woman left.

Rabbi Zafrani returned to tell Hacham Mordechai Eliyahu that the woman left, but when he entered the room, he saw that the Hacham had already sensed her departure.

The Righteous Decree and G-d Fulfills

After Rabbi Mordechai's passing, David Vazana, a neighbor of the Eliyahu family and the head of the Bank of Israel Employees' Union, said, "As a neighbor, I saw how people would come to Hacham Mordechai's home at all hours of the day, from all walks of life and of all different types, with questions and requests and problems — and he would receive all of them happily and graciously."

Mr. Vazana described how "there were so many times when we saw the realization of the Talmud's words, 'The righteous man decrees and G-d fulfills.'[17] Once, the son of one of the employees at the Bank of Israel was critically wounded in a car accident, and was unconscious in Hadassah Ein Kerem Hospital. We came to the rabbi, telling him that the doctors said he has only a few hours left.

"The rabbi waved his hand in dismissal and instructed them to perform a *kapparah* [atonement] with money for charity, saying that if he still doesn't open his eyes, they should do the same with a chicken. We did the first, and the boy started to move his arms and legs. The doctors happened to be there and said, 'It's nothing, just his last-minute palpitations before death.'

"We went back to the rabbi, and he said we must immediately do the *kapparah* with a chicken. We did that, and the boy opened his eyes the next day. ... He later made a full recovery and was even able to enlist in the Israeli army... There were many other stories like this, as well."

---

17. This concept is discussed in several places in the Talmud, including *Moed Katan* 16b, *Ta'anit* 23a, *Ketubot* 103b, *Chullin* 60b, *Shabbat* 63a, as well as in the Midrash (*Bamidbar Rabbah* 14), the *Zohar*, and in *Iyov* 22:28.

Rabbanit Tzviyah Eliyahu, Hacham Mordechai's wife, and their daughter, spoke about their correspondence with the rabbi during his hospital stay toward the end of his life. She related one remarkable incident that involved a woman who had conceived triplets. The doctors told this woman that since two of the fetuses were sharing the same placenta, one was leaching strength from the other, and therefore, one or both of the girls would, in the doctors' words, have "serious problems."

The pregnant woman wept bitterly, feeling that she would not be able to raise a child with such a serious defect. She went to Rabbi Eliyahu.

He told her, "I promise that all three girls will be fine, and if something is not fine, bring them to me. I only have one daughter…" Several months later, she gave birth to three perfectly healthy girls. The doctors were in disbelief.

Suffering for the Jewish People

Rabbanit Tzviyah recalled an instance when, while in poor health himself, the rabbi gave a blessing to a man who was deathly ill. She turned to Hacham Mordechai and asked, "There is someone who looks like he is on his way to the Next World, while you, by contrast, look healthy, but could also use a recovery. Why don't you pray for yourself?"

"No, no," the Hacham replied. "I need to annul the *gezerot* [harsh decrees against the Jewish people]." He explained that his illness was serving as a *kapparah* for the Jewish nation.

The next day, the Israeli Navy discovered and captured a ship carrying 500 Grad rockets being smuggled to Palestinian terrorists.

During Hacham Mordechai's illness, the *rabbanit* further recalled, she pleaded with her husband to pray for his own recovery. "When I told him, 'Enough! Get out of this situation. You could free yourself!' he signaled *no* with his hand, whispering, 'Thousands could be killed, thousands could be killed.'

"I asked him, 'Maybe all this suffering is because of me, maybe because of the children or the grandchildren, or someone in the family did something [wrong]?'

"He responded, 'Ribbono Shel Olam! No, no, because of Klal Yisrael.' I asked him, 'At least you could tell me what this process will bring?' He wrote, 'Mashiah.'

"'Nu, when?' I wrote this three times but the rabbi did not answer me. I asked, 'What do we need to do?'

"The rabbi wrote, '*Teshuvah* [repentance].'

"I asked, 'For what?' The rabbi answered by citing the verse, '*Ve'ahavta lere'acha kamocha* — Love your fellow as yourself.' What is hurtful to you do not do to your friend. Even during the time of [king] Ahav,[18] they worshipped idols, but because there was no baseless hatred, there was no war for forty years. Because there was unity in *Am Yisrael*, there was no war. So we should be concerned that everyone should accept this upon themselves.

"The community has an important job," explained the *rabbanit* during her husband's illness. "The rabbi will not nullify what he took upon himself. He suffers because of Klal Yisrael, and Klal Yisrael needs to act for him. He told me explicitly, 'I will not pray [for my recovery]; the community should pray.'"

The Jewish Nation Loses a Leader

On Monday, 25 Sivan 5770 (June 7, 2010), Hacham Mordechai's soul departed from this world, representing an incalculable loss to the Jewish people. Rabbi Yona Metzger, then Ashkenazi chief

---

18. A wicked king who ruled the land of Israel from about 871 to 852 BCE.

rabbi of Israel,[19] spoke to the *Jerusalem Post* shortly before the funeral, saying, "This is a huge loss to the Torah world and the rabbinate. Rabbi Mordechai Eliyahu was a pillar of Israel's chief rabbinate. He started off as the country's youngest rabbinical judge, and worked his way up to the High Rabbinical Court through his greatness in Torah, from where he was appointed Sephardic chief rabbi of Israel.

"I owe him a personal debt; I received so much from him. He was unparalleled in his human relations, loved by all, and Jews of all types — hassidim, Lithuanians, settlers, Ashkenazim, and Sephardim — would convene in his house to hear Torah from him."

Over 100,000 people came from near and far to pay their last respects to this outstanding Torah personality, whose prominence crossed the religious and social lines that divide the Jewish people, as evidenced by the cross-section of Jews who joined the mourners in their sorrow and pain. The eulogies were short, as the family was determined to complete the burial before midnight, in accordance with the rabbi's wishes that the burial not be delayed.

The Mashiah Watch

Rabbi Mordechai left us not only with a trove of valuable Jewish works and a family of Torah scholars following his example, but also with a powerful sense of hope. Israel's Channel 1 News aired a short piece in 2008 regarding the "Mashiah Watch," explaining that Baba Baruch Abuhatzera[20] had a dream in which his father, the Baba Sali, instructed him to give Hacham Mordechai a special

---

19. He served as the Ashkenazi chief rabbi from 2003 to 2013.

20. A kabbalist, rabbi, and spiritual leader living in Netivot.

watch. He said that when the watch's hands are on 12:00, Mashiah would arrive.

In an interview given about two years before his death, Rabbi Eliyahu commented, "I don't touch the watch. I am afraid to open it. It remains untouched by me."

The dream first spoke of a gold watch, then a silver one. The time on the watch was originally 3:00, and at the time of the interview, the time was 11:45.

The rabbi explained that the hour indicates that the redemption is underway. He added that the gold watch is underneath the silver watch, and silver represents *rahamim* (mercy) whereas gold is *din* (judgment). "I wanted the silver to be on top so Hakadosh Baruch Hu will ensure that the redemption will be rapid.

"We must believe that Mashiah will come, and through our *ma'asim tovim* (good deeds), he will come even sooner!"

Introduction

Boundless Love

They stood on the balcony of Hechal Yaakov, the study hall and synagogue where Rabbi Mordechai Eliyahu had spent countless hours praying, learning, and receiving the thousands who sought him out.[1] They stood, and they watched as the procession carried their beloved rabbi, leader, and *hacham* out of the building and into the massive crowd that had assembled there. He was leaving his much loved *bet midrash* for the last time.

Thousands reached out arms and hands, wanting to be close one last time, wanting to accompany him on this, his final journey. The pallbearers finally reached the waiting vehicle, and even as it attempted to pull away toward the cemetery, the hearse was swallowed by the accompanying masses.

"You see the thousands there?" someone asked his mourning family. "They're your brothers, too. All of them. They're tearing their clothes, too — as though they're his sons. They're crying, too — as though they're his own family. Each person down there feels like a son, maybe even an only child..."

The tangled mass of people, packing ever closer, reaching out in love and desperation, crying and rending their garments, was a fitting closure for a life lived with so much love. Indeed, Rabbi Mordechai Eliyahu typified boundless love — and his students, community, and countless visitors loved him endlessly in return.

---

1. The Hechal Yaakov synagogue and study hall, founded by Rabbi Eliyahu, is located in Jerusalem's Kiryat Moshe neighborhood.

He had given them so many hours, so much attention, so many heartfelt prayers, so many of his own tears, and so much hope. And they were there to embrace that ceaseless love one last time.

Roots and Beginnings

Rabbi Mordechai Eliyahu's father was Rabbi Salman Eliyahu, a great *talmid hacham*. Torah was not an inheritance in this family — though, perhaps, love of Torah *was* a birthright. Hacham Salman was a *ba'al teshuvah* who had returned to Jewish observance at the tremendous price of financial comfort and an academic career. Nevertheless, he saw remarkable success in his life — but it was success of an entirely different nature: the success of a life lived for Torah.

Hacham Salman's love of Torah came from his hard work to acquire it. When he was around twenty,[2] his parents sent him — their only son — from their home in Iraq to England's prestigious Oxford University, where he had enrolled to study finance and business. Their hope was that he would return full of knowledge and expertise, ready to manage and develop the family's business, turning it into a cosmopolitan, multinational firm. But G-d had other plans. Hacham Salman decided to study the teachings of Hillel and Shammai[3] instead of Shakespeare, and those of Rabbi Akiva[4] instead of algorithms.

Torah enraptured him, and he applied his genius to it, learning with diligence until he had made his way through all of the Talmud,

---

2. This was around 1892.

3. Two leading sages of the last century BCE and the early first century CE, they founded two opposing schools of Jewish thought, which came to be known as *Bet Hillel* and *Bet Shammai*.

4. Rabbi Akiva was a *Tanna* of the latter part of the first century and the beginning of the second century, and his teachings are frequently referenced in the Talmud.

the *Zohar*, the *halachot* and the *aggadot*, literal commentaries and esoteric teachings — accomplishing all of that in only about two years. Such an achievement was incredible, even in the eyes of the venerated Ben Ish Hai, Rabbi Yosef Haim.

Rabbi Yehudah Tzadkah, *rosh yeshivah* of Yeshivat Porat Yosef from 1970 until his death in 1991, and a brother-in-law of Hacham Salman, later recalled that it was on the Ben Ish Hai's suggestion that Hacham Salman was inspired to move to the land of Israel, where he would ultimately make his home and pursue a life of Torah.[5]

When Hacham Salman moved to Israel, he married Mazal Tzadkah, a relative of the Ben Ish Hai. Having grown up in a home where there was a constant awareness and sense of the Divine Presence, where G-d's Hand was tangible, Mazal brought a spirit of holiness, purity, and respect for Torah into her marriage. She and Hacham Salman built a life modeled on what she had seen and absorbed from the Ben Ish Hai and his family.

Rabbi Yehudah Tzadkah remembered how Hacham Salman would take his "breaks" from studying: He would sit at the entrance to the study hall, rising for each student who passed through its door — even the first-year boys. He wanted the young yeshivah men to realize how honored, valued, and appreciated they were for who they were, what they represented, and what they were doing. Hacham Salman's love of Torah made him love people.

Hacham Salman merited writing scholarly works, including a commentary on the teachings of the Arizal, the great kabbalist, Rabbi Yitzhak Luria. Many scholars and rabbis would flock to him with their questions — and, of course, laymen would as well.

---

5. Hacham Salman also served as the personal secretary to Lord Herbert L. Samuel, the high commissioner of the British Mandate for Palestine from 1920 to 1925, thanks to the Western education he had received.

His writings revealed the depth of his wisdom and total mastery of his studies.[6] When the eminent kabbalist Hacham Haim Shaul Dweck[7] was nearing the end of his days, Hacham Ezra Attiya[8] asked him, "Who will answer our Kabbalah questions after you pass away?"

Rabbi Dweck responded that though there were many scholars who could be asked, the clearest answers would come from Hacham Salman. And that's how Hacham Salman came to be crowned the leader of Jerusalem's kabbalists. That's the stock Hacham Mordechai came from.

Revealing the Hidden

During the days of the *shivah* for Hacham Mordechai, thousands of people came to comfort the family. But the family felt like their visitors were talking about someone they didn't even know. So many stories were related that they had never heard, that Hacham Mordechai had hidden from them. The stories spanned the breadth of his life, from his childhood to his later years. There were stories of Torah learned in poverty; stories of advice and guidance that saved people; stories about blessings that came to fruition; stories about his sensitivity, love of, and consideration for every Jew; stories about his uncanny ability to see into the future; stories about miracles that came to pass through his hand. The *shivah* revealed a life lived even more fully than anyone had imagined.

---

6. A portion of his work was published in *Kerem Shlomo*.

7. Hacham Haim Shaul Dweck lived from 1857 to 1933.

8. Rabbi Attiya was the *rosh yeshivah* of Porat Yosef for forty-five years. He lived from 1885 to 1970, and was one of the greatest Sephardic Torah leaders of the twentieth century.

Divine Inspiration

After their father passed away, the family heard scores of stories that confirmed something the rabbi's children had never dared verbalize during his lifetime: Rabbi Eliyahu clearly had Divine inspiration, but he had concealed it. Because Hacham Mordechai had revealed similar things about his own rabbis and teachers after their passing,[9] his sons felt they could share their father's special gift after he left this world. Of course the fact that he had this Divine inspiration had mostly been hidden from even his own family during his life.

A Talmudic story describes how even renowned holy men can conceal the extent of their righteousness. The Talmud says, *Come and see the difference between the powerful men of Israel and the pious men of Babylonia.*[10] The passage goes on to relate that when there were troubles in Babylonia, like a drought, Rabbi Huna and Rabbi Hisda, the pious men there, would say to one another, "Let's go and pray together and ask for mercy, and perhaps the Holy One blessed is He will hear us and send us rain."

In comparison, the powerful men of Israel, like Rabbi Yonah, father of Rabbi Mani, said to his household, "I'll take my coat and buy some grain for a dinar." And then he went to a hidden place to pray, where he covered himself with sackcloth and begged for mercy. Then the rain would come. When he returned home

---

9. The rabbi himself had frequently told a story about Rabbi Avraham Ades, who was known to have Divine inspiration: After his passing, Rabbi Ades appeared in a dream to the *rosh yeshivah* Rabbi Ezra Attiya, saying, "Tell people — in the Next World there is no vanity!" That is to say, after someone's passing it's permissible to relate stories of his Divine inspiration, even though during his lifetime it was forbidden. The stories serve as a form of eulogy, with no fear of affecting the person's ego or pride.

10. *Ta'anit* 23b.

without grain he would say, "I saw that it was starting to rain, and of course the price of grain will drop, so I didn't buy."

Even the most spiritually powerful men of Israel, the best-known rabbis, didn't reveal that G-d answered their supplications — not even to their own household. These people concealed themselves to such an extent that no one knew the power of their prayers. The pious of Babylonia were at least aware of each other's holiness, but the powerful of Israel's holy men remained completely hidden, even from their own families.

Although Rabbi Eliyahu spoke about Rabbi Ades's special spiritual powers, Rabbi Attiya did not. When Rabbi Attiya eulogized Rabbi Ades, he hinted to Rabbi Ades's Divine inspiration by repeating the verse, *The spirit of G-d spoke through me, His word is on my tongue.*[11] Those who were aware of the implications understood the true meaning of those words, and those who were not aware simply didn't grasp what he was saying. Thus, Rabbi Eliyahu's family were left unsure of what — and to what extent — they could reveal of their father's greatness. Should they go ahead and publicize detailed revelations of his Divine inspiration or should they leave those special memories and incidents to those who had experienced them?

His sons had typed a number of these amazing stories and saved them in a special computer file. That way, they were written down and safe, and the family could decide later whether or not to print them. As the publication date for the Hebrew volume drew near, Hacham Mordechai's sons decided they *did* want to include the stories of their father's Divine inspiration. But when they tried to pull up the files for editing, something strange occurred. Although the computer was in good working order and no complete folders

---

11. *Shmuel II* 23:2.

had been deleted, those stories of their father's Divine inspiration were all missing. They had somehow been erased.

As no other stories had gone missing, just those of Hacham Mordechai's Divine inspiration, his sons decided not to try to resurrect them. They had experienced so much Heavenly help in compiling the book that they felt that if there was a problem with these particular stories, it was perhaps a message from their father, sent from the Next World. Maybe he didn't want those stories publicized even after his passing…

Thus, although the other stories in this book appear as they were originally told, some of the stories about Hacham Mordechai's Divine inspiration have been edited and do not include the full details of what occurred.

A Life in Book Form

When Hacham Mordechai's family initially conceived of the idea of writing a book about him, they were understandably intimidated. They felt there was no way his life could be laid out in black and white, confined to words and pages, and pressed between the covers of a book. His days were so full, his time so rich, his greatness so incomprehensible, that Hacham Mordechai's family worried that even ten volumes wouldn't do him justice. With new stories and memories being shared on a steady basis, the book would need constant expansion. Nevertheless, his sons felt they had to try.

As Hacham Mordechai himself had once written in an approbation for a book,[12] "The author is fulfilling the verse,

---

12. From his 1986 approbation for Rabbi Binyamin Refael Cohen's *Malchei Tarshish*, a book of stories on the holy men of Tunisia.

Remember the days of old, understand the years of all generations.[13] That is to say, there is reason to reflect on the actions of our ancestors and perpetuate their deeds from generation to generation."

His family felt that by relating stories about him, his life, and his deeds, they would be inspiring people to live better lives themselves by improving their character traits, working on their service of G-d, and, of course, learning Torah. The book was written not just to remember the incredible *eved Hashem* (servant of G-d) that Rabbi Mordechai Eliyahu was, but also to spread the greatness of G-d's Name through his memory.

Living in Our Time

Hacham Mordechai loved to share stories of righteous individuals — especially incidents he had witnessed personally. When he would talk about the Baba Sali, he would always finish by saying, "The Baba Sali lived in our generation. We saw him with our own eyes — these are not faraway tales of people long ago — we actually saw and knew him ourselves."

The same applies to these stories about Rabbi Eliyahu. His family witnessed them personally, or they were shared as first-person accounts by those who had experienced them. Rabbi Eliyahu's prayers were immensely powerful. He seemed to have true Divine inspiration. His actions made him a living *mussar sefer* (ethical work). Yet, he lived in our time. These are not bedtime tales. These stories are meant to teach, inspire, increase faith, and offer encouragement along the lengthy, often convoluted path to self-improvement. And they're only a drop in the ocean, as so many stories remain untold...

---

13. *Devarim* 32:7.

A Note on the Book's Structure

Like the original five-volume Hebrew series on Hacham Mordechai, *Father of Israel*,[14] this English version is written and organized according to the teaching of Rabbi Pinhas Ben Yair[15] as it was brought down by the Ramhal, Rabbi Moshe Haim Luzzatto,[16] in his seminal work, *Mesillat Yesharim (Path of the Just)*. As this book is intended to inspire people to self-improvement, character-building, and personal elevation, following the path laid out by a classic ethical work is only fitting. Thus, this book about Rabbi Mordechai Eliyahu is meant to read less like a biography and more like a book of moral and inspirational teachings.

Path of the Just was a book Rabbi Eliyahu particularly loved and one that he studied frequently. As related by Rabbi Alon Ben David,[17] he was once in the rabbi's study and had the privilege of tidying up the many *sefarim* piled on Hacham Mordechai's desk. When he reached the bottom of the stack, he found *Path of the Just*, and he offered to put it back on the shelf as he had just done with so many other books.

"No, not that," Hacham Mordechai said. "I always need that beside me."

The stories here are intended not only to share sparks of the rabbi's greatness but also to outline and model a path every person can strive toward, just as Hacham Mordechai was constantly striving. The book is therefore structured according to Rabbi Pinhas Ben Yair's formula: *Torah leads to caution; caution leads to alacrity; alacrity*

---

14. Rabbi Shmuel Eliyahu, *Avihem Shel Yisrael* (Jerusalem: Hotzaat Darche Horaah L'Rabbanim, 2011).

15. A fourth-generation *Tanna* who lived during the mid-to-late second century CE.

16. He was a prominent Italian rabbi and kabbalist, and lived from 1707 to 1746.

17. One of Rabbi Eliyahu's close students and followers, from the Ben David family of jewelers.

leads to cleanliness; cleanliness leads to separation;[18] separation leads to purity; purity leads to piety; piety leads to humility; humility leads to fear of sin; fear of sin leads to holiness; holiness leads to Divine inspiration; and Divine inspiration leads to the resurrection of the dead.[19]

Just as the course laid out by *Path of the Just* involves intense, consistent, systematic effort, day after day, Hacham Mordechai's life was one of steady, solid work. There was no magic, no special blessing. As Hacham Mordechai used to tell his children, when Hacham Eliyahu Kanush[20] approached the Ben Ish Hai for a blessing for success in his Torah studies, the Ben Ish Hai replied that a blessing would not help him. He explained that if one did not study, the blessing would be useless. And if one did study, he wouldn't need a blessing.

Indeed, Rabbi Mordechai Eliyahu toiled long and hard to reach the level he attained. From working on his character traits, including anger and pride, to toiling in Torah and *tefillah* (prayer), Rabbi Eliyahu led his life along a path of unswerving diligence, beginning in the wee hours of the dawn and lasting far into the night. Though he always focused on himself in terms of personal improvement and character building, he was at the same time also always focused on everyone around him, giving time, love, caring, and attention to the crowds who sought him wherever he went.

A Prayer

Master of the Universe, behold we are ready and willing to remember and praise Your virtuous servant, the holy Rabbi

---

18. *Prishut*, in Hebrew.

19. Rabbi Moshe Haim Luzzatto, quoting the Talmud (*Avodah Zarah* 20b) in his introduction to *Path of the Just* (*Mesillat Yesharim*).

20. He was a scholar from Baghdad about whom little is known.

Mordechai ben Hacham Salman. It is Your will to relate praises of the righteous; their praise is Your praise, and their glory is Your glory. Find us deserving, so that the holiness of our parents, Mordechai ben Hacham Salman and Rabbanit Tzviyah, should continue to rest upon us, purifying our thoughts and souls. Like them, may we merit the intellect and intelligence to elevate ourselves.

Help us attain greatness in Torah and service of G-d. And please help us cleave to You and Your Torah always, with holy and pure thoughts, fitting and beautiful prayers, the ability to learn and teach Torah, and the blessing to observe, perform, and fulfill all the words of Your Torah with love, joy, and resolve.

May the expressions of my mouth and the thoughts of my heart find favor before You, G-d, my Rock and my Redeemer. May the pleasantness of the L-rd, our G-d, rest upon us and our handiwork always.

Rabbi Shmuel Eliyahu, Safed

Translator's Foreword

I was not privileged to know the rabbi personally, although I, along with millions of others, came to know and love him through his warm (and sometimes fiery) words, and his trademark smile — a smile of pure holiness that radiates out of every photograph of him. And I came to know him better through translating and reviewing this stunning collection of stories about him.

These stories uncover the breadth of Rabbi Eliyahu's astonishing grasp of Torah, both revealed and hidden; his uncompromising stance on Jewish law; and the lengths to which he was prepared to go to avoid sin. There are also plenty of anecdotes that describe the wonders and miracles that happened in the merit of this holy man, the greatness of whom we shall never truly know. But perhaps more than anything, these stories show his humility and his humanity. Rabbi Eliyahu was a man who loved his fellow man as himself. And, even more so, he consistently disregarded his personal honor so that he could do the right thing for every person who asked for his assistance — and even for those who did not ask.

This book is not a biography in the conventional sense; it does not follow the rabbi's life in chronological order, nor does it offer a comprehensive overview of his life and work. It's simply a loving tribute from his children — the Jewish people — to their father, a father who they instinctively knew loved them, as a father loves his children, unconditionally, from the depths of his great heart: Rabbi Mordechai Eliyahu, father of Israel.

Shira Yehudit Djalilmand, Safed

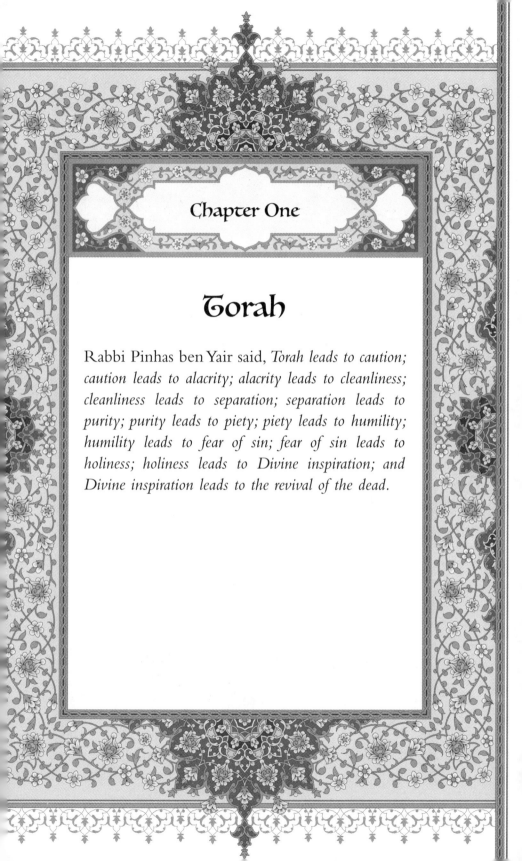

Chapter One

Torah

Rabbi Pinhas ben Yair said, *Torah leads to caution; caution leads to alacrity; alacrity leads to cleanliness; cleanliness leads to separation; separation leads to purity; purity leads to piety; piety leads to humility; humility leads to fear of sin; fear of sin leads to holiness; holiness leads to Divine inspiration; and Divine inspiration leads to the revival of the dead.*

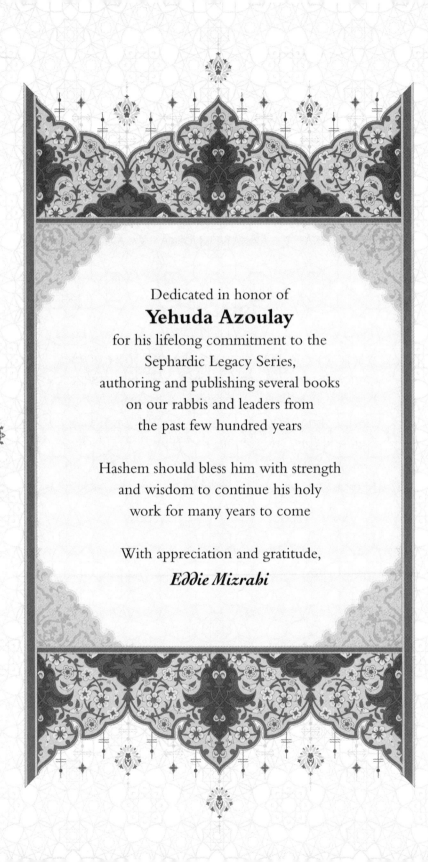

Dedicated in honor of
Yehuda Azoulay
for his lifelong commitment to the
Sephardic Legacy Series,
authoring and publishing several books
on our rabbis and leaders from
the past few hundred years

Hashem should bless him with strength
and wisdom to continue his holy
work for many years to come

With appreciation and gratitude,
Eddie Mizrahi

BREAD WITH SALT

Continuing a Legacy

Although Hacham Mordechai's father, Rabbi Salman Eliyahu,[1] had grown up in a materially wealthy home in Iraq, his family had lived in spiritual poverty. When Hacham Salman discovered the depth and beauty of Torah, and he began making religious changes in his life, his family was dismayed, as they had hoped for their son to become a scholar at Oxford.[2] Following the Ben Ish Hai's advice, Hacham Salman decided to spend his life in the land of Israel.

Rabbi Salman Eliyahu
(credit: Eliyahu Family)

In the Holy Land, Hacham Salman settled in Jerusalem, where he was able to study Torah in peace. His intelligence, wisdom, and spiritual devotion soon became evident to all who interacted with him. His transition into a life lived solely for Torah, in the Holy Land, was not an easy one. But he accepted the challenges with love. Indeed, Hacham Salman truly personified the credo of Rabbi

---

1. Rabbi Salman Eliyahu, sometimes referred to as Rabbi Suleman Eliyahu, passed away in 1940.

2. *Kerem Shlomo*, vol. 1, pp. 25–31.

Shimon bar Yohai,[3] that the gifts of Torah, the land of Israel, and the World to Come are acquired only through suffering.[4]

When Hacham Salman passed away in 1940, he left a rich legacy of Torah scholarship. Among his writings was a six-volume masterpiece, *Kerem Shlomo*. His *sefarim* focused on wisdom from the Kabbalah, elucidations of the holy Arizal's words, and explanations of Rabbi Haim Vital's *Etz Haim*.[5]

Sadly, Hacham Salman passed away when his son Mordechai was only eleven. All the responsibility for the family fell on Rabbanit Mazal, Hacham Salman's widow. She had no way to provide for her family, as she was busy caring for her young children.

The *kever* of Rabbi Salman Eliyahu on the Mount of Olives (credit: Moshe Afnezer)

Although he was only eleven years old, the young Mordechai was compelled to help support the family by selling *turmesin*, a

---

3. Also known by his acronym, Rashbi, Rabbi Shimon bar Yohai was a renowned second-century *Tanna*.

4. As quoted in the Talmud, *Berachot* 5a.

5. Rabbi Haim Vital was the main disciple of the Arizal. He lived from 1542 to 1620.

Rabbi Mordechai Eliyahu as a little boy, with his parents
and older sister, 1929 (credit: Eliyahu Family)

specially prepared legume eaten as a snack.[6] He spent his days
selling the paper-wrapped *turmesin*, returning home at night to
delve into his Torah studies.

Rabbi Shimon, one of Hacham Mordechai's brothers, later
related that the entire family shared one room as their humble
home. At night, they would spread mattresses across the floor,
where they slept two to a bed. Shimon and Mordechai were
"mattress partners," but Mordechai often used his nights to study
Torah, leaving the mattress to his brother. Mordechai would

---

6. *Turmesin*, known as lupin or lupini beans in English, have been eaten as a snack since
   ancient times. They are mentioned in the Mishnah, and they must undergo an extensive
   process to prepare them for consumption, including soaking, cooking, and salting or
   pickling over the course of several days.

Rabbanit Mazal Eliyahu with her children, 1940. Hacham
Mordechai is sitting, first from left. (credit: Eliyahu Family)

take his candle under the table, where he would study without disturbing the rest of the family as they slept.

The special candles Mordechai used enhanced his learning. As his brother later recalled, Mordechai would end his *turmesin* sales by making the rounds to all the local synagogues and study halls, collecting candle remnants from them. He would then melt those stubs down, shaping the soft wax around a wick, forming a new candle for himself.

His older brother, Rabbi Naim, related that in those days, some of Jerusalem's more financially stable residents sought to encourage children to pursue their Torah studies despite the grinding poverty so many of them were living with. They would occasionally give out monetary prizes to boys who could pass Torah tests.

While most of the children used their prize money to buy *helkum*, a candy made from flour, corn, and sugar, Mordechai used the money for something of an entirely different nature: ice. He would buy half a block of ice, which he would then place in a bowl of water. And that's where he would put his feet at night so he wouldn't fall asleep while he was learning Torah.

Walking with Hacham Ovadia

"Some people make it sound like there's a rivalry between Rabbi Ovadia Yosef and me," Hacham Mordechai once said.[7] "But when we were young, we would go for a walk together every evening — from Yeshivat Porat Yosef, where we were both learning, to Yeshivat Hevron."[8]

Porat Yosef was then in such a bad financial state that the administration could not afford to fix the lighting. Since the young scholars wanted nothing more than to study Torah, the two would go for a long walk each night to Yeshivat Hevron, which was well lit. "I was nine years younger than Rabbi Ovadia, so I would carry

Rabbi Mordechai Eliyahu in his youth, in conversation with Rabbi Bentzion Abba-Shaul and Rabbi Ovadia Yosef (credit: Eliyahu Family)

7. He was likely referring to their differences in opinion as to how halachah should be decided: according to the Ben Ish Hai or the *Shulhan Aruch*.

8. This was probably in the 1940s. Yeshivat Porat Yosef was located in the Old City, while Yeshivat Hevron was in the Geulah neighborhood of Jerusalem.

the books and a candle, and we'd take a friendly walk together all the way to the newer part of the city."

✦

TORAH, MY DELIGHT

Learning under Fire

During the War of Independence, Rabbi Eliyahu — then known as just Mordechai — was a young man. He, along with everyone else, spent the day cowering in bomb shelters. The Jews were terrified of the Arabs, who were known for their depravity. The Jews in the fledgling state knew that the Arabs ruthlessly slaughtered everyone they could, wherever they were — even women and children. The Jews of Jerusalem knew that what had happened in Hevron[9] and Safed[10] could happen to them — or could happen anywhere. Everyone remembered the events of Tarpat.[11] The Jews were a bundle of nerves, and the atmosphere was extremely tense.

Rabbi Moshe Tzadkah[12] recalled that most people were not in the state of mind to learn much in the shelters. Yet, every time they so much as glanced in the young Mordechai's[13] direction, they would see him sitting there, learning diligently. It was as if nothing was happening beyond the pages of his *sefer*. He never lifted his head, never took breaks. He just studied continuously, concentrating so

---

9. Arabs massacred nearly seventy Jews in Hevron in 1929. Dozens of others were wounded.

10. Arabs massacred around twenty Jews in Safed just a few days after the Hevron massacre. Homes were looted and torched.

11. This is the Hebrew term for the 1929 massacres, during which 133 Jews were killed and between 198 and 241 others were injured by Arab rioters.

12. Rabbi Moshe Tzadkah is the current *rosh yeshivah* of Yeshivat Porat Yosef in the yeshivah's Geulah branch.

13. Rabbi Eliyahu was around eighteen or nineteen years old at the time of this story.

deeply, concerning himself neither with the turmoil inside the shelter, nor the terror beyond its walls.

"When Hacham Mordechai saw me there, watching him," Rabbi Tzadkah said, "he looked at me and said, 'Come, let's learn together!' And so we sat and reviewed the laws of blessings in great depth. I still remember those laws, which we learned in that terrible time."[14]

Rising with Respect

Rabbi Shabtai Yudelevitz became acquainted with Rabbi Eliyahu in 1950, when the young Shabtai was learning at Yeshivat Kol Torah,[15] and the young Mordechai was learning in Yeshivat Porat Yosef. A learning partner of Shabtai's introduced them when that boy transferred from Kol Torah to Porat Yosef.

Rabbi Mordechai Eliyahu in his youth, giving over a *shiur* at Yeshivat Porat Yosef, Jerusalem (credit: Rabbi Shmuel Zafrani)

14. Rabbi Moshe Tzadkah's recollections were shared in a eulogy he delivered at Rabbi Eliyahu's funeral.

15. Founded in 1939 by Rabbi Yehiel Michel Schlesinger and Rabbi Baruch Kunstadt, Kol Torah is renowned for its high standards of Torah study and the famous Talmudic scholars it has produced. It is located in the Bayit Vegan neighborhood of Jerusalem.

At the time, tens of thousands of new immigrants were coming to the newly formed State of Israel from all over the world. When they arrived in the country, they were placed in government-run absorption camps. The fledgling country's leaders saw these camps as an opportunity to "reprogram" the new immigrants. This way they could be turned into "model" secular citizens, if only they had assistance in shedding their old and outdated religious way of life — or so that was the plan.

In this desolate environment, countless vulnerable immigrants and refugees were persuaded to abandon the faith of their fathers and head in a new direction. They were often led astray by those who came to "help" them adjust to life in the new land.

Many young yeshivah students wanted to get involved in assisting the immigrants, both materially and spiritually. Indeed, these yeshivah boys saw it as their duty to do whatever they could to help the new immigrants remain on the path of their ancestors. And this was how the young Shabtai came to be acquainted with the young Mordechai: Both were enthusiastic young yeshivah boys reaching out to immigrants in the camps. They set up together to work as partners.

The young Mordechai Eliyahu and Shabtai Yudelevitz would visit the camps together, teaching Torah and spreading its light. The government authorities were putting so much pressure on those poor people to work and make a living that it was hard for the two yeshivah boys to accomplish anything. When the establishment moved people to kibbutzim and separated the children from their parents, the situation grew even more difficult.

This was a painful time in Israel, and the two boys were disappointed that the Torah leaders weren't doing more to save the immigrants and help them hold fast to their roots. They approached the *gedole Yisrael* (leading Torah sages of the generation) with hard questions. The young Mordechai, who was then only just out of his teens, approached Rabbi Yaakov Moshe Harlap,[16] the *rosh yeshivah* of Yeshivat Mercaz HaRav, and rabbi of Jerusalem's Shaare Hesed neighborhood, with his queries and concerns.

The young Mordechai asked Rabbi Harlap numerous questions. When Rabbi Harlap finished answering, Mordechai thanked him and bade him farewell. Although he was quite ill and weak at the time, Rabbi Harlap stood and escorted the young Mordechai to the door.

When his family asked Rabbi Harlap why he had done so, when it was so taxing for him, and his visitor was just a young yeshivah student, he responded, "The young man in question is actually a great scholar, and it is a mitzvah to accompany him."

Spreading Torah behind Bars

In a world rife with fake news and media so biased that it cannot be trusted or considered remotely objective, people would be forgiven for thinking that yellow journalism is a modern-day plague. But the term itself has been around since the 1890s — and the problem has existed even longer. And it even affected Rabbi Eliyahu numerous times over the years...

When he was involved with his work in the immigrant camps, the young Mordechai joined an underground group[17] of youthful, idealistic religious activists who sought to stem the growing tide of secularism in the country. The newspapers made a big ruckus about the young "fanatics," describing them like quasi-terrorists. The articles "exposed" the group's plans to make all kinds of trouble, insinuating that they wanted to go so far as to blow up the Knesset. Before long, the group was arrested and its members thrown in

---

16. Rabbi Harlap lived from 1882 to 1951.

17. Their group was called Brit Hakana'im, and it operated from 1949 to 1951.

prison, including the young Mordechai, who was sentenced to nine months in jail.

Rabbi Yehudah Tzadkah, Rabbi Mordechai's uncle, later recalled that the prison's leadership even posted special guards to be on duty when the young "terrorists" arrived. These burly, truncheon-bearing policemen surrounded the prison gates, awaiting the arrival of the young "terrorists." But when the prisoners were brought in, the authorities saw a group of scrawny yeshivah boys with friendly-looking faces. These were the radical activists making headlines? These were the thugs bringing the country to its knees?

The prison warden made it his business to get to know the boys, who certainly didn't look like hardened criminals. He wanted to hear their stories and find out where they were coming from and what made them do what they did. Over the course of their imprisonment, the boys explained to the warden — and whoever else would listen — that their actions just came from a love of the Jewish people and out of a desire to preserve the holiness of the Land.

The boys truly inspired the warden. He learned about the responsibility of one Jew for another, about the beauty of caring for one another, and about the importance of performing acts of loving-kindness. Through them, the warden discovered the meaning of the mitzvot and, by the time the group was released, the warden was so inspired that he had decided to do *teshuvah*, to return and repent. The warden eventually became fully Torah-observant.

Years later, when discussing his imprisonment, Hacham Mordechai said, "If we went to prison just to help the warden do *teshuvah*, it was worth it!"[18]

---

18. Rabbi Baruch Shraga, rabbi of Jerusalem's French Hill neighborhood, and head of one of the financial claims rabbinical courts in Jerusalem, related this story.

Making an Impression

The young Mordechai was incarcerated in the Jalami prison[19] for nine months, where he was held along with Jewish delinquents and Arab criminals. The conditions were deplorable, and even though he had a special relationship with the prison's warden, the young Mordechai faced regular violence and beatings from the guards, along with everyone else.

Nevertheless, the young rabbi didn't stop learning and sharing Torah within those walls. On his first day in jail, he arranged a Torah class for the prisoners, and he was always diligent about maintaining his own learning. He later told his friend Rabbi Tufik[20] that the best Torah learning he did in his entire life was in that prison.

The young Mordechai's studies had an effect not just on the warden and the other Jews around him, but even on the Arabs. Most of the Arab prisoners were incarcerated for severe and violent crimes, and it was considered a danger to interact or get involved with them in any way. But the Muslims saw Mordechai's holiness and devotion, and they approached him with a question. They wanted to know when the upcoming month of Ramadan would begin — and they knew that this young rabbi would be able to calculate the timing of the new moon, and thus, the beginning of their holiest month.

The young Mordechai told them that according to his calculations, Ramadan would begin on a Wednesday. Several days later, word

---

19. Jalami was a popular name for the Kishon Detention Center, located near the Jalami Junction, north of Haifa. The Kishon Detention Center is still in use as a prison today.

20. It is unclear which Rabbi Tufik related this. Rabbi Eliyahu was close to several Rabbis Tufik, including Rabbi Tufik of Betar and Rabbi Tufik of Jerusalem's Kiryat Moshe neighborhood.

came out that the qadi[21] of Egypt had decreed that Ramadan would begin on a Thursday. The Muslim prisoners returned to the young Mordechai, telling him about the contradiction.

The young Mordechai answered, "You're Muslim, and he is the qadi. I'm Jewish. You should follow your qadi and do what he told you."

A few days after that, the qadi issued a correction. He had miscalculated the new moon, and Ramadan would begin on a Wednesday, not on a Thursday, as he had originally publicized. The Muslims came running back to the young rabbi. "Our qadi, who is Muslim, made a mistake, and you, who are Jewish, got it right!" From that day on, they showed the young rabbi the greatest respect, polishing his shoes, making his bed, bringing him his food, and, most importantly, protecting him from anyone who sought to bother him.

Proving the Power of Torah

A young family's little girl had been diagnosed with a brain tumor, and they were advised to seek treatment in Boston, Massachusetts. But much to the family's dismay, the doctors in Boston didn't seem to have any better treatment methods to offer than there were in Israel. They returned home disappointed and full of fear.

After reviewing the results of her MRI, the girl's Israeli medical team told the family that the tumor could be surgically removed, but that such an operation would be extremely risky. The family was understandably quite nervous about the surgery and decided to seek the advice and blessings of Rabbi Eliyahu.

---

21. A Muslim judge who administers the religious laws of Islam, similar to (l'havdil) a *dayan* in Judaism.

He immediately asked the parents for their names, including their mothers' names, and for their daughter's name. After some thought, he looked through several *sefarim* and then announced, "Your daughter doesn't have a tumor."

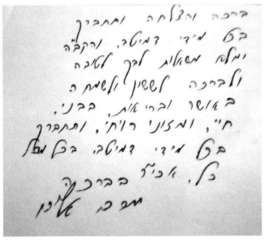

Blessing and signature of Rabbi Mordechai Eliyahu (credit: Havradim)

The confused parents told Rabbi Eliyahu that that was not the case, as they had the MRI scans right in their hands. The tumor was there. Rabbi Eliyahu picked up his *sefarim* again and then said, "No. There is nothing wrong with her."

The young mother asked if there was something she needed to do or take upon herself as an additional merit. Rabbi Eliyahu explained that there was no need for her to commit to anything extra, but said that if she wanted to undertake something, she could light an additional candle every Shabbat. He emphasized that he was sharing this with her only because she had asked.

The parents left feeling quite confused by their bizarre meeting with the rabbi. But just two weeks later, they got total clarity: The department head at Hadassah Ein Kerem Hospital called them, saying that after reviewing their daughter's brain scans, they saw that she did not have a tumor after all. What they were seeing was a particular structure of the brain. She didn't need surgery — or treatment of any kind — in the end.

The girl's father went back to Rabbi Eliyahu, asking him how he had known all this. He motioned to the many *sefarim* that surrounded him. "That's the power of Torah. As our Sages said, *He looked in the Torah and created the world.*[22] And that's what happened, in reality. When you learn Torah, you create reality."

"I'm a teacher in a *hesder* yeshivah,"[23] the girl's father said. "When I want to tell my students a story about the power of Torah, I share this one. I still have the scans and test results in my hands. But reality is in the 'hands' of Hashem."

Meriting Sons

Rabbi Eliyahu valued Torah and Torah study above everything else. Torah rolled off his lips, comprised his conversations, and punctuated his sentences. He would go to great lengths to spread and share that love.

Every Tuesday evening, Rabbi Eliyahu gave a Torah class, and after that class, a few students would write down whatever he had

Rabbi Eliyahu during a Kol Tzofecha Torah class

22. *Midrash Rabbah, Bereshit.* This concept is also brought down in other sources, including the *Zohar.*

23. A *hesder* yeshivah combines Talmudic studies with military service in the Israel Defense Forces.

taught. They would print these
Torah teachings in a newsletter
called *Kol Tzofecha*, which they
would then distribute.

One day, a man from Efrat
approached one of Rabbi Eliyahu's
close students, seeking a meeting
with the rabbi to get his blessing.
The student agreed to help the other man, and took him to the
rabbi. There, he explained to Rabbi Eliyahu that he was an only
son from a family of six daughters, and that he himself had four
daughters and no sons. He desperately wanted a son to carry the
family name.

"Are your daughters healthy?" Rabbi Eliyahu asked.

"Yes!"

"Whole?" the rabbi continued.

"Yes!"

"So what do you want?" Rabbi Eliyahu asked.

"A son to perpetuate my name."

Rabbi Eliyahu smiled, and then said, "Help distribute the *Kol
Tzofecha* sheets for a while, and then your prayers will be answered."

The idea made sense, as the man had a truck, so he volunteered
to distribute the sheets. Of course, he also ended up reading the

newsletters and began really connecting to the whole idea of spreading Torah among the Jewish people.

One day, on his way to distribute the newsletters in Kiryat Arba with a close student of Rabbi Eliyahu's, the driver passed by Hevron. There was an exchange of fire while they were in the area, and they heard gunshots to the left and right. They were completely in range. While Rabbi Eliyahu's student was used to being under fire from his army training, his friend — the truck driver — sat frozen in the driver's seat, holding the steering wheel for dear life — and not budging a bit.

While they escaped healthy and whole physically, their relationship was destroyed. The truck driver shouted, "Have you gone crazy? What kind of places are you taking me? In the end, I won't have sons or daughters. I'm done with this! You can do whatever *you* want, but *I'm* not coming anymore."

Indeed, from that very week, he stopped coming, and the *Kol Tzofecha* team had to find other distributors. Not long after that incident, the truck driver's wife gave birth to twin girls. The man almost lost his mind. He so badly wanted a son and he got two girls. He came back to Rabbi Eliyahu's student, infuriated. "What is this? I never saw such a thing! What happened to the rabbi's blessing?"

"You stopped distributing the sheets," the student answered. "That's what happened."

"Well, I'm not traveling another meter — I'm not going to endanger myself."

"Go tell that to Rabbi Eliyahu," the student suggested.

He agreed, and off they went.

Rabbi Eliyahu asked him, "Do you know what a great mitzvah it is to spread Torah? People take these sheets and learn from them. And then they share some of this Torah with other people, and all that merit goes to you. No harm comes to people who are involved in doing a mitzvah. Why are you scared? Don't be afraid!"

In the end, Rabbi Eliyahu won him over. He told Rabbi Eliyahu, "From now on I'll travel to wherever I'm directed. I won't be afraid anymore."

Shortly thereafter, he mentioned that his wife was expecting again, and he requested a private audience with Rabbi Eliyahu. The student brought him to Rabbi Eliyahu; afterward, he happily shared that the blessing had worked. The ultrasound showed that they were expecting a son.

"I'm in shock," he told the rabbi's student. "I heard about the miracles Rabbi Eliyahu can bring about. It's amazing to see his blessings at work."

An Overflowing Desk

Rabbi David Kaduri[24] once related that he saw Hacham Mordechai sitting at his desk, learning, but the desk was so overflowing with books that there was barely any room on it. He asked Hacham Mordechai if he could put some of the books away to make some  room. Hacham Mordechai refused, saying, "No, that's impossible — I haven't gotten the chance to look at them yet!"

---

24. A noted kabbalist in his own right, he was the only son of renowned kabbalist Rabbi Yitzhak Kaduri. Rabbi David passed away in 2015, at the age of eighty-eight.

Rabbi David looked at Hacham Mordechai, wide-eyed. "And you've looked at all the hundreds of books on your shelves?"

Hacham Mordechai didn't answer.

Making Flies Disappear

Rabbi Eliyahu lived in Be'er Sheva for a time, in the early 1960s. In those days, Be'er Sheva wasn't the urban, developed city it is today. Camels wandered the dusty streets, and flies and mosquitoes plagued the residents all summer long. But there was one place where there were no flies or mosquitoes: in the room Rabbi Eliyahu rented from a landlord named Mr. Weinberger.[25] It was something the property owner always remembered.

The absence of flies and mosquitoes in that room made such an impression that Mr. Weinberger even asked his tenant about it.

"Look, all the windows are closed," Rabbi Eliyahu said, by way of explanation.

At first, Mr. Weinberger believed him. But he later saw that even when all the windows were open, the flies and mosquitoes stayed away. It was one of Rabbi Eliyahu's many secret wonders.

Rabbi Eliyahu's grandson Yinon had a similar experience. He noticed that there were no flies, ants, or other insects in his grandparents' home. At first, he thought it was just coincidental. But over time, it really made an impression on him, especially since every other house in Israel seemed to get plenty of six-legged visitors. Yinon finally asked his father about it.

"I noticed it, too," his father confided, "but I was afraid to say anything."

The next time they visited Rabbi Eliyahu's home, however, they

---

25. First name unknown.

noticed that the miracle had ceased. Some things are not meant to be revealed so openly.

Shedding Tears with the Head of the Mossad

Rabbi Yisrael Gliss[26] was an adviser to Professor Shimon Sheetrit,[27] the minister of religion, and on the side, he worked as a businessman, entrepreneur, and journalist. Rabbi Gliss heard about a clothing factory in Jordan that manufactured suits for a great price. By purchasing these suits wholesale and reselling them to the religious public, he could turn a nice profit and help *haredim* by dramatically reducing the price of menswear.

Rabbi Gliss traveled to Jordan, where he visited the factory, bringing along two suits from Israel to use as examples of what he wanted. The factory manager told Rabbi Gliss to come back a week later. When he returned, Rabbi Gliss saw that the factory had already created a number of suits according to the requested style. He negotiated a good price for them and was going to sign a contract for more with the manufacturer. As Rabbi Gliss sat there, holding the pen, the manager said he wanted to show him something: He had forty Torah scrolls he was willing to sell for a thousand dollars apiece.

Right then, Rabbi Gliss recalled a story he had heard from his parents, when he was only a young child. When the Jordanian Legion conquered Jerusalem in the War of Independence,[28] Rabbi Gliss's relatives were among the people they captured and took as prisoners. As they were transported to Jordanian territory, the prisoners saw a Jordanian truck stuffed with Torah scrolls.

---

26. He is today a well-known Israeli journalist.

27. Sheetrit held the portfolio from 1995 to 1996.

28. 1947–1949.

The Torahs had once been used in synagogues in the Old City, but they were now jammed in a truck, traveling toward Jordan. Realizing Torah scrolls had economic value, someone had decided to take advantage of the situation by pilfering some for later resale.

Rabbi Gliss felt that somehow, he was an important link in the chain of his parents' story and the current one, and he hoped he would participate in closing this circle. He wanted the honor of returning the Torah scrolls to their original homes.

Following the factory manager to a side room, Rabbi Gliss watched as he opened a chest and displayed what he had: one Torah scroll, cut by hand into forty pieces. He must have thought that if he presented each of the pieces as an individual Torah scroll, he could get a lot more money. Rabbi Gliss was in complete shock and distress at seeing a Torah desecrated like that, and making matters worse, it was quite clear that the chopping had taken place quite recently. He assumed that the factory manager had done it himself.

Rabbi Gliss decided then and there that there would absolutely not be a deal — not with the Torah scrolls and not with the suits. He felt that he could not do business with a dishonest person who so ruthlessly defiled holy Jewish objects.

Rabbi Gliss turned to his contacts in the government and the Mossad, asking if they could ascertain where the factory manager had obtained that Torah scroll. After some research, they told him there really were forty scrolls, and they were available for sale. More of the story was soon revealed.

During the Gulf War,[29] Saddam Hussein ordered a certain Iraqi air force officer to blow up Baghdad's Great Synagogue. He thought it would somehow discredit American forces in the eyes

---

29. 1990–1991.

of the Jews. The officer visited the site before bombing it to see what was there. He found numerous Torah scrolls inside, which he then moved to a storeroom off-site. Several days later, he blew the synagogue to smithereens.[30]

After the war ended, the officer was obviously not able to return the Torahs to the synagogue. So he decided to do business with them. The Torah scrolls found their way to book dealers — and into the Mossad's purview.

Upon hearing this account, Rabbi Gliss went to Professor Sheetrit, whom he was working for at the Religious Affairs Ministry. He told Sheetrit the whole story, and they approached the ministry's legal team about reclaiming the scrolls. They gave Rabbi Gliss the green light to go ahead and work to bring the scrolls back home.

Rabbi Gliss began making numerous trips to Jordan, bringing Torah scrolls back with him each time. They were the scrolls from synagogues in the Old City, as well as from Babylon (now modern-day Iraq). The Torahs were then taken to Machon Ot,[31] where Rabbi Yitzhak Steiner[32] carefully and lovingly repaired and restored them.

When Rabbi Gliss finally brought back the last Torah, he went to see Rabbi Yosef Shalom Elyashiv,[33] bringing this Torah along with him. Rabbi Elyashiv took the opportunity to examine and

---

30. The synagogue was one of the oldest in the world and was supposedly so large it could seat 20,000 people.

31. The world's leading authority in Torah scroll repair, restoration, and maintenance. It is located in Jerusalem.

32. One of the founders of Machon Ot.

33. 1910–2012. He was one of the foremost rabbis of the generation and was regarded by many Ashkenazi Jews as the world's leading authority on halachah.

learn from the Torah scroll, making observations about the spacing between the lines, the shape of the letters, and more.

Afterward, Rabbi Gliss took the same Torah scroll to the Vizhnitzer Rebbe.[34] When the rebbe saw the Torah and heard the story of its rescue, along with the other Torah scrolls that had been saved and returned to the Jewish people, he became quite emotional. He wept so much that he needed a towel to dry his tears.

Finally, Rabbi Gliss went to visit Rabbi Mordechai Eliyahu with the Torah. He hadn't even managed to open it when Rabbi Eliyahu said, "That scroll belonged to Shaul Tzadkah's[35] family. The Torah was in the *genizah*[36] closet above the ark."

He went on to describe a second Torah scroll that had belonged to the same family, explaining that it had been sitting in the ark itself. He wanted to know where that Torah was, as it was kosher for ritual use. Rabbi Eliyahu knew so much about that Torah, including who had financed it, which scribe wrote it, and other tidbits of its history. But the best was yet to come.

He said there had been a third Torah scroll there, too, which had been written by the Ben Ish Hai himself. Rabbi Eliyahu mentioned that the Ben Ish Hai had signed the scroll, at the very end, on the back of the last piece of parchment. Rabbi Eliyahu wanted to know if that scroll had been among those that had been rescued — and if so, he wanted to know where it was. Rabbi Gliss promised to do his utmost to find it.

When he investigated the matter, Rabbi Gliss discovered that

---

34. Rabbi Moshe Yehoshua Hager, the fifth Vizhnitzer Rebbe, lived from 1916 to 2012.

35. Shaul Tzadkah was Rabbi Yehudah Tzadkah's father. He immigrated to the land of Israel from Baghdad around 1900.

36. Written holy works require ritual burial when they are no longer usable. They are kept separate, in *genizah*, until they are ready for burial.

the scroll in question had indeed been recovered — and that it was currently in the hands of the Mossad. After the Mossad had helped locate and retrieve the Torah scrolls, the security agency had received one of them to use in their synagogue for the weekly readings. As it turned out, the Torah in the Mossad's synagogue was the very one Rabbi Eliyahu wanted to see: the Ben Ish Hai's scroll. There was just one problem: the Mossad was — and still is — one of the most guarded, enigmatic organizations in the world.

The secret underground base, where the synagogue and Torah scroll were located, is known as "the Hole." No one knows where the Hole is — unless he needs to know. But Rabbi Gliss was able to arrange[37] for Rabbi Mordechai Eliyahu to visit the synagogue in the Hole and see the Ben Ish Hai's Torah scroll.

The Mossad agents were delighted by his visit, and the agency's heads even came to greet him. When Rabbi Eliyahu opened the scroll and revealed the Ben Ish Hai's signature, he began to tremble and weep at the sight.

Everyone stood there, dumbstruck — and then joined in Rabbi Eliyahu's tears. They believed that the Ben Ish Hai's soul had guided the Torah scroll to where it needed to be. The head of the Mossad, who was not a demonstrative man, was standing there crying, too — unabashed tears of joy and emotion. The Torah scroll was finally home.

---

37. Rabbi Zafrani helped coordinate this visit. Rabbi Zafrani served as Rabbi Eliyahu's personal secretary during the time Rabbi Eliyahu was the chief rabbi of Israel. He stayed on as the head of Rabbi Eliyahu's office when Rabbi Eliyahu retired from the position of *Rishon LeZion*. Rabbi Zafrani was — and still is — the *rosh yeshivah* of Yeshivat HaMeiri in Jerusalem's Kiryat Moshe neighborhood.

SHARP MIND, SOUND WISDOM

Outdoing the Computer

When programmers at Bar-Ilan University developed a program that compiled thousands of halachic questions and answers, they wanted to demonstrate their new software to Rabbi Eliyahu. They longed to show him how a computer could be used to almost instantaneously find the source of any question presented to it.

While they were at Rabbi Eliyahu's house, a *dayan* (rabbinical judge) called with a question regarding a particular ruling of the Rashba's.[38] Although the response was quoted in the Rashba's name, the *dayan* was unable to find it recorded in any of the Rashba's *sefarim*.

Rabbi Eliyahu, in turn, presented the question to the programmers and asked if they would be able to find the source using their new software. While they were typing the question into the program, the rabbi was searching his own *sefarim*. Not surprisingly, Rabbi Eliyahu found the mistake

A younger Rabbi Eliyahu giving a Torah lecture (credit: Eliyahu Family)

even before the computer did. The ruling was in the Ritva's[39]

---

38. Shlomo ben Avraham ibn Aderet, commonly known as the Rashba, was an outstanding Torah scholar of the medieval period. He lived from 1235 to 1310.

39. Rabbi Yom Tov ben Avraham Asevilli, the Ritva, lived from 1260 to 1320. He was *rosh yeshivah* of the Yeshivah of Seville, in Spain, and was famous for his commentaries on the Talmud. He was a student of the Rashba (above).

---

work, and had mistakenly been quoted as having been decided by the Rashba.

Saving *Shidduchim*, Where It Counts

Rabbi Eliyahu was acquainted with a certain rabbi who liked to check the suitability of *shidduchim* (marriage matches) based on the couple's names. If their names didn't match according to his method, he would advise them to separate — even if they were already married. To say this brought about a lot of distress is a great understatement. As the Talmud relates, *When a couple divorces, even the altar sheds tears.*[40]

Rabbi Eliyahu warned the rabbi how dangerous and problematic his method was, begging him to cease and desist, but the man paid no attention. Rabbi Eliyahu finally came up with a solution. He asked if he could check the names of the rabbi and his wife. When he made the calculations, he discovered that the couple — this name-checking rabbi and his wife — were completely unsuitable for one another. When Rabbi Eliyahu showed the rabbi his calculations, he told him he must divorce his wife because the numbers just didn't match up.

The rabbi was understandably shaken to the core. He clutched his head, crying, "How can I do that? I have eight children! How can I divorce my wife?"

Rabbi Eliyahu answered, "You don't need to divorce her — but you can't continue to tell other couples to get divorced based on arbitrary, meaningless numbers and calculations." This time the rabbi listened.

Another time, an engaged couple approached Rabbi Eliyahu in tears. They had planned to marry, but their parents had sent them to a certain "rabbi" to have their names checked. The rabbi did so,

---

40. *Gittin* 90b.

announcing that the young people weren't suited to one another. He advised them to break their engagement. The couple was completely distraught; they liked one another and truly believed they had found the right one.

Rabbi Eliyahu was terribly distressed and immediately summoned the rabbi and the parents of the bride and groom. Despite the other rabbi's discomfort, he refused to retract what he had said. So in the presence of the couple, the rabbi, and both sets of parents, Rabbi Eliyahu took the names of the young man and woman. Then he asked the girl's mother if her daughter had another name. She said that when her daughter was very young they had called her by a different name.

The rabbi who had forbidden the marriage meanwhile went pale. "Wait," he said, making calculations with pen and paper, "I didn't realize she had another name! If that's the case, then the formula is completely different and they *can* marry each other."

Like Waiting for a Bus

Members of the Maayane Hayeshua organization,[41] a Jewish outreach group, once held an interview with Rabbi Eliyahu. They discussed how the idea of waiting for Mashiah often seems like more of an abstract concept than a reality, and they wanted to hear how a person can wait for Mashiah, practically speaking.

Rabbi Eliyahu, in his signature style, answered, "We know that we'll be asked in Heaven if we anticipated the Redemption. And we know that if a person answers, 'Of course,' he will be asked how he did so. If he says, 'Oh, I prayed for it in *Shemoneh Esreh*,' they will tell him it wasn't enough. A person has to anticipate Mashiah like a person waiting for the bus: He's sitting at the bus

---

41. Founded in 2000 by Avihai Buaron, this organization seeks encounters with average Israelis in their day-to-day lives.

stop, knowing that the bus is coming, and he jumps up to check if each approaching bus is the one he's waiting for. Now *that's* anticipation."

The Beggar's Children

In the early 1960s, a beggar woman would wander the streets of Tel Aviv, telling anyone who would listen that her son had been stolen from her and sold to other people. She looked so disheveled, neglected, and deranged that no one paid attention to her ramblings, taking her for a mentally ill individual.

That woman also had a daughter who had distanced herself from her mother, trying to get an education and build a normal life for herself. When this daughter got engaged, the rabbinate asked for proof that she was single and Jewish. She brought her mother to the *bet din* in Be'er Sheva, where Rabbi Eliyahu was serving as the *dayan*.

He immediately recognized the beggar woman, and remembered meeting her in Tel Aviv in the past. Recalling her story about her stolen son, he gently asked, "Do you remember your son?"

"Of course I remember," the mother said, starting to cry. "I remember like it was yesterday." She pointed to a spot on her right shoulder. "He had a mole on his shoulder, in this exact spot." She went on to describe the unusual shape of the mole.

The other *dayanim* looked at Rabbi Eliyahu in surprise. "Do you really believe this woman?"

Rabbi Eliyahu responded, "The verse says, *A fool does not stay on one topic.*[42] That means that a fool wouldn't keep repeating the same

---

42. This possibly refers to the verse in *Mishle* 18:2, *A fool has no delight in understanding, but only in revealing his own opinion*, or to the Talmudic discussion of that verse, as seen in *Bava Metzia* 85b: *Ulla said: This explains the adage that people say, "A small coin in an empty barrel calls kish, kish,"* i.e., *it rattles loudly, whereas a coin in a barrel full of coins is not heard.*

nonsense his whole life. If this woman says the same thing all the time, there must be some truth to what she's saying."

The rabbi asked one of the groom's friends to go with him to the *mikvah* (ritual bath) before the official engagement and wedding, instructing him to look for a mole on the groom's right shoulder in the place the woman had described. The friend reported to Rabbi Eliyahu that not only did the groom have a mole in that exact spot, but it also had a peculiar shape. The shape he described precisely fit the woman's report.

Rabbi Eliyahu summoned the groom and asked him who his parents were. The young man immediately gave the names of the parents who had raised him. "Did they adopt you?" Rabbi Eliyahu asked.

The groom responded in the negative.

"Do you look like your parents?" Rabbi Eliyahu asked.

"No, not at all," he answered.

Rabbi Eliyahu immediately called for the boy's parents. "Your son is about to get married. I need you to answer me truthfully. This is very important. Is your son your biological child?"

The people who had raised him shook their heads. "No. He's actually adopted, but there are no official records of the adoption."

Rabbi Eliyahu then summoned the bride and groom. "You're not the son of the people who raised you," he said to the young man. "You're the son of another woman." The young man was obviously deeply shocked and upset by what he had heard, and he refused to believe it.

"Wait just a moment and you'll see for yourself," Rabbi Eliyahu said. He then called in the boy's adoptive parents.

"Did you give birth to this boy?" he asked.

"No," they said, much to the boy's surprise.

The rabbi then summoned the beggar woman. "Tell us about

your lost son," he said. In front of all those assembled there, she related how she had had a son who was taken from her many years ago and that she had had no peace of mind ever since.

"Did your son have any marks on his body that would identify him?" Rabbi Eliyahu asked gently.

The woman nodded, describing the mole on his right shoulder.

The groom blanched.

"And how was that mole shaped?" Rabbi Eliyahu asked.

She described the exact shape.

The groom-son fainted and the beggar woman became completely distraught. The *bet din* broke into total pandemonium. The boy was then revived and seated on a chair, his face as white as snow.

Rabbi Eliyahu then asked the beggar woman for other identifying marks that only she would know about. She described some other marks on her lost son's body.

The boy confirmed that she had indeed described him.

"Well," Rabbi Eliyahu said to the woman, "here's your son. He almost married your daughter! But because you didn't give up on your motherhood, he was saved from marrying his sister and he was returned to you."

Controlling Flights, Directing Journeys

Rabbi Eliyahu had an incredible knack for answering people on their level and in a way they could understand. Whenever he would meet people who were far from observant Judaism, he would search for some common link between himself and them, be it from their community, family, or interests. Rabbi Eliyahu would use this as a point of connection, making people feel comfortable with him and like they could relate to him.

During his time as chief rabbi, Rabbi Eliyahu was invited to tour

Ben Gurion Airport. One of the airport's directors participated in showing the dignitaries around. When the group stopped for a break, this director approached Rabbi Eliyahu, wanting to know if he could ask a question. "It won't let me rest..." the man said, explaining why it was so urgent for him to discuss this now.

"Please," Rabbi Eliyahu said with a smile.

"So," the director began, "why does a person who asks a rabbi a halachic question have to act according to what the rabbi tells him?"

Before Rabbi Eliyahu had even gotten more than a few words out, the director interjected, "Don't rabbis make mistakes sometimes?"

"Of course," Rabbi Eliyahu answered. "Everyone can err. But it's still worthwhile to listen to a rabbi, because he often has a broader perspective and a deeper base of knowledge on a topic, and he can see and know things a regular person doesn't."

The director's face clearly betrayed his dissatisfaction with that answer.

Rabbi Eliyahu continued, "Even though a person has free will, it's a good idea to seek — and heed — the advice of a rabbi, rather than acting arbitrarily."

The director wouldn't let it rest. "But why is someone *obligated*? I don't understand. Let the rabbi say whatever he says and the questioner do whatever he wants."

Rabbi Eliyahu just smiled. "Wait. You'll soon understand."

The next stop on the tour was at the control tower. "This control tower is the height of a fifteen-story building," the guide informed the group. "The air-traffic controllers sit at the top, supervising all the take-offs and landings."

The group looked out the windows that surrounded the room. The runways were spread out on the ground below. "The air-traffic controllers use the height and the wide field of vision to see all the planes taking off and landing. The pilots can only see what's right in front of them, so they must follow the instructions of the air-traffic controllers, of course."

Rabbi Eliyahu turned to the airport director who had just been asking him questions. "Let's imagine a pilot sees a clear runway and requests permission to land, but the controller denies the request. Instead, he sends the pilot to a different runway. Can the pilot ignore him, do what he wants, and land on the first runway?" Rabbi Eliyahu asked.

"G-d forbid!" the director cried. "The pilot has to listen to the directions of the controllers. Their perspective is much broader. They see and know things the pilot can't possibly see from his position!"

"Listen to your words, straight from your own mouth," Rabbi Eliyahu responded with a smile.

HARMONY AT HOME

Shouting for *Shalom*

Rabbi Eliyahu always put great effort into making peace and promoting *shalom bayit* between couples.

On one occasion, Rabbi Dov Bigon, the *rosh yeshivah* of Machon Meir,[43] sent a couple to him for some counseling. They were engaged to be married, but there were numerous differences between them. The girl seemed much more boisterous and loud,

---

43. Machon Meir is a yeshivah and outreach program in Jerusalem's Kiryat Moshe neighborhood. It was founded in 1973.

and somewhat bad-tempered. The boy, on the other hand, seemed very quiet and gentle. Rabbi Bigon wasn't sure what to do with the couple and whether or not they should even get married, so he brought them to Rabbi Eliyahu.

As soon as they came into Rabbi Eliyahu's office, the rabbi began yelling at the boy, shouting loudly. Rabbi Bigon was shocked, as he had known Rabbi Eliyahu for many years and had never heard him raise his voice in such a way. Rabbi Eliyahu finally stopped shouting and said to the couple, "It's fine, you can get married."

The next day Rabbi Bigon approached Rabbi Eliyahu for an explanation. "The girl has a tendency to shout, so I wanted to see if her groom could withstand it without getting upset. I saw that he stood up to it well, so I told them they could get married."

Identifying a Woman of Valor

Rabbi Eliyahu once related that when he was serving as a *dayan* in the Be'er Sheva *bet din*,[44] a couple approached him regarding their personal conflict. The husband and wife each had a number of lawyers in tow.

"When the hearing began," Rabbi Eliyahu said, "I asked the lawyers to leave the room. They insisted on staying, saying they had to be present, but I refused. They threatened to go to the Supreme Court over it — so I said, 'Go right ahead. Why not go right now?'"

They left. Then Rabbi Eliyahu asked the husband what had happened. He said that his wife had thrown a plate of salad at him. Then Rabbi Eliyahu turned to the wife, asking for her version of events. She said her husband had thrown a pot of soup at her. Rabbi Eliyahu asked them what had triggered all this.

---

44. He served as a *dayan* in Be'er Sheva from 1960 to 1964, and was the youngest *dayan* in the country at that time.

The wife said, "My husband comes home from synagogue on Friday night and sings 'Shalom Alechem,' but never 'Eshet Hayil,' even though I've asked him to!"

"That's because you're not a woman of valor," her husband retorted.

That was the crux of the whole argument. After the hearing, Rabbi Eliyahu asked the bet din's secretary to set up an appointment for them to continue the case the following day. That evening, Rabbi Eliyahu was pondering the song and the meaning of "Eshet Hayil." He took out the text and reviewed it, reading all the commentaries on it, too. In the course of his learning, he saw that Shlomo Hamelech[45] had penned the song's verses about his mother — and that gave Rabbi Eliyahu a flash of inspiration.

The following day, when the couple returned to the bet din, Rabbi Eliyahu first invited the husband for a private audience. "In your opinion, who is a real woman of valor?" Rabbi Eliyahu asked him.

"My mother," the man said. "She respects me."

"Good," Rabbi Eliyahu said. "You should start singing 'Eshet Hayil' every Friday night and think about your mother when you sing."

The man agreed.

Rabbi Eliyahu then summoned the wife. He explained to her that he had spoken to her husband and that he was prepared to sing "Eshet Hayil" each Friday night, as is customary. She was placated, and the couple returned home.

Just two weeks later, the husband was back at the bet din. Rabbi Eliyahu immediately assumed the suggestion hadn't worked, and he asked the man what had happened.

"Since I started singing 'Eshet Hayil' on Friday nights, my wife

---

45. King Solomon.

started being more considerate of me. She cooks the food I like and she speaks to me more kindly. I see that she really is a woman of valor sometimes. Can I think about her, too, when I sing?"

Rabbi Eliyahu nodded. "Sing *'Eshet Hayil'* and think of both your mother and your wife!"[46]

LEADERS OF GENERATIONS

The Lubavitcher Rebbe's Passing

When the Lubavitcher Rebbe, Rabbi Menahem Mendel Schneerson,[47] had to start limiting his public speeches and begin medical treatment, he personally called Rabbi Eliyahu sometime close to midnight. The rebbe was not known to call anyone on the phone, but that night he called Rabbi Eliyahu, opening his conversation with the question, "Is the honored rabbi before or after *Tikun Hatzot?*"[48] Other than the beginning, no one knows the content of the conversation between the two great men.

Sometime later, Rabbi Eliyahu traveled to the United States, where he spoke at an event in San Francisco. It was just two days before the Lubavitcher Rebbe's passing, but of course no one knew that at the time of his speech. On the day of the rebbe's death,

---

46. From *B'sha'ar Hamelech*, a booklet of Rabbi Eliyahu's prayers and *segulot*. It also contains personal stories and recollections. The pamphlet was privately published in 2010.

47. 1902–1994.

48. A collection of prayers traditionally recited nightly after midnight as an expression of mourning over the destruction of the Temple in Jerusalem.

still in California, Rabbi Eliyahu cut his public appearances short, hurrying to New York for the funeral.

Rabbi Eliyahu's on-time arrival for that funeral is another story in and of itself — and a miraculous one at that, especially considering that given the events over the course of the day he should have arrived long after the funeral ended. But the main point was that he was there, both to accompany the rebbe's funeral procession and to eulogize him.[49]

Are You Eliyahu Hanavi?[50]

Rabbanit Tzviyah, the rabbi's wife, once related that when her husband was a *dayan* in Jerusalem, someone from southern Israel came to visit the Eliyahus' home. As the man was preparing to leave, Rabbi Eliyahu thought of joining him in his car to go visit the Baba Sali. He broached the topic with his wife, saying they could return by bus.

She checked the bus schedule and saw that it would work if they could be in Ramle on time to catch the eleven o'clock bus back to Jerusalem. Catching that Ramle bus meant, however, that they would have to leave Netivot on an eight o'clock bus. They decided to make the trip, riding with their visitor.

They arrived at the Baba Sali's home, which at the time was in a regular apartment block. The Baba Sali's wife greeted them at the door, apologizing that she couldn't invite them in to see her husband. Rabbanit Tzviyah was deeply disappointed that they had made the whole trip in vain. But her distress was short-lived: The Baba Sali called to his wife, instructing her to let the Eliyahus

---

49. Rabbi Eliyahu was the only person to eulogize both the Lubavitcher Rebbe and the Baba Sali.

50. Elijah the prophet.

enter. "I've been waiting for Hacham Mordechai for days already!" he exclaimed.

The Baba Sali's wife opened the door, waving them in. Rabbi Eliyahu went into the Baba Sali's room and Rabbanit Tzviyah sat down with the Baba Sali's wife, who began to weep. "My husband hasn't eaten this entire week — since the end of Shabbat. He said there's a terrible, heavy decree hanging over the Jewish people, and he's been fasting to annul it. Please ask your husband to persuade him to eat. He hasn't eaten for five days already!"

The Baba Sali blesses Rabbi Mordechai Eliyahu (credit: Rabbi Shmuel Zafrani)

After some time had passed, the door to the Baba Sali's room opened, and the two rabbis came out. The Baba Sali's face was shining as he said to his wife, "The decree has been canceled! Let's eat with our guests."

His wife immediately set the table and served a beautiful meal. The two rabbis sang and praised G-d. But at seven-thirty Rabbanit Tzviyah began to signal to her husband to finish and say *Birkat Hamazon* (the blessing after meals); they needed to leave in time to catch the eight o'clock bus out of Netivot.

Although the Baba Sali was sitting far from Rabbanit Tzviyah, he seemed to know what she was saying. He instructed Rabbi Eliyahu, "Tell your wife not to worry. You'll get back to Jerusalem in good time." He continued the meal for another hour, singing and praising the Holy One. They finally said the blessing after meals and finished the meal. It was eight-thirty at night, long after the bus to Ramle had come and gone.

When they left the Baba Sali's house, Rabbi Eliyahu said to his wife, "Come, we'll take the late bus to Ramle and see what we can do from there."

"The bus that leaves now doesn't get to Ramle until eleven-thirty — half an hour *after* the last bus from Ramle departs for Jerusalem," she said.

"Never mind," Rabbi Eliyahu replied. "At least we'll be closer to Jerusalem."

They took the eight-thirty bus to Ramle, arriving there at eleven-thirty. "Let's see what's happening with the bus to Jerusalem," Rabbi Eliyahu suggested.

"It was supposed to leave at eleven," his wife responded. "I don't think we should bother."

But Rabbi Eliyahu was insistent. They went to the bus stop and saw that, lo and behold, the bus to Jerusalem was sitting there, full of passengers.

"Can we board?" Rabbi Eliyahu asked the driver.

"There's no point," he answered. "The bus won't start."

"So what are all the passengers doing here?" Rabbi Eliyahu asked.

"Well, they already paid, so they're waiting it out. But there's no point in boarding. The bus has broken down."

"We're getting on anyway," Rabbi Eliyahu said, climbing onto the bus with his wife. They settled into their seats and then Rabbi Eliyahu said to the driver, "Try starting the engine again."

The driver turned his key in the ignition — and to everyone's amazement, the bus started right away, even though it hadn't worked for the past half hour.

"What, are you Eliyahu Hanavi?" the driver exclaimed, eyeing his passenger warily.

"No," the rabbi said. "I'm Eliyahu Mordechai."

Concealing Kabbalistic Wisdom

Rabbi Eliyahu never spoke about the Kabbalah he learned. He never shared from who he learned it, when he learned it, or any other details. Only in his last days, before he was admitted to the hospital, did he even mention Rabbi Menahem Menashe,[51] widely known as "the Tinsmith."

Describing him, Rabbi Eliyahu referred to Rabbi Menashe as one of the *lamed-vav tzaddikim*,[52] saying he was possibly even the first of them. Given how careful Rabbi Eliyahu was to measure and consider every single word he uttered, his making such a statement about someone was absolutely astounding. He related that Rabbi Yehudah Tzadkah had once asked the Tinsmith to teach in his yeshivah when he was the *rosh yeshivah* of Porat Yosef.

"Who am I?" Rabbi Menashe asked, by way of response. "I'm nothing but a tinsmith." Although Rabbi Menashe was indeed a metalworker, Rabbi Tzadkah saw his greatness and brought him to teach in the yeshivah.

Rabbi Eliyahu spoke about the Tinsmith with deep awe and respect, impressing and inspiring his family with stories he had concealed all his life. He said that Rabbi Menashe would imbue

---

51. 1892–1968.

52. One of the thirty-six hidden righteous men discussed in the Talmud and mystical sources, like the *Tikkune Zohar*.

his students with a love for the land of Israel, instilling in them a feeling of responsibility for the Jewish people, and teaching them to spread Torah in *Am Yisrael*.

Rabbi Eliyahu considered himself one of the Tinsmith's students, and in their younger years, they would travel together to the absorption camps for new immigrants and other places where they needed to spread the Torah's light. Some say it was from the Tinsmith that Rabbi Eliyahu learned the wisdom of the Kabbalah — and how to conceal his mastery and understanding of that mystical knowledge.

The Light of Youth

Rabbi Eliyahu was once on a trip abroad. He arrived for prayers at a large synagogue in the community he was visiting. Although the time for Shabbat evening prayers had arrived, there were no children present among the congregation. Rabbi Eliyahu knew that some of the people in the congregation must have had children, but he figured they probably left them all at home. Perhaps they didn't think it was important or appropriate for them to attend?

After *Kabbalat Shabbat*, the community asked their honored guest to come and grace them with a few words. Rabbi Eliyahu climbed the steps to the dais and then stood in silence for a moment. Then he burst out, "Oy, what darkness rests in your synagogue!"

Everyone sat in shock, stealing glances at one another. Then someone in the audience called out, "Maybe the *gabbai* (synagogue assistant) should turn on the big chandeliers we use only for Yom Kippur?"

Paying no heed to the ignorant remark, Rabbi Eliyahu continued. "I see a terrible darkness here, gentlemen. It's hard for me to describe."

Someone in the congregation got up from his seat and

approached the dais. He presented himself as an ophthalmologist. "If the respected rabbi sees terrible darkness, I suspect he may be experiencing an urgent and serious eye condition. I'm prepared to immediately refer the rabbi to my eye clinic and perform an exam…"

And it was there in that tense atmosphere that Rabbi Eliyahu cried out, "In a synagogue empty of children, where children are not invited and encouraged to attend, a deep darkness resides."

He then began a discourse on the importance of educating children about coming to the synagogue, where they learn to pray and become familiar with the service. He explained that not only do they need to know this for their own future as Jews, but for the future of the entire community. Children are the future. They are the next generation of G-d-fearing Jews.

When Rabbi Eliyahu finished and returned to his seat, there seemed to be a new light shining in the building.

A Choice Made in Heaven

When the suggestion was first made that Rabbi Eliyahu should run for the position of chief rabbi of Israel, his wife objected. Rabbanit Tzviyah felt it was difficult enough as it was for him to cope with the crowds who gathered on their doorstep each morning with questions, let alone the unceasing telephone calls at all hours of the day and night. Making matters more complicated, she knew that Rabbi Eliyahu wouldn't turn anyone away, no matter what he was in the middle of doing.

No matter how simple, small, or trivial a question was, Rabbi Eliyahu would drop whatever he was involved in to try and answer it. Rabbanit Eliyahu just didn't know how her husband would manage to keep up with the even greater demands of the position — and she feared that he would never have a free moment again.

When Rabbi Eliyahu heard that his wife was opposed to his

appointment, he immediately rejected the idea to those who were suggesting it. But then Rabbanit Eliyahu started contemplating the proposal, eventually concluding that helping the Jewish people was an essential role of theirs. She felt that if people were advocating her husband's candidacy so strongly, she wouldn't stand in their way.

Rabbi Eliyahu finally agreed — and then nearly backed out again shortly thereafter, on the advice of his wife, who had once more fallen into doubt, beset by reservations and uncertainty. The situation was especially complicated, as right after his candidacy was announced, all kinds of people began coming out of the woodwork with memories of the rabbi's time in prison and so on. The *rabbanit* worried about him being in a position that would put him under so much public scrutiny, in addition to the huge toll it would take on his time and energy.

One Erev Shabbat, Rabbanit Tzviyah poured her heart out to her husband, sharing all her hesitations. On Motzae Shabbat, she started receiving phone calls. The first was from the Baba Sali, who told her that Rabbi Eliyahu's candidacy was from Heaven and she shouldn't fight it. The Gerrer Rebbe[53] called next, saying the same thing. A short time later, an emissary of the Lubavitcher Rebbe arrived with the same message: "In Heaven they chose you."

She believed that these messages were truly Heaven-sent. It was as if those righteous men had sensed the doubts plaguing her heart and then reached out to reassure her — each using the exact same wording to encourage and support her.

The following Monday, Rabbanit Eliyahu went to visit Rabbi Yitzhak Kaduri[54] to ask him a question about a personal matter.

---

53. Rabbi Simhah Bunim Alter, the Lev Simhah, 1898–1992.

54. A renowned and widely sought-after kabbalist, originally from Baghdad. His birth year is disputed, usually estimated between 1898 and 1902. He passed away in Jerusalem in 2006.

He asked her why she was asking him when she could ask her own husband. She responded that while her husband was a rabbi who gave halachic rulings, she was seeking a kabbalist to give her a blessing. Rabbi Kaduri laughed, saying that her husband was also a

Rabbi Mordechai Eliyahu sitting beside Rabbi Yitzhak
Kaduri at a *simhah* (credit: Eliyahu Family)

kabbalist and that he could also give blessings that would be fulfilled. He added, "And all the Kabbalah I know I learned from Rabbi Eliyahu's father. So how could it be that he doesn't have the power to give blessings?" He then asked her if the three rabbis had sent their messages to her on Motzae Shabbat.

Invitation to the inauguration of Rabbi Mordechai
Eliyahu as *Rishon LeZion*, 1983 (credit: Eliyahu Family)

When she confirmed that they had, Rabbi Kaduri nodded, affirming their words. Rabbanit Eliyahu recalled wondering how he could know all of this, as she couldn't imagine the rabbis calling and telling him what they had done and said — but she didn't ask. She just knew that all her objections had vanished. She could — and would — support her husband as chief rabbi of Israel.

After Rabbi Eliyahu's inauguration as *Rishon LeZion*, on
the way to the Kotel (credit: Eliyahu Family)

After her husband's passing, she recalled this story. "When I think back to all that happened during that time, I wonder what I was thinking. How could I not have seen the greatness of my husband in those days? He managed to conceal himself even from me. And perhaps even today, even after so many stories have been shared, he's still concealing himself?"

PUTTING JEWISH LAW INTO PRACTICE

Taste — and See

Rabbi Eitan Eizman[55] was elected to be the rabbi of the Shadmot Mahola moshav in the Jordan Valley. It was all new to him, as prior to that, he had been a *rosh yeshivah* and was busy with educating young men, and all the issues that accompanied that. He was intimately familiar with the topics learned in the Talmud and all the theoretical matters that arise in its study, but now that he had joined the rabbinate, he had entered the realm of the practical — and he felt he needed guidance. Rabbi Mordechai Eliyahu helped him enormously during the period in which he was learning how to rule on all manners of applied halachah.

The moshav was facing very complicated agricultural questions, including dealing with settlements that were located close to the halachic boundaries of the land of Israel; farming in accordance to Jewish law; and so many more related topics. Rabbi Eliyahu instructed Rabbi Eizman to come see him early in the morning, right after Shaharit and before he left for the rabbinical court. Rabbi Eizman would come, worried that he was stealing the rabbi's time, and not wanting to use up the rabbi's short allotment for breakfast, which he usually ate in great haste.

"But he always received me with a smile," Rabbi Eizman recalled. "When I asked if I was taking away from his time at the *bet din*, he would always reassure me, saying that questions about

---

55. Rabbi Eizman is the director of the Tzviyah network of educational institutions, was a former director of the chief rabbinate of Israel, and was the former rabbi of the Shadmot Mahola moshav.

settling and living in the land of Israel *are* Torah, and I had nothing to worry about."

On a number of occasions, Rabbi Eizman needed to verify whether a particular fruit was *orlah*, a fruit produced by a tree within the first three years after planting, which is forbidden to eat. Rabbi Eliyahu would travel with Rabbi Eizman and other area rabbis to the Jordan Valley to visit the orchards. If they were inquiring about *kilayim*, hybrid species, Rabbi Eliyahu would actually taste the leaves in order to know whether they were one species or two.

One time, Rabbi Eliyahu wanted to see if the small leaves on a grafted tree were the same as those on the original tree. He crawled under the tree, took the leaves from the branches of the grafted tree, and compared them to the leaves of the original tree. By observing Rabbi Eliyahu's investigations, Rabbi Eizman learned how to do his own practical rabbinic work.

"When it came to matters of *taharah* (states of ritual purity), I really sensed that he was ruling according to some kind of Divine inspiration," Rabbi Eizman recalled. "I asked him once if that was the case, but he didn't respond. Another time, he jokingly answered that he was. After the fact, I realized it wasn't a joke, but the truth — it was just that the way he said things made it seem as if he had denied it."

Situation by Situation, Case by Case

Rabbi Eliyahu was known for considering everything when he issued a halachic ruling, from the timing to the circumstances to the people involved. If a woman approached him on Thursday, wondering about the kashrut of a particular chicken, he might say that it wasn't permissible, but if she brought that same chicken to him on an Erev Shabbat, he might permit the use of that chicken. He wasn't being lenient or compromising his standards or Jewish law in any way; it was just that he knew the halachah so thoroughly. On one occasion, something was acceptable, and on another occasion, it was not.

One time, Rabbi Eliyahu was asked about the acceptability of high school girls performing in front of their parents, both the mothers and the fathers. The school had apparently been holding such performances for many years. *Little by little, I shall drive them away from you,* Rabbi Eliyahu said, quoting the Humash.[56] He explained that even though the situation was less than ideal and compromised the girls' modesty, there were lenient opinions to rely on for that year. But, just a year later when the same principal approached him regarding the same issue, Rabbi Eliyahu said the time had come to stop.

He also permitted that same principal to be present when the girls in his high school were singing Shabbat songs, even though the other staff members and guests would need to leave the room during the singing. It wasn't a matter of leniency. Rabbi Eliyahu simply knew the halachah and understood the spirit of the Torah, applying it appropriately to each person in his or her role. He truly fulfilled the verse, *After Hashem, your G-d, you should walk.*[57]

Rabbi Eliyahu was also known for issuing rulings that promoted unity between Jews, especially between Sephardim and Ashkenazim. Although he wrote an entire book of Jewish law based on the rulings of the Ben Ish Hai,[58] which followed the Sephardic approach to halachah, he later published Sephardic guidelines to

---

56. *Shemot* 23:30.

57. *Devarim* 13:5.

58. After Rabbi Eliyahu's passing, his assistants noted how much he revered and loved the Ben Ish Hai. "He would mention the Ben Ish Hai numerous times during the day, every day, and would always refer to him as Morenu V'Rabbenu Ateret Roshenu HaBen Ish Hai

Rabbi Mordechai Eliyahu with the Klausenberger Rebbe,
Rabbi Yekusiel Yehudah Halberstam

the *Kitzur Shulhan Aruch*, which is based on Ashkenazi custom. He wanted there to be at least one volume of Jewish law that could be used by both Sephardim and Ashkenazim.

Although Rabbi Eliyahu definitely had one hand in the world of Kabbalah, he always ruled according to halachah.[59] He was known for saying, "Rabbi Shimon bar Yohai ruled like this, and so did the Ari…"

He explained that taking Kabbalah into account in modern-day halachah was possible in part because of the needs of the generation. Jews of all stripes — both Sephardim and Ashkenazim

---

every time," his former secretary, Mrs. Naomi Knobel, related (via e-mail to the editor, April 10, 2019).

59. This was similar to the style of the Ben Ish Hai and the Hida, Rabbi Haim Yosef David Azoulay, 1724–1806. When issuing halachic rulings they would take the Arizal's opinions into account.

— are searching for the Tree of Life (*Etz Haim*) that's found in the Torah, in addition to the Tree of Knowledge (*Etz Da'at*), he would explain.

Rabbi Eliyahu felt that modern-day Jews are more open to the inner wisdom of Torah, viewing the people as living in the generation of the Redemption. He felt that the search for deep and internal insight is vital for people and it must be taken into account, even in halachic rulings. Of course, he also strongly believed that every decision depended on *siyatta d'Shmaya* (Heavenly help) — not in place of learned, informed conclusions, but alongside them.

Rabbi Eliyahu was known for his open discussions about Divine inspiration. He regularly told people that when Jewish law and Divine inspiration conflict, one should rule according to halachah, but should still strive for the truth. In one such instance, a rabbi approached Rabbi Eliyahu with a stained garment, seeking to clarify whether or not the stain was *tahor* (pure). "According to halachah," Rabbi Eliyahu said, "the stain is pure. But really, the woman is impure."

The questioner asked Rabbi Eliyahu how he should rule. Rabbi Eliyahu said that the woman was pure — but that her rabbi should keep in mind the truth. The rabbi returned to the woman's husband and shared the seemingly confusing and conflicting decision. The husband said it was no longer relevant. Clearly, Rabbi Eliyahu had a broader perspective, seeing beyond the stain.

In another circumstance, a *kohen* called Rabbi Eliyahu with an emergency. He had been working at the Sugat[60] factory, where his hand was severed. He had been advised to wrap the severed hand in ice and race to the hospital, where they might be able to reattach it. The *kohen* wanted to know if he was allowed to travel

---

60. An Israeli brand known for the sugar and other food items they produce.

in the ambulance with the hand, as it might be impure and he was a *kohen*.[61]

"It's permitted!" Rabbi Eliyahu said. "And go fast!"

Later, when Rabbi Eliyahu told this story, he explained that he didn't actually know at that moment why it was permissible for the *kohen* to travel in the ambulance. But he later learned that the severed hand was pure. He cited the story of *Bene Yisrael* standing at Har Sinai: Their souls departed at the moment that G-d began to speak, yet they were not considered as actually being dead. After their souls were restored, they did not need to purify themselves in a *mikvah*. Rabbi Eliyahu viewed the severed hand in the same way.

On another occasion, Rabbi Eliyahu had to decide on a case where, according to the details that had been presented to him, a particular woman's children all seemed to be *mamzerim* (children of a forbidden marriage).[62] He prayed and prayed, begging for Heavenly help in finding a way to permit the children according to Jewish law. That Heavenly help soon materialized: He discovered a book on his own shelves that held the answer. And when he opened it, the answer was on that exact page. It discussed the sordid secret of a man who wanted to declare his own children *mamzerim* because of a financial conflict with his wife.

These stories aren't just about a great and righteous rabbi. They're a guide for all rabbis, everywhere, in knowing that G-d is with them at every moment, guiding every decision. As the verse says, *G-d stands in the Divine assembly.*[63]

---

61. *Kohanim* strive to maintain their ritual purity so that they will be able to serve in the Temple when it is rebuilt.

62. According to Jewish law, such children would be forbidden from marrying other Jews.

63. *Tehillim* 82:1.

LOVING YOUR FELLOW

Being a Friend, Halachically Speaking

People often assume that detail-oriented, fastidious people are less personable or dynamic than their more carefree peers. Rabbi Eliyahu defied that stereotype. Although he was extremely careful with every facet of Jewish law, he was renowned for his friendliness and vibrancy. His understanding of and empathy for others was extraordinary.

Rabbi Eliyahu's capacity to identify with, consider, and appreciate

others was all encompassing. He was able to see situations — and the people involved in them — from both a personal perspective and a more general standpoint — simultaneously. Though Rabbi Eliyahu was one of the busiest people, often coping with sleep-deprivation and a gamut of urgent and difficult issues, he always had an aura of affability and happiness, displaying astonishing tranquility and calmness in the face of all manner of situations.

Rabbi Eliyahu blessing one of his congregants

Moshe Cohen, a resident of Bet El who frequently consulted Rabbi Eliyahu, credited the rabbi with teaching him to think ahead as a matter of course. Whether it was to plan for whatever situations in kashrut might arise at an event, to arrange for a *minyan* in some far-off location, or to take into consideration who would be attending a particular affair, he taught people to be prudent in their preparations.

Mr. Cohen once remarked, "If you look at any kind of catered event in a hall, from the side and from afar, everything appears to flow smoothly. But, in truth, everything was very precisely thought-out — and everything was done with happiness and care. That was all Rabbi Eliyahu; it was his legacy."

A Quarter and a Third

For nearly ten years after his marriage, Rabbi Eliyahu sat and studied Torah from morning to night, while his wife, Tzviyah,

Rabbi Mordechai Eliyahu at his wedding to Rabbanit
Tzviyah (Credit: Eliyahu Family Archives)

supported the family. They lived very modestly during this time, spending only what was absolutely necessary. During those first years, they didn't even have the money to buy a refrigerator. Instead, they would purchase ice from a supplier who passed through the streets with his horse and wagon, selling ice to those who had no refrigerator.

Whenever the *rabbanit* would purchase the ice, she would buy a quarter of a block, but when the rabbi would be the one to make the purchase, he'd request a third of a block. When the vendor asked Rabbi Eliyahu why he took a third of a block while his wife would only purchase a quarter, the young rabbi answered, "I want to make things easier for my wife, so she won't have to go without."

Rabbi Eliyahu told him that the Talmud says that whoever honors his wife will become rich in the end.[64] The ice-seller saw the respect with which Rabbi Eliyahu treated his wife and it made quite an impression on him.

Years later, when Rabbi Eliyahu became the chief rabbi of Israel, that same ice-seller was hired to guard the entrance to the chief rabbinate. The guard immediately recognized Rabbi Eliyahu as the same young man who used to take a third of a block of ice instead of a quarter. And Rabbi Eliyahu, in turn, recognized him, and immediately went to shake the man's hand.

The guard was so overcome and emotional, he couldn't get more than a few words out of his mouth: "Ah, a quarter and a third!"

High on Life

There was a very serious and devoted young man who used to be a heavy drug user. He had started out with recreational drugs and then moved on to successively harder and heavier drugs, seeking more intense experiences. He had tried nearly every combination out there until there was only one thing left to try: a drug that sends users into powerful, very long-lasting hallucinations.

---

64. See *Bava Metzia* 59a.

It wasn't easy for him to access this drug: Not only did he have to work and save money to buy it, this boy had to make special connections with dealers who could acquire it for him. When he finally had the drug in his possession, he decided that the best, loftiest place to try it was at the Kotel. And the greatest, most ideal time? Shabbat.

He figured that by swallowing the drug at the Kotel at that time, he would get as close as he possibly could to G-d. He waited until Erev Shabbat to take the drug, and entered Shabbat high and flying. The hallucinations made him feel tremendously joyful and radiant, and they imbued him with strong feelings of holiness. He desperately wanted to share his experience with someone, to describe his emotions and the sensations he was feeling. But, looking around, he knew no one there would understand him. Everyone around him, everyone he knew, even his family and friends, wouldn't be able to relate to him. He felt they were on far too low a level. However, there was one person he believed *could* understand: Rabbi Mordechai Eliyahu.

The young man immediately left the Kotel plaza and started walking to Rabbi Eliyahu's house. When he finally arrived, Rabbi Eliyahu opened the door, took one look at the boy, and immediately understood what kind of condition this kid was in. "What you're feeling now is nothing. It's not real," Rabbi Eliyahu said, waving his hand in dismissal. "When you come off the drug, come back to me. I'll teach you how to reach a much higher place. But just know that it's a 'long shortcut.'"

The young man did indeed return after Shabbat, and Rabbi Eliyahu sat down with him, true to his word. He understood and recognized the emotions the boy was experiencing and was able to help him attain those feelings through a kosher means: Torah study and mitzvah observance. Nevertheless, Rabbi Eliyahu kept emphasizing that the road one must travel to get there is "the long path that *is* the short path."

The boy took it all upon himself, donning *tzitzit* right then and there — and making a *Sheheheyanu* blessing on his new garment. He went on to study in Machon Meir, where he delved into Torah and Talmud. And yes, he eventually reached higher places than he ever had with the drugs.

Today that young man is married, with a family, and he has made it his life's mission to spread the light of Torah in all the darkest places, never forgetting that someone once did the same for him.[65]

Tithing Time

Rabbi Eliyahu became quite active in drawing people closer to Torah. He would frequently quote the Talmudic saying that "whoever teaches Torah to his friend's son merits to sit in the Heavenly yeshivah, as it is written, *[Thus G-d said] … If you repent I will bring you back and let you stand before Me.*"[66]

Rabbi Eliyahu giving a lecture

---

65. As heard from Rabbi Nehemiah Tau, son of Rabbi Tzvi Tau of Yeshivat Har Hamor, and *rosh yeshivah* of Midbarah K'Eden.

66. *Bava Metzia* 85a, quoting *Yirmiyahu* 15:19.

Rabbi Eliyahu would explain that whoever teaches Torah to the son of an unlearned man receives incredible blessings; G-d even cancels decrees on his behalf. He cited the verse in *Yirmiyahu, If you bring forth the precious from out of the vile, then you will be like My own mouth.*[67] He would say that if it wasn't written in the Talmud, a person couldn't possibly say such a thing. To compare oneself to the "mouth" of the Holy One blessed is He? "Would could say such a thing?" Rabbi Eliyahu would ask. Then he would explain that the value of spreading Torah is far greater than a person could ever imagine.

He would often discuss the pain Rabbi Yehudah Tzadkah, his uncle, would feel when he contemplated the sorry state of the Jewish people. He related that once, Rabbi Tzadkah was passing a retirement home on Jerusalem's Jaffa Road, and he saw elderly men sitting outside engaged in some heated debate. Some were saying "seven," while others were saying "eight."

Rabbi Tzadkah stopped to ask what they were arguing about. The men answered that they had counted the various vehicles that had driven by and they were in disagreement over whether there had been seven or eight.

"Perhaps a tow truck drove by, hauling a car, and some of you counted one vehicle while others counted two?" Rabbi Tzadkah suggested.

"How did you know?" one of the men asked.

Rabbi Tzadkah didn't answer. Instead, he asked them a question, "Why is this so important? Why do you need to know how many vehicles passed by?"

"We're bored," they answered.

---

67. 15:19.

"So let's go inside and learn some Torah," Rabbi Tzadkah proposed.

They took him up on the offer. That study session led to more learning sessions. The men found it to be truly enjoyable. Rabbi Tzadkah returned every day to teach them a class. He eventually sent one of his students to teach the elderly men, explaining to his *talmidim* that even though it might have felt as if they were taking time away from their own studies, this was something absolutely necessary and important, justifying any time they were losing from their own Torah learning.

"This was how our father Avraham spread Torah," Rabbi Eliyahu concluded when he related this tale. "Just as a person has to tithe his money, he has to tithe his time. That's how important it is to teach Torah to others."

Rebuke Wrapped in Candy

A Safed resident approached Rabbi Shmuel Eliyahu, Hacham Mordechai's son and the current chief rabbi of Safed, with a story about Hacham Mordechai. He had been in Hacham Mordechai's Torah class and, once, he did something so out of place that he deserved a severe censure.

Indeed, Rabbi Eliyahu called him over, rebuked him, and even raised his hand, giving him something between a slap and a caress. With his other hand, Rabbi Eliyahu presented him with a candy. "Take it and make a blessing."

"I have received more than a few reprimands and smacks in my life," the man said. "But I never received a rebuke that affected me like the one I'd gotten from Rabbi Eliyahu. He knew how to deliver a rebuke with such love and care; it touched the deepest, most inner parts of my being."

Chapter Two

Caution and Vigilance

Every person should engage in self-contemplation, pondering what his next step in his service of G-d should be, according to the Torah's path. Afterward, a person must reflect on his actions, asking himself whether he indeed followed the right course. By doing this, a person can sanctify himself and his actions. As it is written, *Give careful thought to the path of your feet and all your ways will be established.*[1] And, as it is said, *Let us search and examine our ways and return to Hashem.*[2]

---

1. *Mishle* 4:26.
2. *Eichah* 3:40.

In loving memory of
Aaron Newman

לעילוי נשמת
אהרן יצחק בן שלום הלוי

Steve and Daniele Delouya Newman
Josef and Leslie Newman
Nissa, Natalie, and Jonah Newman

THE HONOR OF OTHERS

A Matter of Life and Death

Rabbi Shmuel Eliyahu recalled that when he was young, his father would receive the public at their home. As soon as Hacham Mordechai returned from his morning prayers, there would already be people lined up waiting for him.

Rabbi Eliyahu speaking to congregants after prayers

He would sit with them, answering their questions and helping them until he had to leave for the *bet din*. That was his schedule day in and day out: Rabbi Eliyahu would receive visitors until the very last minute and then have a bite of breakfast. Hacham Mordechai was very careful about leaving the house on time so that he would not keep people waiting for him at the *bet din*. To get there promptly, he had to end his receiving hours by nine o'clock.

One morning, the young Shmuel heard someone shouting in the area where the visitors would sit as they waited to be called. When he went to investigate, he saw a woman arguing with Rabbi Yehudah Mutzafi,[3] Rabbi Eliyahu's assistant. Rabbi Mutzafi was telling her that Rabbi Eliyahu had to leave and that she should come back the following day. But the woman was insistent, explaining that her question was concerning a matter of life and death.

Hacham Mordechai heard the shouting and came out of his room,

---

3. Rabbi Yehudah Mutzafi passed away in 2017.

telling the woman she could enter. She went in and consulted with Rabbi Eliyahu for some ten minutes — a considerable delay when he had already planned to leave. When she finally left the room, Rabbi Eliyahu called after her, "If that doesn't work, come back to me."

After she had gone, Rabbi Mutzafi asked Rabbi Eliyahu if it had really been a matter of life and death.

"Not exactly," Rabbi Eliyahu said. "But it was a very important question."

Rabbi Mutzafi asked what the very important question was, to which Rabbi Eliyahu responded, "The woman has a cat that hasn't eaten for several days. She's worried that it's going to die and she came to ask me what to do."

The young Shmuel couldn't help but smirk as he asked his father, "What did you answer her?"

"I suggested that she change the cat's food and take it outside. I gave her a few suggestions, and I told her she should come back if none of them work."

"And *that* was the question that was so urgent that the rabbi had to miss his breakfast and will go hungry to the *bet din*?" Rabbi Mutzafi asked.

Rabbi Eliyahu nodded. "That was actually the most significant question asked to me this entire morning. The cat is the center of that woman's life. She was so distressed by her pet not eating. If her cat would die, she would be in tremendous anguish. We need to help each person in his or her place, wherever he or she is holding in life."

Years later, Rabbi Shmuel reflected on this story, saying, "At that time, this story confused me. But it has accompanied me through the years, and I preserve the memory of it as an important reminder to conduct myself with sensitivity, even to those who are so different from me."

Making Peace between the Bedouin

The Be'er Sheva rabbinical court used to be situated adjacent to the Muslim religious court. Muslims from the surrounding area, mostly Negev Bedouin, would bring their conflicts to their court to get them adjudicated according to shari'a law (derived from the Koran).

There was once a serious and intense clash between a number of lower-level sheiks and the son of the Negev's most prominent sheik. Blood revenge was quite common among the Bedouin, and if a person was killed — accidentally or deliberately — his family could avenge his death through reciprocal murders.

Given that both sides of the quarrel involved prestigious Bedouin families, they sought a quick resolution at the Muslim religious court. But even choosing the presiding judge became a battle...

Rabbi Eliyahu was serving on the Be'er Sheva *bet din* at that time,[4] and he was still quite young — around thirty-one at most. As he was walking to the *bet din*, he saw the large crowd gathered

Rabbi Mordechai Eliyahu receives his *semichut* to become a *dayan*, in the President's house, 1960 (credit: Eliyahu Family)

---

4. He served on the Be'er Sheva *bet din* from 1960 to 1964.

outside the Muslim court. There was quite a tumult, as both sides had brought along numerous friends, family members, and supporters.

Rabbi Eliyahu meanwhile saw some bread lying on the street; he picked it up, kissed it, and laid it on a ledge where it wouldn't be stepped on.[5] Suddenly he noticed a sheik running after him, along with two Israeli police officers. The sheik called to Rabbi Eliyahu in Arabic, shouting, "Hey, you!"

Pretending he didn't understand Arabic, Rabbi Eliyahu tried to continue walking, but the sheik wouldn't let him go. The police officers explained to Rabbi Eliyahu that this Bedouin sheik wanted Rabbi Eliyahu to officiate in the case between the Bedouin clans. They said that the sheik had seen Rabbi Eliyahu pick up the bread from the ground, and it had made quite an impression on him. He now wanted Rabbi Eliyahu to arbitrate his son's case.

Rabbi Eliyahu politely explained that he received a salary to mediate cases at the rabbinical court and had no jurisdiction on the Muslim court. The verses from the morning prayers came to his mind, *May it be Your will, O L-rd my G-d, and G-d of my forefathers, that You rescue me today and every day from brazen men…and from a harsh trial and a harsh opponent, whether he is a member of the covenant or whether he is not a member of the covenant.*[6] But Rabbi Eliyahu soon saw there was nothing he could do; if the other side agreed, he was going to have to serve as the arbitrator between the two sides.

The Bedouin sheiks unanimously agreed that Rabbi Eliyahu would make a first-rate intermediary. As he went to judge their case, he thought, *At least this will make a bit of a* kiddush Hashem *(a sanctification of G-d's Name). When non-Jews recognize the righteousness*

---

5. Many observant Jews are careful to treat bread with respect.

6. From the *yehi ratzon* at the end of *Birkat Hashahar.*

of the Torah and its followers, it elevates Hashem's greatness in their eyes. After all, as the verse says, *You shall safeguard them and perform them, for it is your wisdom and discernment in the eyes of the nations who shall hear of these decrees and who shall say, "Surely a wise and discerning people is this great nation."*[7]

So Rabbi Eliyahu heard their case, and instead of issuing a judgment, he managed to arrange an apology and a compromise between them, and everyone went away satisfied.

Setting Priorities Straight

When the chief rabbinate moved into new quarters,[8] it was a very hectic time. Unfortunately, many of the letters that had been sent to Rabbi Eliyahu piled up during that time and sat unanswered. The secretary there, Mrs. Naomi Knobel, was distressed to think of so many people waiting to receive responses to their questions, many of them pressing.

Rabbi Mordechai Eliyahu's official stamp as a member of the Bet Din Hagadol (credit: Eliyahu Family)

---

7. *Devarim* 4:6.

8. This was in 1992.

She called Rabbanit Eliyahu, asking her if it would be possible to give at least several of the most urgent letters to her husband. There were hundreds waiting in the office, and he was understandably quite busy, but if he could answer even a few, it would alleviate at least some of the backup and pressure. The *rabbanit* told Mrs. Knobel that her husband had said she should bring the letters right away.

The secretary sat and worked with Rabbi Eliyahu for two and a half hours. He was interrupted numerous times with urgent telephone calls, but each time after giving his ruling, advice, or blessing, he would instantly return to the exact subject at hand, picking up just where he had left off in the letter. While this was going on, the *rabbanit* came in and said they would need to complete their work quickly, as a prestigious rabbi had arrived with a whole entourage and wanted to speak with Rabbi Eliyahu.

Rabbi Eliyahu asked if he had made an appointment, to which

his wife responded in the negative. "So then let him wait," Rabbi Eliyahu said.

The secretary was surprised, but didn't comment about it. When the *rabbanit* returned several minutes later to ask what she should do, as they were pressuring her, her husband answered, "The senders of these letters have been waiting an extremely long time for an answer. I must first finish this work. If the rabbi can't wait, he should make an appointment for another time."

He sat with the secretary for another forty-five minutes, working on the letters.

Care for the *Kohanim*

Rabbi Eliyahu never set limits on synagogue cantors — not about the length of prayers nor about the tune or style used.[9] There was just one place in the prayer service where he was strict: with *Birkat Kohanim* (the Priestly Blessing). When it came to *Birkat Kohanim*, Rabbi Eliyahu would warn cantors not to draw out the melody too long. He explained that the *kohanim* were standing

9. As heard from Rabbi Ezra Barnea, cantor in the Hechal Yaakov synagogue.

with their arms raised and their muscles could start to ache if the cantor prolonged the prayer.

He would also caution the cantor against changing the tune while pronouncing the Priestly Blessing. Rabbi Eliyahu explained that while cantors are professionals who can move seamlessly from one melody to another, even within a single blessing, *kohanim* aren't professionals and they can't switch tunes so quickly. They need to follow the cantor's lead while making blessings — and if the melody changes, they're liable to lose their concentration and get confused.

Advance Apology

Rabbi Eliyahu was renowned for his sensitivity to others. The *rosh yeshivah* of the Maale Ephraim yeshivah, Rabbi Ariel Farjun, had the privilege to work with Rabbi Eliyahu on the rabbi's halachah book. From their very first meeting about the book, Rabbi Eliyahu said to Rabbi Farjun, "Before we begin, I want to ask your forgiveness in advance if I offend you during the work."

Rabbi Farjun later remarked, "And, as could be expected, that didn't happen even once." He recalled that in one of the files he gave to Rabbi Eliyahu, there was a section he had meant to delete prior to sharing the text. It was neither clear nor logical, but Rabbi Farjun had overlooked it and mistakenly given it to the rabbi. Nevertheless, Rabbi Eliyahu read the passage again and again, trying to make sense of it, even though Rabbi Farjun had explained that the whole section was there by mistake. Rabbi Eliyahu was just that careful about the sensitivities of others.

"*Shalom*, Mordechai Speaking"

When Mrs. Naomi Knobel, Rabbi Eliyahu's secretary, was still new on the job in the rabbi's bureau, Rabbi Eliyahu called the office. When she answered the phone, he identified himself as "Mordechai" and asked for the phone number of a particular individual.

As Mrs. Knobel was a beginner, she didn't know who that person was, and she told Rabbi Eliyahu she didn't know anyone by that name. Of course, she had no idea it was Rabbi Eliyahu himself on the line...

The rabbi called again and asked to be transferred to the other secretary in the office. It was only then that Mrs. Knobel realized just who was calling. She was deeply embarrassed and went to ask Rabbi Eliyahu for forgiveness the next morning. Instead, Rabbi Eliyahu responded, "But I'm the one who needs to ask forgiveness — from you, for causing you such embarrassment."

She added another, similar memory. "I'll never forget asking his forgiveness before Yom Kippur one year, for things such as wasting his time with typos and such, but he stopped me with his hand, brushing off my entreaty with a nod and smile. Then he left the office and started down the stairs, only to come right back and say to me, 'And I forgot to seek forgiveness from you for all the troubles I bothered you with,'" she recalled. "I nearly fainted!"

Rain of Tears

Although Rabbi Eliyahu was very careful to honor every individual, he was especially cautious when it came to children. His driver, Mr. Roni Levi, shares that Rabbi Eliyahu was once invited to the bar mitzvah of an orphan, but the rabbi couldn't attend, as he was scheduled as one of the keynote speakers at a rabbinical conference at one of the Dead Sea-area hotels.

The driver and Rabbi Eliyahu set out for the conference, but while they were on the road, a tremendous downpour began. The rain was so heavy that streams in the Judean Desert overflowed

Rabbi Eliyahu testing a young student

and flooded the roads to the Dead Sea. The route to the hotels was completely blocked, and Roni was forced to turn around and head back to Jerusalem.

As they drove, Rabbi Eliyahu suddenly turned to his driver and said, "Please take me to the bar mitzvah. All this water is the tears of the bar mitzvah boy." Roni wondered how the rabbi could know that the young boy was really crying. He thought that perhaps the rabbi was exaggerating just a tad.

When they arrived at the bar mitzvah, everyone was surprised and delighted to see Rabbi Eliyahu, as he had already informed them that he wouldn't be able to attend. Much to the family's great pleasure, Rabbi Eliyahu stayed a great deal longer than was his usual custom. As Rabbi Eliyahu and his driver finally rose to depart from the hall, the bar mitzvah boy accompanied them out. The young man told Roni, "When Rabbi Eliyahu said he wouldn't be able to come to my bar mitzvah, I cried all night. And now I'm so happy that he attended and blessed me."

Roni later remarked that he felt the boy's words were meant especially for him. "I lacked faith in the rabbi's overarching vision. The young bar mitzvah boy's story set me straight."

Great Rabbi, Great Teacher

Rabbi Shmuel Katz, the principal of a school[10] in Har Nof, Jerusalem, recalled that year after year, his first-grade students were privileged to receive their first siddur and Humash from Rabbi Eliyahu in a beautiful and moving ceremony. For over twenty years, Rabbi Katz had been bringing his first-grade students to Rabbi Eliyahu for this momentous occasion in their lives.

One year, when the students and their parents arrived at Hechal Shlomo, the seat of the chief rabbinate, the children and their parents went to sit in the synagogue, waiting for the ceremony to begin. Meanwhile, Rabbi Katz went up to the third floor, where Rabbi Eliyahu's office was located, to tell Rabbi Shmuel Zafrani, the office manager, that they had arrived.

When Rabbi Katz entered the office, he felt as if the world was falling apart right before his eyes. There were many prominent rabbis, yeshivah heads, municipal chief rabbis, and more, all waiting to speak to Rabbi Eliyahu. Rabbi Katz greeted Rabbi Zafrani with a heavy heart. He was sure Rabbi Eliyahu would first receive all the rabbis and only then come down to the school event. It could take hours. Rabbi Katz worried that the children would never be able to wait so long, but he figured he had no other option but to try.

As Rabbi Katz turned to leave and go back downstairs, Rabbi

---

10. He is the principal of Bet Hasefer Hamossad Mamlachti-Dati Torani Har Nof.

Zafrani motioned for him to wait. "Rabbi Eliyahu is coming down to the event right away," he announced.

Rabbi Katz was shocked and delighted. He ran down the steps while Rabbi Eliyahu took the elevator.

The students and their parents were very excited to see Rabbi Eliyahu. They stood up immediately upon his arrival and began to sing. Many even managed to kiss his hand. Rabbi Eliyahu took a seat in the place that had been prepared for him, and Rabbi Katz went up onto the dais. He announced that he would not begin the ceremony with the usual greetings and blessings, as Rabbi Eliyahu was in a great hurry.

Rabbi Eliyahu giving a blessing to children (credit: Eliyahu Family)

"Who told you that?" Rabbi Eliyahu asked in surprise. "You should speak!"

Rabbi Katz had just seen it with his own eyes — the waiting room was full of prominent rabbis waiting to consult with him. But if Rabbi Eliyahu was telling him to speak, he would.

After he finished, Rabbi Eliyahu came up to the dais and blessed the students. He spiced his words with *midrashim* and stories, keeping the students and their parents entranced. He finished by asking them to never discard their siddur or Humash, even if it was no longer usable, but to save it to show their grandchildren one day.

When it was time to distribute the Humashim, Rabbi Katz again apologized to the students and parents about having to hurry. The presentation of the Humashim and the requisite picture taking would have to be carried out quickly, as the rabbi was in a rush to get back to his office. But, once again, Rabbi Eliyahu rejoined, "Who said I'm in a hurry?"

The Humashim were given out as if Rabbi Eliyahu had all the time in the world. He patiently presented each child with a Humash, asked each one to kiss his hand, and then placed his hand on each boy's head to give him a blessing. After this, he shook the boys' hands and then smiled patiently while their parents snapped photos.

When a six- or seven-year-old child receives his first Humash

Rabbi Eliyahu cutting a child's hair

and siddur from such a dignified rabbi — wearing the special garb of the chief rabbi of Israel — it makes an impression. Rabbi Katz believed Rabbi Eliyahu devoted so much time and energy to the ceremony because he saw it as a true investment in the next generation.

The Rabbi Makes Repairs

One Purim night, a number of people arrived at Rabbi Eliyahu's house to sing and dance as part of their Purim festivities. Around midnight, Rabbi Eliyahu's family began hinting that it was getting late, as the rabbi was planning to rise early the next morning to pray at sunrise. Everyone began to leave.

Suddenly, Rabbi Eliyahu noticed a young boy, around seven years old, crying. He called the boy over to him, asking, "Why are you crying? It's Purim. We're supposed to be happy!"

"The sword from my costume broke," the boy answered between sobs.

Rabbi Eliyahu led him to the kitchen. "Don't worry; I'll fix it." The rabbi walked over to the stove, lit the flame, and heated up both edges of the sword. He then placed a clip between the sides and stuck the plastic sword back together.

When he later recalled this story, Rabbi Eliyahu's son Rabbi Yosef noted that his father appeared completely relaxed the whole time, despite the fact that it was so late at night and the repair took at least fifteen minutes. But, he added, his father always felt that everything and anything the Jewish people were going through was important to him — even part of a child's costume.

SAVING LIVES — BODY, SOUL, AND SPIRIT

Treating the Mentally Ill with Love

No matter how much prestige or prominence Rabbi Eliyahu earned, he always maintained his quiet patience and simple humility. One of the rabbi's many petitioners suffered from serious clinical depression. This woman experienced terrible insomnia because of it, as well as other debilitating symptoms, and the woman eventually ended up in a psychiatric hospital.

This depressed young woman would frequently call her brother, who had a relationship with Rabbi Eliyahu, and ask him to have the rabbi pray for her to get well. She would also call the rabbi's home or office — sometimes as often as four or five times a day — seeking the rabbi's blessings. Rabbi Eliyahu always listened and gave her the blessings she sought.

During this time, this woman compulsively gave money to charity. She was obsessively worried that she perhaps had an obligation to donate money, so she gave without limits and without considering her personal financial state. She would call Rabbi Eliyahu for reassurance, and Rabbi Eliyahu always answered her with patience, encouragement, and blessings.

One Motzae Shabbat, the sick woman was feeling particularly low. She called her brother, and asked him to call Rabbi Eliyahu. Rabbi Eliyahu said that he would like to see the two of them and they should come over right then. The pair went and stayed with Rabbi Eliyahu until almost midnight, getting his blessings. The depressed woman left feeling a bit lighter and happier.

From then on, she would go often to the rabbi's home for his encouragement and blessings, and each time she would leave feeling stronger and more emotionally regulated. Her obsessive fretting abated and her depression subsided. She began to sleep deeply and soundly once again. She felt she had finally recovered.

After she was well, the woman discovered that Rabbi Eliyahu had been mentioning her name in his prayers as many as five or six times a day. Not only that, he would also frequently pray for her at the tombs of the righteous and at the Kotel.

People with complicated medical histories often experience difficulty in finding a marriage partner, and this woman was no exception. One day, she was at a memorial service for a prominent Moroccan rabbi, Rabbi Moshe Vizgon.[11] Rabbi Eliyahu was also there, as he had been invited to speak about the deceased.

After his talk, this woman approached Rabbi Eliyahu, saying, "I'm feeling so, so bitter inside."

"Why? What happened? What's making you so resentful and angry?" he asked.

"Lavan, the Aramite, was totally evil, and he wanted to kill our forefather Yaakov. Yet, this great sinner merited such a righteous *chatan* for a son-in-law! How is that possible?"

Rabbi Eliyahu smiled and blessed her, understanding that she was thinking about herself and her own future. "May it be G-d's will that you, too, should have a *chatan* (a bridegroom) as righteous as Jacob."

Almost immediately thereafter, the woman was introduced to the man who would become her husband. And he had every character trait she had sought and desired: he was a scholar, a G-d-fearing individual, and someone full of love for G-d and the Jewish

---

11. Rabbi Vizgon was born in 1904, in Mogador, Morocco — modern-day Essaouira. He served as a rabbinical judge there, later becoming the head of the rabbinical court in Marrakech. He passed away in Jerusalem in 1996.

people. He was compassionate and considerate and had many other wonderful qualities.

Even today, she still feels that this wonderful gift was no accident. "I know it is all in the merit of Rabbi Eliyahu's many, many prayers for me," she said. "They went straight up to Heaven."

War Is War

Many IDF soldiers would come to Rabbi Eliyahu before their official induction, seeking his blessing. On one such occasion Rabbi Eliyahu told the young soldiers about a time when Rabbi Shimon bar Yohai was trying to save the Jewish people from terrible Roman decrees. Rabbi Shimon asked G-d to send an angel to help him. But instead, G-d sent a demon known as Ben Tamalion.[12]

Rabbi Shimon was hurt, asking G-d, "Is this what I deserve? Even Hagar, Abraham's concubine, merited having an angel sent to her three times. But for me You send a demon?"

Finally, Rabbi Shimon calmed down and said, "Let a miracle happen anyway." And he agreed to the demon's mission.

"But really," Rabbi Eliyahu asked, "why did the Holy One blessed is He send a demon and not an angel?" He looked at the young soldiers. "The answer is that in wars against the enemies of Israel, sometimes a demon is better than an angel. The angel must do precisely as he is told, performing his mission without veering left or right. But in war, you need to be like demons. To save lives you may need to do things and act in ways that are not exactly according to instructions." The soldiers took his words to heart.

Feeling Everyone's Pain

Rabbi Eliyahu was the kind of person who felt everyone's pain.

---

12. This story is found in the Talmud, *Me'ilah* 17b.

He carried it in his heart, worrying over everyone's worries, and truly feeling the pain and heartaches of all those who shared their troubles with him.

One time, Rabbi Eliyahu's brother Rabbi Shimon was feeling severely ill, and he was admitted to Jerusalem's Hadassah Hospital for testing. When all was said and done, the doctors prescribed a headache medicine and sent him on his way. Though he took the pills as instructed, the pain did not diminish.

Finally, he went to see his brother, Hacham Mordechai. "The problem is with your heart, not your head," he said. "You need to see a cardiologist."

Rabbi Shimon took his brother's advice and made an appointment to consult with a specialist. But the doctor didn't find anything amiss. "It's all in your head," he said. "I think everything's fine." He suggested that it could be anxiety-related, saying that Rabbi Shimon was perhaps not really feeling pain in his diaphragm.

But all through the following Shabbat, Rabbi Shimon had tremendous discomfort and pain. He went back to his brother and related what the doctors had said.

"I'm telling you, it's a heart problem," Hacham Mordechai said. "You need to hire a doctor privately and have him perform a cardiac catheterization."

Rabbi Shimon repeated what the cardiologist had told him, but Hacham Mordechai only repeated himself. "You need to engage a private doctor and have him do a catheterization."

Rabbi Shimon followed his brother's directions, hiring a cardiologist to do the catheterization. He found that Rabbi Shimon's arteries were almost totally blocked, with 99 percent obstruction. The doctor was completely dumbfounded. How could it be that the other doctors hadn't seen such a dramatic blockage? He arranged an emergency bypass surgery for Rabbi Shimon.

The doctor said that the initial surgery would take four and a half hours, but that Rabbi Shimon would need to remain unconscious for about two and a half weeks following the operation. Because the blockage was so extensive, they would have to perform a number of bypasses during that time.

Before the surgery, Rabbi Shimon went to see his brother Hacham Mordechai to apprise him of everything that had transpired. "Don't worry," Hacham Mordechai said. He instructed his brother to go to the Mount of Olives to pray at a particular grave for a complete and quick recovery.

Rabbi Shimon did as he had been told and then went into heart surgery. The bypass took only half the time the doctors had expected, and he regained consciousness within only a day of the surgery — and not the anticipated two and a half weeks. The surgeons claimed it was an open miracle. During the surgery, Rabbi Shimon had seen his brother's face the entire time, and he knew that his brother was praying for him and blessing him. Perhaps that had something to do with it…

While Rabbi Shimon was recovering, Hacham Mordechai came to visit him every single day, even though he was so busy and had numerous obligations. On every visit, he shared a story and gave his brother blessings, leaving Rabbi Shimon and his family full of belief, trust, and hope.

After his release from the hospital, Rabbi Shimon spoke with Rabbanit Tzviyah. She shared that on the day of the surgery, Hacham Mordechai didn't receive anyone, canceled all his meetings, and closeted himself in his room. He spent the day praying and reciting Tehillim on his brother's behalf. Even though Hacham Mordechai felt the pain of all those around him and truly cared for each person's suffering, he always remembered his own family, looking out for them, too.

When Rabbi Shimon recovered, he asked his cardiologist how it was possible that other doctors hadn't seen the obstruction initially. "A mistake like that is one in a million," he replied. Not with a brother like Hacham Mordechai...

What Did You Eat in Morocco?

Rabbi Yaakov Shkenazi, who served on the Sephardic Edah Haredit,[13] once said that Rabbi Eliyahu had learned the trait of *emet* (truth) from Rabbi Shkenazi's father-in-law, Rabbi Yehudah Tzadkah, as well as from Hacham Ezra Attiya. Both rabbis were *roshe yeshivah* in Yeshivat Porat Yosef. He shared a story to illustrate his point.

Hacham Ezra Attiya in the center, sitting with other great *mekubalim* of Yeshivat Porat Yosef

Once, a student approached Rabbi Tzadkah, asking him to sign a certificate on his behalf, but Rabbi Tzadkah said he could not.

"Why can't the Rosh Yeshivah sign?" the student complained. "Rabbi Bentzion Abba-Shaul signed. Can't the rabbi sign as well?"

---

13. Today he is a *posek* and author living in Jerusalem.

Rabbi Tzadkah pointed to the date on the document and explained, "The certificate is dated with yesterday's date, not today's. So it would be dishonest for me to sign something today that was dated for yesterday."

A similar incident occurred with Hacham Ezra, when a student sought his signature for a teaching certificate and Hacham Ezra refused. Hacham Ezra clarified that the document listed the location as being in the "Old City of Jerusalem," but seeing as they were in the new part of the city, signing it would be dishonest.

Hacham Ezra Attiya at the laying of the cornerstone for Yeshivat Porat Yosef

The student begged him to go ahead and sign it, saying it was urgent.

"If that's that case, then come with me," Hacham Ezra said. He put on his rabbinical robe and walked with the student from the new section of Jerusalem to the Old City, even though he was already aging and it was difficult for him to traverse such a distance on foot. There, in the Old City, he signed the certificate.

Rabbi Eliyahu loved his teachers very much and was inspired by their example. He strived for truth and worked to emulate them, unafraid of others' reactions or judgment of him. On one of his trips abroad, he visited a nursing home where the *mashgiah* (kashrut supervisor) was not doing his job properly. The facility's manager was taking full advantage of the *mashgiah's* negligence and was serving non-kosher food to the residents.

When Rabbi Eliyahu arrived at the old-age home, he asked the *mashgiah* to give him a tour. During the tour, the two of them met one of the residents. Rabbi Eliyahu asked the elderly Jew where he was from.

"Morocco," the old man answered.

"Did you keep kosher in Morocco?" Rabbi Eliyahu asked.

"Of course, Rabbi! Everything was kosher — our great rabbis supervised the slaughtering, and all the meat was *glatt kosher.*"

"And what do you eat here?" Rabbi Eliyahu asked him.

"I don't know. There's a *mashgiah,*" answered the elderly man.

The *mashgiah* heard and remained silent.

Rabbi Eliyahu turned to another resident, an elderly Algerian man, and asked him the same questions. Again, the *mashgiah* heard that this Jew had been very strict about kashrut, though he now relied on the *mashgiah.* Again, the *mashgiah* heard and remained silent.

Then the *mashgiah* tried to cut the tour short, offering some excuse, because he clearly saw where it was heading. But Rabbi Eliyahu wasn't deterred. He called the owners of the home and informed them that the entire place was not kosher, and that they would need to *kasher* all the utensils and appoint a G-d-fearing *mashgiah.*

There was obviously no limit to this *mashgiah's* chutzpah, as he later called Rabbi Eliyahu and protested. "Look what you've done to me!" he shouted. "You've shamed and embarrassed me. You've ruined my career!"

"You shamed yourself — and you *should* be feeling embarrassed,"

Rabbi Eliyahu responded. "You fed Jews non-kosher food. And now, instead of running away, you're complaining?"

The *mashgiah* finally got the message.

In Caution's Merit

Moshe Yaakov Luxenberg, who used to translate the *Kol Tzofecha parashah* sheets into French, once witnessed an interesting event in Hechal Yaakov, Rabbi Eliyahu's synagogue, on the night of Hoshana Rabbah. It was Rabbi Eliyahu's custom to spend the holy night learning in the study hall. He would take a few breaks

Rabbi Mordechai Eliyahu on Hoshana Rabbah

throughout the night to drink something, which he would do in the synagogue's sukkah. There, in the sukkah, was a table laden with all manners of delicacies and treats.

Mr. Luxenberg had the privilege of sitting directly opposite Rabbi Eliyahu. While he was sitting there, someone passed the rabbi a drink, on which he stood up to make a blessing. But as he watched, Mr. Luxenberg noticed the rabbi looking at something: a plate of salted peanuts.

Rabbi Eliyahu whispered something to one of the synagogue attendants. After a brief investigation, the rabbi said something, and all the peanuts were immediately removed from the table. Apparently, there was a problem with the kashrut of those peanuts, and Rabbi Eliyahu had somehow been able to discern it.

If Mr. Luxenberg hadn't witnessed this personally, he wouldn't have believed it, he said. After all, it was mindboggling to him that Rabbi Eliyahu could simply *feel* that there was something off about those peanuts. Mr. Luxenberg instantly thought of *Path of the Just*, which discusses the traits of caution and cleanliness. He knew that he had just seen that concept manifest before his eyes, something very few have seen — and something even fewer have succeeded in attaining.

THE POWER OF POSITIVITY

Good Signs

The last night of Pesah, a young boy, then around ten years old, became very irritable and upset, though he later could not recall why. He crawled under the table and sat there, angry and frustrated. His family thought it was best to give him space, letting him stay there to calm down.

Meanwhile, the boy's mother began to serve the fish, and something very bizarre occurred. The fish platter suddenly shattered in her hands, and shards flew everywhere. More pieces fell on the boy's empty chair than anywhere else. Just a moment later, the glass saltshaker shattered, too. It had just been sitting on the table, and it wasn't hot or close to anything hot. No one had touched it. It just exploded.

The whole family was quite disturbed by these uncanny events, and right after the holiday, the boy's father called Rabbi Yehudah Mutzafi, Hacham Mordechai's personal assistant. Although Rabbi Mutzafi attempted to calm them down and offer reassurances, the man wanted to speak with Rabbi Eliyahu to hear what he had to say on the matter.

The Sages say, *All dreams go after the mouth,*[14] suggesting that a dream's interpretation goes according to how one analyzes it. Rabbi Eliyahu, who always maintained a positive outlook in life, told the family that they could look forward to two pieces of good news in the near future. He asked the family to be in touch when those good things occurred.

It was only a few days later when the man called Rabbi Eliyahu

---

14. *Berachot* 55b.

back. They'd just purchased a new apartment and they had also celebrated the birth of a baby girl.[15]

Calming Down the *Rabbanit*

The *rabbanit* had very difficult pregnancies, during which she was mostly confined to bed and kept under close medical supervision. During one of the pregnancies, she required hospitalization. The other children were home with their father. It was wintertime, and as often happens at that time of year, the children got sick.

Rabbi Eliyahu didn't want to tell his wife about their illnesses because he feared that she would leave the hospital and rush home to take care of them. But one of the neighbors who went to visit her innocently mentioned it, not imagining that her children's fevers were being kept secret from her.

When Rabbi Eliyahu came to visit her, she was so worried that she begged him to let her leave the hospital and go home to take care of everyone. He knew very well that getting out of bed and going home would endanger her and the pregnancy, so he tried to dissuade her by saying that the children were really feeling okay.

But she wouldn't be convinced, and begged to see the children herself. In the end, Rabbi Eliyahu suggested that he bring their children to the hospital so she could see with her own eyes that they were fine. She agreed.

He went home, called a taxi, and loaded everyone inside. They then drove off to the hospital, where Rabbi Eliyahu asked the driver to park outside her window. Then he instructed the children to stay in the taxi and watch their mother's window. He told them that when they saw her window open, they should wave hello from their taxi window.

---

15. As heard from Ariel Even Daniel, who was the young boy in the story.

Rabbi Eliyahu then went up to his wife's room. When she saw him come in without the children, she cried, "I knew they were sick! You kept them home because you didn't want me to see them!"

Rabbi Eliyahu shook his head. "I brought them, and they're in a taxi right outside your window. But because it's so cold outside, I didn't want the children to leave the car. They could get sick."

The rabbi went over to the window and opened it. The children began to wave. When she saw the children happy and "healthy," she calmed down and agreed to remain in the hospital.

Years later, when Rabbi Eliyahu would retell the story, he'd ask with a twinkle in his eye, "So, what do you think? Should the neighbor who told my wife they were sick have to pay for the taxi?"

Chapter Three

Alacrity

Know that the angels are praised for this good trait, as it is said of them, *The strong warriors who do His bidding, to obey the voice of His word.*[1] And it is said, *And the* chayot *ran to and fro like the appearance of a flash of lightning.*[2]

Man is just a man, and not an angel. It is not possible for him to reach the height of an angel. But, certainly, he should do all that he can to get closer to the level of the angels. As David Hamelech would say, *I hastened and did not delay to keep Your commandments.*[3]

---

1. *Tehillim* 103:20.
2. *Yehezkel* 1:14.
3. *Tehillim* 119:60.

In loving memory of

Simone Delouya

לעילוי נשמת
שמחה בת אהרן

Steve and Daniele Delouya Newman
Josef and Leslie Newman

In loving memory of

Joseph and Annette Newman

לעילוי נשמת
יוסף בן זאב הלוי
חנה בת יצחק

Steve and Daniele Delouya Newman
Josef and Leslie Newman

READY FOR ANY MITZVAH

Jumping through the Window

A beloved congregant at one of Jerusalem's synagogues passed away. Shortly before he died, he had the opportunity to fulfill the positive commandment of writing a Torah scroll, despite the fact that he had never trained or worked as a scribe. There were many mistakes in the scroll, but the congregants decided that they would use his Torah scroll throughout the year of mourning for him.

One of the synagogue members was concerned that the congregation was not actually fulfilling their obligation to read from the Torah when they used the scroll this man had written. He turned to Rabbi Shaul Tzemah for guidance. Rabbi Tzemah suggested that the two of them visit Rabbi Eliyahu to discuss the matter.

Although it was after eleven o'clock at night, Rabbi Eliyahu received them warmly and listened with patience. After hearing them out, he asked, "Are you here with a car?"

The men nodded.

"Then let's go to the synagogue so I can see the Torah myself," he said.

And so, at that late hour, they drove with Rabbi Eliyahu to the synagogue to check the kashrut of the Torah scroll. When they got there, they found the building locked. The men figured they had no other option but to turn around and drive Rabbi Eliyahu back home. But, to their surprise, Rabbi Eliyahu suggested that they look for a window that had been left unlocked. A quick check revealed one unlocked window.

"So let's go in!" Rabbi Eliyahu said. With that, he jumped through the window, with the two men quickly following him inside.

He opened the Torah scroll and saw that it was indeed full of mistakes. He then said aloud, "To the honored deceased, this scroll needs checking. At this moment it cannot be used for Torah readings." Rabbi Eliyahu then took out a piece of paper and wrote, "This scroll may not be used for Torah readings until it has been inspected completely." He signed the note, attached it with paper clips, and left the building.

The next day, when the congregation opened the Torah scroll and saw the note, they immediately took it upon themselves to send the scroll for a full examination and correction.[4]

Swift to Console

Mrs. Naomi Knobel, the rabbi's secretary, was thrown into mourning when her father passed away one Motzae Shabbat. Right after Shabbat, she had called Rabbi Eliyahu to let him know that her father's situation was grim, as his body systems were shutting down. Although she did not reach Rabbi Eliyahu himself, she gave the message to one of his assistants and hung up.

Within moments, her phone rang. It was Rabbi Nissim Lopes,[5] one of Rabbi Eliyahu's assistants. He spoke with urgency. "Do kapparot[6] right now over your father's head! Now!"

She was confused and started asking all kinds of questions. But Rabbi Lopes cut her off, saying, "Rabbi Eliyahu said to do it right away. Now!"

She rushed to his bedside and performed the kapparot ritual,

4. This story was heard from Rabbi Eliyahu Farjun, a student in Rabbi Eliyahu's bet midrash and employee of the publication and distribution department at Hechal Yaakov.

5. Rabbi Lopes was close to the Eliyahus from the time he was a child and became an unofficial assistant to the rabbi when he got older.

6. A customary ritual atonement usually practiced before Yom Kippur.

holding money above his head. As soon as she had finished, her father passed away.

The next morning, around seven o'clock, just as she'd finished saying the morning blessings, the phone rang. Rabbi Eliyahu was on the line, consoling her according to the Ashkenazi custom and then according to the Sephardic tradition.[7] Mrs. Knobel was stunned and moved by his call, and she was deeply touched to receive him during the *shivah*. In fact, Mrs. Knobel and her family considered it the height of the entire *shivah*.

When he sat with them, Mrs. Knobel asked Rabbi Eliyahu to pray for her mother, asking that she get the strength and inner fortitude to carry on. But Rabbi Eliyahu asked, "Who am I to pray? Your father is now beside the *Kise Hakavod* (G-d's throne). He will pray!"

The family felt that no one had consoled them as deeply or given them such a good feeling as Rabbi Eliyahu and his wife. After the *shivah*, Mrs. Knobel asked the rabbi's assistants why he had called so early that first morning.

"Rabbi Eliyahu had to go to the hospital for some tests that day and he was worried that he wouldn't feel well enough to call afterward. He didn't want to put it off." His promptness had made such a difference to them.

The Exchanged Bodies

Rabbi Eliyahu's alacrity was ever-present, even in times of trouble. One of his students recalled a difficult time in Israel, when

---

7. In Ashkenazi tradition, people comfort a mourner by reciting the phrase, *HaMakom yenahem etchem b'toch sha'ar avle Zion v'Yerushalayim*, "May G-d comfort you amidst the mourners of Tzion and Yerushalayim." In Sephardic communities, the practice is to say, *Min haShamayim tenachamu* or *Tenachamu min haShamayim*, "May you be comforted by Heaven."

Rabbi Mordechai Eliyahu with Rabbi Avraham Shapira (credit: harav.org)

Rabbi Mordechai Eliyahu with Rabbi Avraham Shapira on a
visit to Rabbi Moshe Feinstein (credit: Eliyahu Family)

Elhanan Atali, a yeshivah student, was murdered.[8] Both Rabbi
Eliyahu and Rabbi Avraham Shapira[9] asked their student to be

---

8. February 28, 1991. Elhanan Atali was murdered by Arabs as he walked unarmed
through the streets of the Old City. He was twenty-six.

9. Rabbi Shapira was the Ashkenazi chief rabbi of Israel from 1983 to 1993, prior to

present at the Abu Kabir Forensics Institute[10] to make sure that no autopsy would be performed on the body and no dishonor would be brought upon the murder victim.

When the examination was finished, Elhanan's body was brought to the inner room at Jerusalem's Shamgar funeral home to prepare for the burial. As the funeral began, Rabbi Eliyahu's student glanced at the body and was astonished to see that the shrouded form lying there was not Elhanan. Though the body was completely wrapped in burial shrouds, the man immediately recognized that the shape of this body was not the same as that of Elhanan's. It was not the same person he had dealt with.

There were thousands of people gathered there, many in great pain. Their broken cries and sighs of anguish filled the hall. Rabbi Eliyahu's student looked around and found one of the people in charge. "That's not Elhanan!" he exclaimed.

But the man rebuked him, looking at him as if he just didn't understand.

He repeated himself with urgency. "It's *not* Elhanan Atali," he said forcefully.

The other man answered him back just as powerfully. "Yes it is!"

Rabbi Eliyahu was standing nearby and heard the discussion. "Go inside the funeral room and figure out what's going on. Then come right back to me!" he instructed his student.

This man went into the preparatory chamber and saw that, indeed, Elhanan Atali's body was still inside the room and someone else's body had been brought out by mistake. He quickly reported his findings to Rabbi Eliyahu.

---

which he served as the *rosh yeshivah* of Mercaz HaRav in Jerusalem. He lived from 1914 to 2007.

10. Also known as the L. Greenberg National Institute of Forensic Medicine, the facility is located in the Abu Kabir neighborhood of Tel Aviv.

The rabbi immediately took matters into his own hands. "Get ready to exchange the bodies when I tell you," he instructed. Then he told the crowd to turn their backs to him. When everyone had turned, they quickly exchanged the bodies, returning the deceased who had been brought out by mistake and placing Elhanan's body on the bier. The crowd thankfully didn't notice the mistake and the funeral continued on its way.

After the funeral proceeded, Rabbi Eliyahu told his student that the other deceased man must have passed away childless and needed Tehillim recited over his body, as people had done when they mistook him for Elhanan. This student was curious and decided to ascertain just who the other deceased man was. He discovered that he was indeed childless. He must have had some great merit to have the prayers of so many people recited on his behalf at his funeral.

Several days later, Rabbi Eliyahu's student went to the *shivah*. Elhanan's father said exactly the same things to him about the deceased man who had been mistaken for his son and for whom so many people had tearfully recited Tehillim. His father said that just as Elhanan had performed so many acts of kindness in his lifetime, even in his death he continued to do so, performing one final act of loving-kindness for someone who had no one to escort him to his final resting place or even to cry over his death.

Tefillin Shel Rosh

Rabbi Eliyahu was hospitalized in Shaare Zedek Medical Center. After morning prayers one day, Rabbi Eliyahu turned to his assistant, Reb Asaf Aharoni,[11] and said, "Keep my *tefillin* with you." Reb Asaf didn't understand what Rabbi Eliyahu meant, but

---

11. Reb Asaf Aharoni continues to assist in the rabbi's office to this day.

it all became clear later that day, when the rabbi suffered a very serious stroke and was transferred to Hadassah Hospital.

Reb Asaf kept the *tefillin* with him. But, the truth was, at that moment, bringing along Rabbi Eliyahu's *tefillin* seemed unnecessary. Rabbi Eliyahu was unconscious and the chances of him being able to don *tefillin* the next day seemed near to nil. But Reb Asaf always took Rabbi Eliyahu's word as law, so he brought the *tefillin* along anyway.

After completing an extremely complicated treatment on Rabbi Eliyahu, involving a catheterization through the tiniest veins of the brain, Rabbi Eliyahu's doctor exited the operating theater to speak to the rabbi's family and assistants. The neurosurgeon, Professor Jose Cohen, told them that throughout his entire career he had never encountered a case like this one. It was so unusual, in fact, that if he were to relate it to his colleagues and other medical professionals, he was sure they wouldn't believe him and would accuse him of making the whole thing up.

The procedure was carried out under full anesthesia, of course. The doctors said they would have to wait until at least nine o'clock the following morning before Rabbi Eliyahu could be awoken, as the anesthetic they had administered for the brain catheterization was particularly powerful. The atmosphere in the recovery room was quite tense, and the doctors were understandably nervous as they waited to see if Rabbi Eliyahu would wake up at all following the risky procedure. The medical staff was constantly by his side, scrutinizing the equipment that monitored the rabbi's vital signs.

At close to five-thirty in the morning, exactly as the time for sunrise arrived, Rabbi Eliyahu opened his eyes, immediately signaling to Reb Asaf, using hand signs to ask where his *tefillin* were. Reb Asaf showed him the *tefillin*, and then Rabbi Eliyahu used more hand signals to ask if it was time to put them on yet.

Reb Asaf and the others in the room confirmed that it was

indeed the correct time to don *tefillin*, and they washed the rabbi's hands and then put the *tefillin* on him. He prayed the morning prayers and then went back to sleep.

When the doctors heard what had happened, they were in complete shock. And they said that if Rabbi Eliyahu was already in such good shape, he could be sent back to Shaare Zedek to continue treatment there.

Paying the Worker the Same Day

Shalom Konaniyan Cohen, Rabbi Eliyahu's early morning driver, used to be a metalworker and had his own foundry. As per the *rabbanit's* request, he crafted an iron door for the Eliyahus' home. When it came time to fit the door, Shalom wanted the privilege of doing the job himself. So rather than sending one of his workers, he personally went to the Eliyahus to install the door he had made.

Shalom has always cherished the memories of that precious opportunity. While he was at the Eliyahus, he learned numerous *halachot* from the rabbi, including several relating to the placement of the *mezuzah*. But the greatest thing he learned was at the end of the job.

As soon as Shalom had finished installing the door, Rabbi Eliyahu asked him how much he owed for the work. "It's not urgent," Shalom replied. "I'll figure out the bill and let you know."

But Rabbi Eliyahu responded, "A worker's wage must be paid the same day. You did the work; now you need to receive your payment."

That job was the first for which Shalom had received his fee immediately upon completion.

An Unusual Circumcision

One Shabbat, a *mohel* came to Rabbi Eliyahu with a question.

He was supposed to be performing a *brit* that day, but just an hour earlier, the father of the baby told him that his son had been born by Caesarian section. Because the birth was not natural, according to halachah, the *brit* could not be done on Shabbat — but the baby's family was not observant and did not realize this beforehand.

The *mohel* asked Rabbi Eliyahu what to do. Numerous guests had already arrived, including many prestigious personalities. If the circumcision was canceled, the *mohel* worried, it could cause a *hillul Hashem* (a desecration of G-d's Name). But, at the same time, he wondered how he could possibly go ahead and perform such a circumcision on Shabbat.

Rabbi Eliyahu replied, "You're a quick *mohel*. Here's what you need to

Rabbi Eliyahu making the blessing over wine at a *brit milah*

do. Make all the blessings out loud, but instead of saying G-d's Name, say 'Hashem' under your breath. Draw out and emphasize the other words of the blessing. Afterward, open the diaper and pretend to be doing a *brit* until the baby cries a bit. Then quickly dress him with iodine and bandages and close the diaper."

The *mohel* nodded.

"Then tell the parents not to open the bandages and explain that you'll come to check them tomorrow," Rabbi Eliyahu continued. "Tomorrow, start to take off the diaper and then suggest to the parents that they leave the room so they don't get upset or even pass out from the sight of the blood. When they're outside, do the circumcision quickly and bandage the baby up again."

The *mohel* did as Rabbi Eliyahu had instructed. The next day he returned to the rabbi and told him that he had done everything according to Rabbi Eliyahu's word. No one had noticed that the circumcision had not actually taken place on Shabbat. They had been so busy with the food and all the goings-on that they never noticed the *brit* hadn't really been performed. On Sunday, the *mohel* made the blessings himself[12] — and did the real circumcision.

The Holy Mortar

In the days before the War of Independence and the formation of the State of Israel, the British ruled the land. They wouldn't allow Jewish residents to engage in military drills or prepare for war, which was anticipated as soon as the upcoming British withdrawal would occur. Instead, the British helped the Arabs stockpile weapons and fortify key positions, doing whatever they could to thwart the emerging Jewish state.

When the withdrawal finally took place, Jerusalem was immediately under siege. Every able-bodied man volunteered to serve in the war, including the young Rabbi Eliyahu and his brothers Naim and Shimon.[13] Their main work was in the fortifications opposite the Arab positions. During that time, the Jewish fighters smuggled in a mortar that had been purchased abroad and dismantled before being brought to Jerusalem. But the problem was that no one knew how to reassemble it.

---

12. A blessing said by one individual at a circumcision, even without the presence of a *minyan*, is still valid.

13. Rabbi Shimon Eliyahu shared his memories of these events.

The old mortar was liable to be quite dangerous — or, alternately, completely ineffective — if put together improperly, and it was a valuable weapon that no one wanted to lose or waste in the struggle against the Arabs. Of course, there was no instruction manual for it, either. The young Jewish fighters worried that if they didn't succeed in stopping the ever-intensifying conflagration with the Arabs, they could all end up slaughtered, as had happened in Gush Etzion.[14]

When the young Mordechai heard about the mortar, he volunteered to assemble it. He sat with the parts, looking them over like a puzzle, putting them together this way and that, until the mortar was finally reassembled. It took him several hours and he was lacking a number of essential tools, but he managed somehow. His brother Shimon recalled that to complete the job Hacham Mordechai had needed a very narrow screwdriver, but lacking that, he had taken a hammer and removed its head in such a way that he could use that as a screwdriver.

When Rabbi Eliyahu had finally finished, the area commander was summoned to see the mortar. He asked Rabbi Eliyahu how he wanted to be paid for the work. "Last night the Arabs fired from one of their homes and injured my brother Naim. I ask that the first shell be fired on that house," he requested.

The commander agreed — and so it was. They fired on that house and the mortar worked. The house from which the Arabs had injured Naim was blown up. Thus, the verse was fulfilled, *And there is hope for your future.*[15]

---

14. On May 13, 1948, 129 Jewish Haganah fighters and civilian residents of the Kfar Etzion kibbutz were massacred by a combined force of Arab Legion soldiers and local Arabs. Only four Jews survived.

15. *Yirmiyahu* 31:16.

Swift to Give Charity

Shalom Konaniyan Cohen, Rabbi Eliyahu's early morning driver, related a story that he said could never be shared during the rabbi's lifetime. It was about the secret charity missions Rabbi Eliyahu would send him on. The rabbi would give Shalom envelopes with money in them and ask him to clandestinely deliver them to people's homes. "Drop off the envelope at a time when no one will see you," Rabbi Eliyahu would instruct him. Shalom later said that he was sure that none of the recipients ever ascertained the source of the money.

One of the recipients was a Torah scholar who wasn't able to put food on the table. Rabbi Eliyahu regularly sent Shalom to deliver envelopes of money to him, which Shalom would place in the mailbox next to the man's home. That Torah scholar thrived, eventually becoming the head of a yeshivah.

"Rabbi Eliyahu saw the scholar's potential with his 'spiritual eyes,' with his depth of vision," Shalom said. "The Eliyahus' financial support enabled him to continue his studies and become one of the top educators of our time."

But the missions weren't always involving Torah scholars; sometimes Shalom was directed to simple people. One time, he was sent to the Bukharan Quarter with instructions to find a particular woman and accompany her to the butcher shop to purchase meat and chicken. Shalom realized that he couldn't give her the money directly, as she would likely spend it on unnecessary splurges.

Shalom was once tasked with finding out what type of kashrut a particular Torah scholar relied on, as Rabbi Eliyahu wanted to send him a crate of chicken and meat, and he needed to be sure the scholar would be comfortable using it. Shalom knew that Rabbi Eliyahu never expected people to just follow his own opinion or to do as he did. He wanted people to be comfortable, even if it meant doing some detective work to ascertain which kashrut a particular Torah scholar preferred. That's how he gave charity: according to the needs of the recipient.

In that particular case with the Torah scholar and the kashrut, Shalom wasn't successful at determining his preferences. Nevertheless, by the next morning, Rabbi Eliyahu had somehow obtained the information. He was overjoyed. "Now I can send him meat and chicken for Shabbat and the holidays!"

Let's Be Partners

Rabbi Yaakov Shkenazi, a halachic decisor at the Sephardic Edah Haredit,[16] shared a story about a time when a man came to see Rabbi Eliyahu and broke down in tears. "Making a living is tough, and I don't have any way to support my children! What can I do?" he cried to Rabbi Eliyahu.

"What do you know how to do?" Rabbi Eliyahu asked him.

The man replied that he had experience selling produce.

"If so," the rabbi suggested, "what would you think of partnering with me to open a fruit and vegetable stand?"

The man was amenable to the idea, so Rabbi Eliyahu asked him how much money he would need to get his stall established. The man estimated that it would take several thousand dollars, naming a particular sum. Rabbi Eliyahu asked him to wait and then came back with the exact amount of money he needed.

Handing over the money, he said, "Take it, open the stand, and we'll be partners."

After some time had passed, Rabbi Eliyahu contacted the produce seller, asking him how business was going.

---

16. The Orthodox Council of Jerusalem.

"I don't know what to tell you," was his answer. "I have to pay for gas and electricity, and the income is still very tight."

"No problem," Rabbi Eliyahu said, reminding him they were partners. "We're partners not just in profit, but also in expenses. When you start to make a profit and cover the basic operating costs, come back to me and return my investment."

That man eventually became very wealthy. Years later, he came back to Rabbi Eliyahu to repay the rabbi's initial investment. But Rabbi Eliyahu turned him away. "Forget about the money. Keep it. It's all yours!"

A Groom on His Wedding Day

How does a Torah scholar traditionally spend his wedding

Rabbi Mordechai Eliyahu on the day of his wedding (credit: Eliyahu Family)

day, before the ceremony? He learns, prays, and visits the graves of the righteous. And that's exactly what Rabbi Eliyahu did on the day of his own wedding.

He went to the tomb of David Hamelech on Mount Zion to recite Tehillim and prepare himself spiritually for his marriage. Near the tomb, there's a steep ascent up Mount Zion toward the old railway station. As Rabbi Eliyahu was leaving the site, he noticed an elderly porter pushing a heavy load with a dolly. The man was straining to get up the steep hill with the cart. So Rabbi Eliyahu went to help him, in fulfillment

Hacham Shalom Azoulay of Porat
Yosef attending Rabbi Eliyahu's
wedding (credit: Eliyahu Family)

Rabbi Aryeh Levine under the
chuppah at the wedding
(credit: Eliyahu Family)

of the verse, *You shall surely help him.*[17] He even pushed the dolly all
the way up the steep slope until they reached the railway station.

That night, when the time came for the wedding ceremony, that
same elderly man arrived as one of the guests. He was astonished
to see that the young man who had helped him that morning was
none other than the groom himself.[18]

Song of the Secretary: The Mitzvah to Make Others Happy

Mrs. Naomi Knobel, the rabbi's secretary, wanted to give a
concert for women. Though she truly enjoyed singing and felt
that her concert would bring other women much happiness, it was
something she hadn't done for many years and it took a great deal
of energy and effort on her part to get it off the ground again.

---

17. *Devarim* 22:4.

18. This story was related by Rabbi Mordechai Nagari, a close disciple of Rabbi
Eliyahu. Rabbi Nagari has been the chief Sephardic rabbi of Maale Adumim since
1984.

Rabbi Eliyahu gave Mrs. Knobel a lot of encouragement, urging her to continue, and even advocating for her to produce recordings. He guided her every step of the way with regard to the *halachot* of singing for women, including how to work with the recording studio and how to sing when male technicians or audio engineers were present.

When she was in the year of mourning for her father, Mrs. Knobel asked Rabbi Eliyahu for advice. She wanted to know if she should wait until completing the year before performing again.[19] The rabbi told her she could return to it right after the *sheloshim* (initial thirty-day mourning period).

Mrs. Knobel reminded him that this was not her source of income, which is usually the reason why an observant Jew would be granted permission to participate in such an event. But Rabbi Eliyahu responded, "If you succeed in bringing joy to women, then it's not only permitted, but it's also a mitzvah! People aren't coping with the difficulties of life today because they don't have inner joy, and if you manage to give them that, it's important and a mitzvah. Do it, be successful, and find favor in the eyes of all those who come to hear and see you!"

Every time she had a big or important performance, she would seek his blessing. And Rabbi Eliyahu would always respond, "It's important. It's a mitzvah. Do it, be successful, and find favor in the eyes of those who hear and see you!"

Ever since, Mrs. Knobel has felt that her singing and performances are a personal mission and mandate from Rabbi Eliyahu. She gives concerts in many places, and wherever she goes, she knows she's fulfilling his personal directive.

Mrs. Knobel had a show arranged in Nahariya. It was scheduled

---

19. Observant Jews usually do not participate in any joyous events such as weddings, concerts, and the like for the first year after a parent's death.

far in advance, so of course at that time she had no idea that it would end up being a very difficult and painful week during which to perform. Time flew by, and then Rabbi Eliyahu passed away. During the week of *shivah*, Mrs. Knobel realized that her concert in Nahariya was booked for the last night of the *shivah*. There would be many eulogies delivered that night at Rabbi Eliyahu's synagogue — and Mrs. Knobel was his secretary, so she was busy arranging them all.

As soon as she realized that her performance was to be held on the last night of the *shivah*, she tried to rearrange her plans by rescheduling the show or even canceling it. But she quickly saw that the event's organizers were becoming tense and anxious by her attempts to change the arrangements. The show was for an organization that helps bereaved widows, and she felt it was important to keep her commitment.

She left Jerusalem with a heavy heart, not telling anyone that she wouldn't be present at the eulogies. It was very difficult for her, and she also felt that she was missing something she personally wanted to attend. She arrived in Haifa in the late afternoon, stopping by the shores of the Mediterranean to pray Minhah. She looked up toward the heavens and said, "Master of the Universe! You know how difficult it is for me now, how painful, how much my heart is torn. I've lost the rabbi and lost my father. Give me strength! How can I make others happy when I have no joy myself? How?"

In her mind's eye, she saw Rabbi Eliyahu smiling at her like a ray of light. She had clarity: She was going to carry out the orders of Rabbi Eliyahu. She was going to bring joy to people. Besides, she was going to be comforting hundreds of widows…

"I'm not a special person," Mrs. Knobel said. "But I was privileged to receive a blessing and instructions to make others happy. At that moment, the rabbi's blessing turned into a personal mandate for me. I was going to bring a little light and happiness into the lives of people who so badly needed it, exactly on the last day of Rabbi Eliyahu's *shivah*."

The performance was only supposed to be an hour and a half. But it went on and on, and it became the most joyous, exultant show she had ever had. When she finally brought the concert to a conclusion, Mrs. Knobel told the women about her connection to Rabbi Eliyahu and how difficult it had been for her to come. But then she explained her personal mission from Rabbi Eliyahu and asked them to have in mind that all the happiness they felt should be a merit for the elevation of the rabbi's soul.

For a few moments there was stunned, shocked silence in the audience. And then the performance took on a life of its own. She had brought along lots of candles, and they lit them all. The women put their arms around each other and stood, hugging, swaying, and singing together in the candlelight. They carried on singing and praying together with tremendous devotion, togetherness, and sisterhood until nearly two in the morning.

"And that's how I eulogized the rabbi," Mrs. Knobel said.

☙

THE VALUE OF TIME

Every Precious Minute

No matter how busy Rabbi Eliyahu was resolving important issues, receiving visitors, and answering questions until the wee hours of the night, he was always up in time to pray with the sunrise *minyan*. He was such a regular there that if he *didn't* come, it was cause for concern.

Rabbi David Shalom, an educator, once heard that the best time to catch Rabbi Eliyahu was right after the rabbi finished his morning prayers and before he headed home. Once, when Rabbi

After prayers in Hechal Yaakov

Shalom was in urgent need of Rabbi Eliyahu's advice, he left his own neighborhood while it was still dark so that he could get to Rabbi Eliyahu's synagogue, Hechal Yaakov, in time to speak with him right after prayers. Rabbi Shalom was sure that he wouldn't have to wait too long to speak with Rabbi Eliyahu and get his counsel, but he was sorely mistaken.

Rabbi Eliyahu answered the questions of no fewer than eighteen different people from the moment he exited the building until he entered his car. Each one received the rabbi's complete attention and a quick, clear response — and all this was before six in the morning.

When Rabbi Eliyahu saw Rabbi Shalom waiting but wasn't able to speak with him before he got into his car, he told Rabbi Shalom to come straight to his house. Rabbi Shalom got there and sat in the living room, but there were already ten questions about family purity waiting for Rabbi Eliyahu to decide on. Finally, after all that, he was available to speak to Rabbi Shalom.

During the few minutes they were speaking, they were

Accompanying Rabbi Eliyahu on his way home from Shaharit

interrupted numerous times by phone calls from people seeking Rabbi Eliyahu's blessing or his advice. It wasn't even seven in the morning, but everyone who needed it had received an answer or a good word, and the rabbi even wrote down the names of several of those in need of prayers.

Rabbi Eliyahu didn't even take his first drink until he had received additional people — and he was over seventy years old at this time. Rabbi Shalom later remarked, "I may not have saved time that morning, but I *did* receive an amazing lesson on dedication and devotion to helping everyone and anyone who needed it, with issues both big and small. He had so much kindness and limitless patience. And I also learned how much can be done before seven o'clock in the morning!"

The Worth of Five Minutes

When Rabbi Eliyahu was ill, there were a number of occasions when he wanted to rest a little — but only a *little*. He would ask his assistants to wake him after just five minutes and no more.

Those in his inner circle would beg him to take just a few more minutes — even if only ten or fifteen — as rest was an essential part of his recovery, especially after his lengthy hospitalization. But Rabbi Eliyahu would never agree. "You know how much a person can accomplish in five minutes?" he would ask. "And you want me to waste them? Five minutes, and no more. That's what I need."

Shortcut to Sunrise Prayers

Rabbi Eliyahu traveled abroad for one of the many public affairs he had to attend over the years. He was accompanied by Itzik Golan,[20] a resident of Givat Shmuel, among others. On the way to the event, they visited the graves of various righteous men who were buried in the area. But on the way home, they split up and returned to Israel on different flights. Some of the group departed on a flight an hour ahead of Rabbi Eliyahu's, with their plane set to arrive at Ben Gurion Airport an hour before his.

Rabbi Eliyahu returning from one of his many overseas visits (credit: harav.org)

---

20. A member of the Ben David family, and a very close follower of the rabbi.

According to the flight schedule, the first group would arrive in Israel two hours before sunrise, which would give them enough time to pass through customs and travel to Jerusalem to pray with the sunrise *minyan*. Those traveling with Rabbi Eliyahu, on the other hand, would have to pray at Ben Gurion Airport if they wished to do so at sunrise. The first group was concerned that there wouldn't be a *minyan* for Rabbi Eliyahu at sunrise at the airport, so some of them decided that they would remain there and wait for the rabbi to arrive. They could then pray together with him when he landed an hour later.

But life takes a different course for the truly righteous. When the first group arrived at the airport, they saw Rabbi Eliyahu ahead of them in line at passport control. The group from the first flight was completely flabbergasted at this miraculous occurrence. There was just no logical explanation for it. Rabbi Eliyahu had taken off from Budapest an hour after them. He had flown in a regular plane, not a Concorde or an F-15 fighter jet. Yet he had arrived before the first group.

Itzik, a business executive who considers himself to be a

After the sunrise *minyan* on a snowy Jerusalem morning

completely rational, down-to-earth person, couldn't believe his eyes. He went back and checked all the details of the flight times, and the only explanation he could come up with was that Rabbi Eliyahu had merited a *kefitzat haderech* (a miraculous shortcut).

Rabbi Eliyahu was always vigilant about praying at sunrise every day in his own synagogue. And the Sages teach that one who sets a place for his prayer will merit Divine help.[21] Rabbi Eliyahu's fellow travelers saw that verse manifest when the land of Israel seemingly reached out to receive the rabbi so he could pray at sunrise in his own study hall, in comfort and peace, as he was accustomed to do with such regularity...

---

21. *Berachot* 6b. *Whoever establishes a fixed place for prayer will have the G-d of Avraham assist him.*

Chapter Four

Cleanliness

A person who completely purifies himself and is clean of all blemishes in thought and spirit will have clarity of vision and purity of understanding. He will not be tempted by even the slightest desire, for he will distance himself from all forms of sin. The Sages thus spoke of the "perfect ones" who purify themselves and all their acts so they won't be tainted by even a hint of sin.

May the merits of
Rabbi Mordechai Eliyahu
protect all Am Israel

From
Amiga Blanga Family

ALWAYS JUDICIOUS

They Pay Me More in Heaven

A prestigious woman came to see Rabbi Eliyahu to give him a substantial financial gift. She viewed it as a kind of "repayment," as he had saved her from death — not once, but *twice*. The rabbi refused to take the money, as he always did, even when the woman begged him to take it. It was clearly her way of exhibiting gratitude to him.

Rabbi Eliyahu told her there were numerous places she could donate the money, but she pleaded with him incessantly, imploring him to just take it. He thought for a moment and then asked, "How much do you want to give me?"

The woman's face lit up and she withdrew a bundle of bills from her pocketbook. Rabbi Eliyahu looked at the wad of cash and then sagely remarked, "That's all? In Heaven they pay me more!" When the woman heard that, she calmed down and finally left.

The Seal of Kashrut — and Honesty

About eight years before Rabbi Eliyahu had his own kashrut seal for certifying food and eateries, there was a particular butcher shop owner who wanted to take all of Rabbi Eliyahu's kashrut stringencies[1] upon himself.

Rabbi Eliyahu told him that he would certify the meat as long as the man kept three additional conditions:

- The meat had to remain at the same price (even after implementing the stringencies) so that full-time Torah scholars would be able to afford it for Shabbat and festivals.

---

1. The details of Rabbi Eliyahu's particular stringencies in kashrut are beyond the scope of this work.

- No water could be injected in the meat.

- No soy could be added to the meat.

The butcher was very successful. Customers were happy with the special kashrut certification and the many stringencies he followed. The meat was of excellent quality. After some time, however, the butcher returned to Rabbi Eliyahu, lamenting that he might have to close his business. His competitors, who had other kashrut seals, were charging higher prices — and adding water and soy fat — and thus were making much more of a profit. The butcher felt it wasn't worth it for him to carry on. He begged Rabbi Eliyahu to allow him to add water and soy to the meat, but Rabbi Eliyahu wouldn't permit it.

When Rabbi Eliyahu was pressed by others about why he was so inflexible on this matter, Rabbi Eliyahu replied, "Let's say that I allow him to add water, and we obligate the butcher to clearly state on the package that there is 10 percent water added. What will happen if the equipment isn't exact, and 12 percent water is added instead of 10 percent? My kashrut signature would be party to theft. No, I'm not prepared to do that..."

A Place in Paradise

Rabbi Eliyahu was always very careful with other people's money. For many years, he would use the Ohale Yaakov siddur during the High Holidays. Compiled by Rabbi Yaakov Midraband,[2] the Ohale Yaakov,[3] it contains Rabbi Yaakov's deep commentaries on the prayers and the Yom Kippur confessions, following interpretations

---

2. More commonly known as Rabbi Yaakov Yitzhaki, he lived from 1846 to 1917. He was the chief rabbi and head of the *bet din* in Dagestan, in the North Caucasus region of Russia. When he came to the land of Israel, he became one of the founders of the Be'er Yaakov settlement and a historian of the nation of Israel.

3. He is also referred to as the Baal Ha'ohalim.

found in the Kabbalah and *midrashim*. Rabbi Eliyahu said that the Ohale Yaakov's greatness in all areas of Torah was revealed through his commentary in the siddur.

He once shared a story that related to both himself and the Ohale Yaakov — and which illustrated with frightening clarity just how careful one must be with others' money.

As a young man, Rabbi Eliyahu taught a Torah class in the Bukharan Quarter that was attended by many regular working men. During one class before the High Holidays, Rabbi Eliyahu discussed a number of the Ohale Yaakov's explanations of the upcoming prayers. One of the participants in the class, an elderly Jew named Reb Yohanan, seemed to be paying extra close attention when he heard the name of the Ohale Yaakov.

After the class, Reb Yohanan came up to Rabbi Eliyahu and said, "Rabbenu, I knew Rabbi Yaakov, and I even have a keepsake from him. He was our neighbor, and he was very, very poor. He once asked me for a loan. I gave it to him, and he gave me a promissory note for it.[4] Rabbi Yaakov tragically passed away and never had a chance to redeem the note. I still have that IOU today, as a memory of him."

When Rabbi Eliyahu heard this, he began to tremble. "Please," he said, "can I ask you a favor? Say right now that you forgive the loan, and then, as soon as you get home, write on the note 'repaid' or 'forgiven.'" The man agreed, but asked Rabbi Eliyahu if he would need to tell his wife about the whole incident.

Rabbi Eliyahu said there was no need to do so.

The next day, after he finished his prayers at sunrise, Rabbi Eliyahu found Reb Yohanan's wife waiting for him by the entrance to the synagogue. She asked to speak with him and then related

---

4. Halachah instructs that a *shtar*, or written document, must be drawn up between the lender and the recipient when money is loaned.

the following story. "Last night I dreamt about Rabbi Yaakov, the Ohale Yaakov, who was our neighbor. In the dream, he told me that since his death, he had been refused entry to Gan Eden, and only that night, thanks to Rabbi Mordechai, he had been allowed to enter. He asked me to come and thank you for the kindness you did for him."

She continued, "I don't know if this dream is real or imaginary, nor do I know why he was telling it especially to me. I don't really know if he was waiting to get into Gan Eden for decades. And I don't know what gave him such difficulty. But he asked me to come, so here I am."

In the meantime, the woman's husband, Reb Yohanan, had exited the synagogue. When he saw his wife talking to Rabbi Eliyahu, he stood off to the side to give her privacy. But then Rabbi Eliyahu motioned for him to come over. As soon as he did, Reb Yohanan burst out, "Rabbenu, I have to tell you about the dream I had last night..." And he went on to relate the exact same dream his wife had dreamed, about the Ohale Yaakov.

Rabbi Eliyahu smiled. "Tell your wife what happened last night after the class."

Reb Yohanan told his wife about the promissory note that he had torn up the night before.

His wife burst into tears. "How terrible that it was because of us such a righteous man was in distress for so many years!"

But Rabbi Eliyahu said, "You're actually blessed. You have a great merit that you lent money to a righteous man when he needed it. It was because of you that he entered Gan Eden. You are blessed and your portion is blessed!"

When Rabbi David Batzri[5] related this story, he added, "As

---

5. *Rosh yeshivah* of Yeshivat Nahar Shalom.

is known, in Heaven great care is taken with the accuracy of someone's name. When the woman told Rabbi Eliyahu that in Heaven they called him 'Rabbi Mordechai,' he was in shock — not only from the whole incident itself, but also from hearing that they had called him 'rabbi' in Heaven."

Of course, when Rabbi Eliyahu would tell this story, he would omit the words "Rabbi Mordechai," skipping that part altogether. He would just tell the story to illustrate the grave importance of being careful with other people's money.

Ten Times as Much

On one of the mornings before his wedding, a groom set out to arrange the musical accompaniment for the event, placing a call to a certain band, asking them to perform at his wedding. He agreed that he would come by later that evening to give them a deposit. But, later that same day, he spoke to his fiancée and discovered that she preferred a different band.

That afternoon the groom called the band again and explained that his fiancée had already chosen another group. But the band manager responded, "I've already written it on my schedule. Canceling will cost you a hundred dollars." The groom refused to pay, and the band manager said he wanted to bring the groom to Rabbi Eliyahu for a Torah judgment.

At Rabbi Eliyahu's house the next day, the groom was told to pay. When the groom sought further explanation, Rabbi Eliyahu told him that the band's manager needed the money. The groom said that he also needed the money and asked if it was according to halachah that he should pay or just a recommendation. Rabbi Eliyahu looked at him and said, "What do you care? Pay, and G-d will give you ten times as much!"

The groom figured that Rabbi Eliyahu didn't want anyone to

hold a grudge or feel resentful toward him on his wedding day — or ever. The groom thus handed over the money. Later that day, he went to the Mercaz HaRav yeshivah to learn. He sat in the library, studying into the wee hours. At one o'clock in the morning, a businessman came in, speaking English. He seemed rushed and somewhat stressed, so the groom directed him to an English-speaking boy who was learning there, too.

The boy spoke to the businessman and then pointed at the groom. The businessman ran back over to the groom and said, "Here!" He pressed an envelope into the groom's palm, shook his other hand, and then ran out to a waiting taxi.

The confused groom turned to the English-speaking boy for an explanation. He clarified that the businessman had just secured an excellent contract and was looking for a needy family, *kollel* man, or bridegroom to donate to in thanks to G-d for his business deal. So the English-speaking boy pointed out the groom, who was just days away from his wedding. The businessman had no time to speak with him, as he was rushing to catch a plane. And that was that.

The groom opened the envelope and counted the money inside. It was exactly a thousand dollars. Rabbi Eliyahu's assurance that "G-d will give you ten times as much" had come true right away, exactly as he had said.

Prepare the Flashlights

Rabbi Eliyahu was so careful to keep everything pure, from the greatest matters to the smallest affairs. He was as cautious about not stealing another's money as he was about not stealing another's sleep.

Rabbi Eliyahu would take his sons to *Selihot* (special prayers of atonement said before sunrise during Elul) when they were young.

The night before *Selihot*, he would tell them to prepare flashlights for the morning. That way, they would already have in their heads before going to sleep that they would be getting up early to go to *Selihot*, and they could get ready to leave easily and quickly.

At the crack of dawn the next morning, Rabbi Eliyahu would wake the boys with a whisper, so as not to wake their mother. He was very concerned about them not stealing her sleep and consequently losing any reward for the mitzvah they were about to do. They proceeded to *Selihot* in absolute silence, being careful not to slam the front door so as not to wake the neighbors, avoiding conversation in the stairwell so as not to disturb anyone, and so on. Rabbi Eliyahu would always remind them that sleep couldn't be returned to a person. His sons never forgot this lesson, even though they had learned it in early childhood.[6]

BETWEEN MAN AND MAN

A Watch on His Right Hand

The vast majority of the world wears their watch on their left wrist, because people tend to put the watch on their non-dominant side and most people are right-handed. It's also easy to see the watch that way and simple to adjust it, and the watch supposedly gets less wear-and-tear than if worn on the right — at least for those who are righties. But Rabbi Eliyahu — a right-handed person himself — always wore his watch on his right hand, with the watch face sitting on the inside of his wrist.

---

6. This story was related by Rabbi Shmuel Eliyahu, Hacham Mordechai's son.

Rabbi Mordechai Nagari once asked Rabbi Eliyahu why he did that.

His answer? "So as not to insult people! Sometimes, you're speaking in public and somebody looks at his watch. You think that perhaps your speech isn't interesting, even though he could well be checking his watch for a different reason. Or you could be talking to someone and see him glance at his watch — and you think that person just wants you to stop talking," he explained.

Thus Rabbi Eliyahu always wore his watch on his right hand, with the face positioned inward, toward his body. That way, he could clandestinely check his watch without insulting the person speaking to him. He also said that wearing the watch on the right gave him an extra minute each day, when he would have had to remove the watch to put on his *tefillin*. Those single minutes could add up to a significant amount of time over a long period, and he could use that time for more important things.

The Rabbi Wins, the Rabbi Pays

The newspapers *Yom Hashishi* and *Erev Shabbat* had religiously oriented content, but nevertheless suffered occasional lapses in *shemirat halashon* (safeguarding speech) when it came to their coverage. Unfortunately, these slip-ups sometimes resulted in the defamation of rabbis, including Rabbi Mordechai Eliyahu. The *lashon hara* (forbidden speech) was not always intentional. Sometimes information, facts, or opinions weren't properly checked or were misrepresented.

One way to deal with such slander-filled articles was to make a claim through the courts. But Rabbi Eliyahu would never agree to do so, though he certainly would have won. He could have perhaps won hundreds of thousands of shekels by making claims on each incident of *lashon hara*. But Rabbi Eliyahu felt that it would be a desecration of G-d's Name to use the civil courts, even in cases where it was technically permitted to do so. He feared that the public would learn from such cases that using civil courts was acceptable, even in cases that should have gone through *bet din* instead. Thus Rabbi Eliyahu bore the insults directed his way, swallowing his pride time and again.

When a new editor, Rabbi Yisrael Gliss, was brought on to the *Erev Shabbat* newspaper staff, he tried to make sure the publication wouldn't err in the realm of *lashon hara*. But one time, when Rabbi Gliss was abroad visiting the States for two weeks, one of the authors penned a negative piece about one of Rabbi Eliyahu's family members. And it turned out to be completely false.

The same son who had just been defamed in the article decided that the time had come to settle this issue once and for all. He sued Rabbi Gliss and the newspaper in the civil court for a large sum. And he won, for the full amount.

Rabbi Gliss had no idea how he would raise such a significant amount of money, which he was expected to pay out of pocket. So he did what he always did when he needed advice: he went to speak to Rabbi Eliyahu.

"You were found guilty in court?" Rabbi Eliyahu asked. "So pay!"

"But I don't have the money," Rabbi Gliss said.

"It's your responsibility to make sure that no *lashon hara* is written in the newspaper that you edit," Rabbi Eliyahu said. "You failed to take that responsibility — so pay!"

He went on to say that the large sum didn't even begin to cover the amount of damage done by *lashon hara* against rabbis. "*Lashon hara* against rabbis can cause serious harm to Jewish law. Just imagine that someone who regularly attends the class of a certain rabbi reads one of these negative articles. He begins to wonder why he should listen to such a rabbi anyway. And then he ceases going to his classes altogether, stops seeking his advice, and so on," Rabbi Eliyahu explained.

He continued, "Or imagine that someone has a question relating to the laws of family purity, Shabbat, or some other area of halachah. He reads that a certain rabbi has done some evil or despicable thing. Whether it's true, completely false, or a half-lie, it doesn't matter anymore. The damage has been done. That man won't go to that rabbi with his questions anymore, and he probably won't go to any rabbi at all. He'll just assume that all rabbis are the same, so he'll follow his own opinion instead of doing what the Torah commands."

Rabbi Gliss began to tremble, feeling the gravity of the situation. When Rabbi Eliyahu saw how affected Rabbi Gliss was, he pulled a checkbook from a drawer and said, "You hurt a member of my family and you should pay. But I know you don't have the money. So take this money and pay. But just make sure that no one finds out you got the money from me."

Rabbi Eliyahu proceeded to write him a check for the full amount. Then he said, "Cash this check at the bank and pay him in cash."

Rabbi Gliss left the Eliyahus' home with the check in hand, but he was still shaking and trembling violently and could barely stand. He sat on the steps outside the Eliyahus' home and began to weep like a little boy. He later said, "I have never seen such greatness of soul or character in all my life."

He did exactly as Rabbi Eliyahu had instructed, and he refrained from telling the family the story until after Rabbi Eliyahu's passing. Rabbi Gliss also learned a lesson about *lashon hara* in his newspaper and took full responsibility from then on.

Everyone Gets a Blessing

A group had traveled from central Israel to pray at Rabbi Eliyahu's synagogue with the sunrise *minyan*. They had come especially to seek the rabbi's blessings, as they had done in the past. But this time, it was Rosh Hodesh, and the synagogue was absolutely packed, way beyond the normal crowd.

Rabbi Eliyahu giving a halachah *shiur* (credit: harav.org)

When the prayers ended, Rabbi Eliyahu taught one halachah, as was his custom, and then one of the people standing next to him stood up and banged on a table. "Today the rabbi is in a hurry," he announced. "Please do not ask him for a blessing."

The group from central Israel was really disappointed. They had gotten up so early and traveled so far. Nevertheless, they didn't want to trouble the rabbi, so they figured they would just leave. But there were lots of disheartened people in the synagogue, and it seemed that the rabbi felt their pain. There was another clap on the table, this time from Rabbi Eliyahu himself.

"I'm not leaving the synagogue until everyone gets a blessing!" he announced. He then sat down on his chair.

Although the synagogue was extremely crowded, and Rabbi

Rabbi Mordechai Eliyahu blessing the congregation

Eliyahu was apparently in a big rush, he sat for over an hour giving each and every person in the synagogue his blessing.[7]

Simple Pen, Great Deed

Eyal Sheli, the director of Safed's community centers, was privileged to receive Rabbi Eliyahu's blessings on numerous occasions. He was also introduced to his wife through Rabbi Eliyahu's intervention, and he considered himself blessed to receive advice on all manners of issues from the rabbi, too.

He recalled that Rabbi Eliyahu not only had a great understanding of Torah and had much life experience, but also had a very astute perception of the human soul. He used that insight to help many people and inspire them to improve.

Eyal once traveled from Safed to Jerusalem to ask Rabbi Eliyahu about a particular issue. A short time later, Rabbi Eliyahu came to Safed to visit his son, the chief rabbi of the city, and he requested

---

7. As heard from Natanel Kahane.

that Eyal be summoned for a visit. When Eyal arrived, Rabbi Eliyahu pulled a pen from his pocket and said, "You were by me a while ago and forgot your pen." He smiled as he handed it over. "Take it, it's yours," he said.

The pen was of the cheapest, simplest variety. Yet Rabbi Eliyahu remembered it, even with the endless issues being brought before him and all the people who needed him. He even remembered to bring it with him to Safed...

Eyal was so moved by the incident that he asked Rabbi Eliyahu to write something in his prayer book using that pen so that he would always remember that moment and it would be inscribed on his heart. "And every time I'm reminded of that pen, it brings me to tears," Eyal said. "It reminds me of the rabbi and what we lost. We miss him terribly."

Newspapers for the Sake of Shabbat

Yiska Buchnik had returned to traditional Judaism, becoming a *ba'alat teshuvah*. She was introduced to — and subsequently married — a boy who wanted to study Torah. After their wedding, her husband decided to start praying in Rabbi Eliyahu's synagogue. At that time, Rabbi Eliyahu was serving as a judge in the Supreme Rabbinical Court in Jerusalem.

Rabbi Eliyahu would frequently give over Torah thoughts and ethical concepts, spiced with humor and stories he had personally experienced. Mrs. Buchnik's husband, who came from a religious background, was truly awed by Rabbi Eliyahu's character. He was great yet humble, noble yet simple.

Mrs. Buchnik's husband suggested to his bride that they take Rabbi Eliyahu as their rabbi, both in matters of halachah and for guidance and advice in life. But she was a new returnee to Judaism, and not being acquainted with Rabbi Eliyahu, Mrs. Buchnik feared that she wouldn't be able to follow the rabbi's rulings or maintain his standards.

However, she very quickly learned how wise Rabbi Eliyahu was. She felt that he not only understood her, but that he completely comprehended the different world she had come from. Looking back, she is amazed at the rabbi's incredible patience for the many "problems" and issues they approached him about, which in retrospect seem so inconsequential. He treated their mundane concerns with total seriousness.

He also knew how to be gentle but firm, and when to be brief versus when to discuss matters in depth. Sometimes he even referred the young couple to other people for advice. They felt that he gave them so much clarity in matters of educating their children, lighting the way for them. "And what was most wonderful," Mrs. Buchnik recalled, "was that we merited to hear the *Shechinah* (the Divine Presence) speak through his mouth not just once, but on several occasions."

Early in their marriage, Mrs. Buchnik asked her husband if he could pick up some newspapers and magazines for her when he was doing his Erev Shabbat shopping. The publications she had requested were all of a secular nature, and her husband explained that he felt uncomfortable buying them, especially with his yarmulke and beard. He didn't want to bring all the nonsense of the world into his home. Yet Mrs. Buchnik did not have time to go out, and she didn't understand why he couldn't just pick them up since he was going out anyway. Besides, she said, he could always explain that he was buying the newspapers for her.

Finally, they decided to take their problem to Rabbi Eliyahu. Mr. Buchnik approached him, discussing the problem. The rabbi listened intently and then asked what kind of home the Buchniks hoped to build.

Mr. Buchnik answered that he wanted to build a Torah home and so did his wife, but she was just not up to a particular level yet.

Rabbi Eliyahu answered, "Buy your wife the newspapers. It will be okay. The day will come when she won't want them anymore."

Mr. Buchnik came home with the shopping — and the newspapers. His wife was quite surprised and asked if he had been to see Rabbi Eliyahu. He shared everything that had transpired. She was so moved by the story and by what Rabbi Eliyahu had said that she announced to her husband, "From today, there won't be such newspapers in our house — let's take them and throw them in the garbage!"[8] And that's exactly what they did.

---

8. Yiska Buchnik was a lecturer at Michlalah Yerushalayim, a girls' college in Jerusalem. She lives in Jerusalem.

Chapter Five

Abstinence and Self-Restraint

The survivors within the nation who wish to draw close to Hashem will raise up all those who depend upon them. They fulfill acts of piety and *prishut* [asceticism] that others could not fulfill.

Because it is not possible that an entire nation can be on the same level, as there are many levels within a people, each person grows according to his understanding. And so there are exceptional individuals who have completely prepared themselves to live a life of serving Hashem. Through those who are ready, those who are not ready will merit the love of Hashem and the light of the Divine Presence.

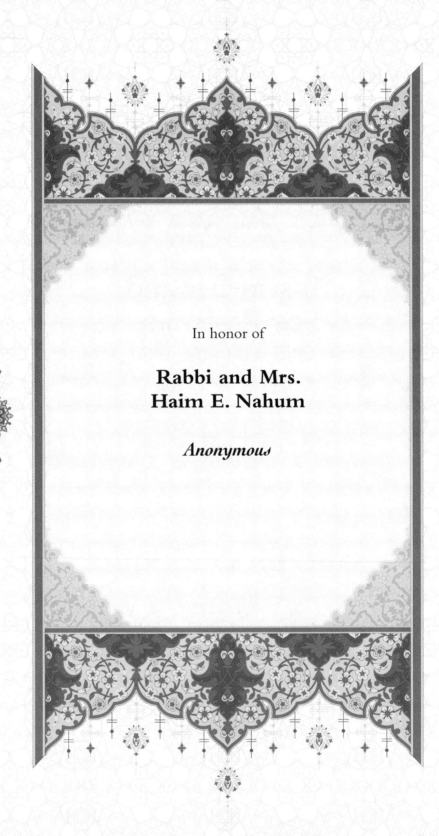

In honor of

Rabbi and Mrs.
Haim E. Nahum

Anonymous

ALWAYS THINKING BIGGER

Charity, Not Candy

Rabbi Eliyahu's brother Rabbi Shimon recalled that when they were young children, their mother would set aside a little money each week for the kids to buy some treats and goodies. The other children in the family would use the coins to buy candies, but the young Mordechai would give the money to a family even poorer than his own.

When his mother noticed that her son Mordechai wasn't eating candies like everyone else, she asked Shimon what was going on. Shimon didn't answer her, but their mother figured it out quickly. And so, from then on, instead of giving Mordechai the money, she would give his coin to Shimon with instructions to buy for him, too. "He needs to say a hundred blessings a day!" she said.

But Mordechai didn't want to eat candies. He would make a blessing on Shimon's candy instead, so that he could fulfill his mother's wishes. Then he'd taste a little and say, "I've had enough already — give it to someone else."

Rabbi Shimon recalled that young Mordechai would spend every waking minute learning Torah, both during the week and on Shabbat. Because the family didn't have any books at home, he would go to learn in the library of the Porat Yosef yeshivah.

There was a tiny lamp in the yeshivah library and the young Mordechai would learn by its light. The *gabbai* (sexton) saw him learning by the small, weak light and said, "What are you doing? You'll ruin your eyesight!"

The *gabbai* went and put a bigger light there so the young Mordechai could see better and therefore learn better. And that's how he was when he was only twelve years old.

His brother recalled that Mordechai also had hands of gold: He

Yeshivat Porat Yosef in the Old City of Jerusalem as it
looked when Hacham Mordechai studied there

could fix anything and everything that broke. In those early days
of home electrical appliances, there weren't many technicians who
knew how to fix them. Somehow, the young Mordechai figured
out how to take all the broken pieces, fix them, and put devices
back together again. He had skilled hands and a big heart.

Until You Walk in His Shoes

When Rabbi Eliyahu was a young boy, he wore through his
shoes, as children are wont to do. His mother saved up money, coin

by coin, to be able to purchase a new pair of shoes for him. When she finally had the necessary sum, she went to the shoemaker, who was also a great Torah scholar,[1] to engage his services in making the young Mordechai a new pair.

The young boy requested that his new shoes be made a little too big so that he could wear them for a long time. He realized he was at a stage of rapid growth, and he thought that it only made sense to buy bigger shoes so that he wouldn't outgrow them immediately. He planned to stuff them with newspaper so they wouldn't be loose on his feet.

The shoemaker soon notified the Eliyahus that the shoes were ready. The young Mordechai went with his mother to pick up the new shoes. She paid the shoemaker half a lira and took the shoes. Mordechai was very pleased with the pair.

But later that same day, Mordechai was walking somewhere and saw the mother of one of his fellow yeshivah students — and she was crying.

"What's wrong?" the young Mordechai asked her. "Why are you crying?"

She explained that her son didn't want to go to yeshivah because he didn't have any decent shoes. The boy was refusing to go in torn shoes.

"So I'll give him mine," Mordechai offered.

She shook her head. "He's bigger than you. Your shoes will be much too small for him."

Without hesitation, the young Mordechai replied, "These shoes are actually a few sizes too big for me, so they should fit your son."

He ran home, got his old shoes, packed up the new shoes, and

---

1. The shoemaker was the father of Rabbi Bentzion Abba-Shaul, who became *rosh yeshivah* of Porat Yosef.

brought them to the boy's mother. Indeed, the shoes were a perfect fit, and he agreed to go to yeshivah to study.

That night, Mrs. Eliyahu saw her son polishing his old shoes. "Why are you polishing them?" she asked, and he told her the story.

Mrs. Eliyahu was thrilled with her son's wonderful character traits and said, "You'll get new shoes anyway!" She took him back to the shoemaker and asked him to make another pair of shoes for the young Mordechai.

"What happened?" the shoemaker asked. "You got new shoes just yesterday! Where are they?"

Mrs. Eliyahu told him the story. The shoemaker, astounded by the generosity of the young boy, told her he was prepared to sell her the shoes at cost price only and forgo his profits.[2]

Retaining Dignity in Trying Times

The situation in Jerusalem during the days of the War of

Yeshivat Porat Yosef under fire during the War of Independence, 1948

---

2. This story was related by Rabbi Shimon Eliyahu, Hacham Mordechai's brother.

Independence[3] was very difficult. The grave shortage of food was nearing catastrophic proportions. Men, women, and children were starving for bread, and meat or fish were distant dreams.

There were days when no one managed to access food at all, and even when food was distributed, it was in scant supply. Of course, when food was delivered to the shelters, people jumped up to get it, pushing, shoving, and scrambling to grab a portion, understandably motivated by fear and ravenous hunger. The distributor had to be very strict and careful when allocating the portions, so as to ensure adequate supplies for everyone. It was total pandemonium and utter chaos.

Those who were with the young Rabbi Eliyahu in the shelter knew that he never rose from his place or went to the corner where the portions were being allocated. If someone managed to save some food for him, he had something to eat, but if they didn't get any for him, he simply went hungry. But to fall upon the food, scuffling with the crowd? That was something he simply wasn't capable of doing.[4]

Don't Wake Anyone

Rabbi Eliyahu's assistant, Rabbi Yehudah Mutzafi, was with the rabbi on a particularly busy day. They had spent the entire day on the road, visiting kibbutzim. Because they were dealing with kibbutzim where the food wasn't kosher, they couldn't eat anything, and by the end of the day they were quite hungry.

They arrived at the Kinar Galil Hotel[5] after midnight, to spend the night there. As soon as they entered the premises, Rabbi Eliyahu instructed Rabbi Mutzafi to go straight to his room to

---

3. 1947–1948.

4. As related by Rabbi Moshe Tzadkah.

5. On the northeastern bank of the Kinneret (Sea of Galilee).

sleep, warning him not to wake anyone to bring them food. A short time later, Rabbi Mutzafi knocked on Rabbi Eliyahu's door, carrying a thermos of hot water.

"I told you not to wake anyone!" Rabbi Eliyahu admonished him.

"Don't worry," Rabbi Mutzafi said. "The hot water was next to the hotel's synagogue, for the guests to use." Only then would Rabbi Eliyahu take the water and drink, even though he had had a full day during which he hadn't eaten a thing.

FOR THE SAKE OF KASHRUT

Personal Supervision

Rabbi Eliyahu was extremely careful with kashrut and would not eat anything if there were any doubts as to its origins. Even when his early morning driver, Shalom Konaniyan Cohen, would prepare the food, Rabbi Eliyahu would check everything and only then agree to eat it.

One day, somebody brought the rabbi a box of herbal tea produced in Holland, praising the brew for its taste and health benefits. The man explained that he thought it would really help the rabbi, so he had gone to some trouble to find and transport it from abroad.

Rabbi Eliyahu thanked him and took the special tea from the man's outstretched hands. This visitor was clearly very pleased. Afterward, Shalom, who had witnessed the incident, asked Rabbi Eliyahu, "What's so special about this tea that we have to bring it from Holland? We have better tea than this in Israel! Why do we have to eat produce from abroad?"

Rabbi Eliyahu replied, "That man went to a lot of trouble, and we have to give him a good feeling and show gratitude for all the trouble he went to. But don't worry! I have a serious *mashgiah* at home," he said, clearly implying the *rabbanit*. "I also have a big garbage bin in the kitchen," he said. "The *rabbanit* checks everything, and every item that doesn't meet with her approval goes right into the garbage."

Shalom Konaniyan Cohen quickly learned that not only was Rabbi Eliyahu extremely cautious in matters of kashrut, he was equally careful in matters of respecting his fellow man.

Rice and Wine

Once, Rabbi Shmuel Eliyahu was sitting with his father when he was served rice. Rabbi Eliyahu didn't want to eat the rice, even though his family and assistants pleaded with him to do so. When Rabbi Shmuel asked his father why he wouldn't eat, Rabbi Eliyahu looked up, took the fork in his hand, and divided the serving of rice into two halves on the plate. There, between the two portions, was a worm.

When Rabbi Shmuel asked his father how he had known there was a worm there, he answered, "It's written that the Holy One, blessed is He, doesn't let people err with non-kosher food. Especially if someone is careful in this world, he is warned from Above."[6]

Rabbi Shmuel sought clarification, asking his father how someone receives such a warning. Rabbi Eliyahu answered that there are several ways. One is that a person has a strong desire to eat that particular food, which can actually be a sign that there's

---

6. See *Chullin* 7a: *Rabbi Zeira answered, "Now, since even with regard to the animals of the righteous, the Holy One, blessed be He, does not generate mishaps through them, is it not all the more so true that the righteous themselves would not experience mishaps?"*

something forbidden in it. The evil inclination tries very hard to make people stumble.

On a different occasion, Hacham Mordechai and Rabbi Shmuel went to visit a major winery with several other rabbis. When the rabbis arrived, they were offered grape juice by the *mashgiah* of the winery. Everyone took a glass, except Hacham Mordechai. Despite everyone's pleading and cajoling, Rabbi Eliyahu simply would not drink.

After the initial refreshments, the rabbis began a tour of the winery during which they were shown all the kashrut procedures and precautions. When the tour came to an end, Rabbi Eliyahu asked the *mashgiah* how the tithing of the wine was carried out. The *mashgiah* explained that they tithed the wine after bottling it.

"And where do you keep the bottles that were already tithed and those that were not?" Rabbi Eliyahu asked.

The *mashgiah* pointed to a particular spot where the tithed bottles were kept and to the place where those that still needed tithing were waiting.

Rabbi Eliyahu then asked another question. "And from where did you take the grape juice that you offered us at the beginning of the tour?"

The *mashgiah* stood aghast, in total astonishment and shock. "Rabbi Eliyahu has Divine inspiration. How could he know three hours ago, at the beginning of the tour, that the grape juice that I brought was *tevel* (untithed)?"

Rabbi Eliyahu demurred. "I don't have plain inspiration, nor do I have Divine inspiration. I'm just cautious. Why wait to tithe grape juice until it's already bottled? Our Sages warn us not to leave fruit or wine in the house that hasn't yet been tithed,[7] so

---

7. This concept is discussed in the Talmud, *Berachot* 35b.

that we shouldn't make any mistake. Whoever leaves wine without tithing it, intending to take care of it at the end, will surely slip up, as he is not following the injunction of the Sages."

Chapter Six

Purity

Purity repairs the heart and corrects the thoughts. And this is the language that we find from King David, who said, *Create in me a pure heart, O L-rd.*[1] A person should not allow the evil inclination any place in his deeds; rather, all of a person's deeds should emanate from a place of wisdom and awe — and not from any sin or desire.

This applies even for bodily and material deeds: Even if a person made abstinence a part of his life and only took what was essential from this world, he still needs to purify his heart and thoughts. He needs to work so that even the little he takes is not intended for personal enjoyment or desire, but rather for the greater good.

---

1. *Tehillim* 51:12.

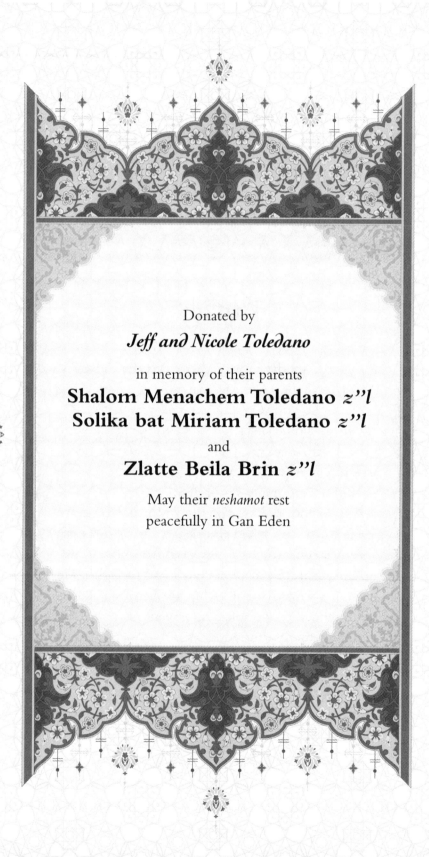

Donated by
Jeff and Nicole Toledano

in memory of their parents
Shalom Menachem Toledano *z"l*
Solika bat Miriam Toledano *z"l*
and
Zlatte Beila Brin *z"l*

May their *neshamot* rest
peacefully in Gan Eden

FOR THE SAKE OF THE MITZVAH

Negatives Destroyed

During one of Rabbi Eliyahu's visits to Jewish communities in Canada, he heard from rabbis and community leaders there that Jews in Quebec had a serious problem regarding the *mikvah*. There was a beautiful, kosher *mikvah* in town, but the keys were unfortunately in the hands of a Reform rabbi. This individual didn't believe in the concepts of purity and impurity, let alone halachah, so he only opened the *mikvah* once a week.

This brief window of availability caused significant distress to many people. Sometimes they had to wait a week or more to visit the ritual bath, due to the callousness of the Reform rabbi who held the keys — and the power.

Rabbi Eliyahu inquired as to how the keys had ended up in this rabbi's hands in the first place, and he soon learned that the *mikvah* had been built with financial assistance from the local government authority. Because the Reform rabbi had close ties to people in the government, he was able to present himself as the representative of all the Jews in the area, and thereby be placed in control of the *mikvah's* keys. He was thus given the jurisdiction to administer the facility on his own terms.

Rabbi Eliyahu called the Reform rabbi and said, "You don't believe in immersing in the *mikvah* anyway, so why not just give the keys to the Orthodox rabbis and they'll operate it on a daily basis?"

But the man replied, "Because the keys and the *mikvah* are in my hands, they need me, and it would be a shame for me to lose that power."

Rabbi Eliyahu then said, "Either you open the *mikvah* daily, or I will go to the mayor and tell him, with the authority of my position as chief rabbi of Israel, that you're not a proper rabbi but an imposter. And I will ask him to transfer the keys to the Orthodox rabbis so they can operate the *mikvah* properly."

Although the Reform rabbi was shocked, he couldn't bring himself to retreat gracefully. Instead, he made his own suggestion. "If that's the case, I want you to come visit me at my house and I'll give you the keys there." Rabbi Eliyahu agreed.

After the conversation, the community leaders and rabbis told Rabbi Eliyahu that the Reform rabbi would surely have newspaper reporters and photographers there to record this big event: the chief rabbi of Israel visiting the home of a Reform rabbi. This public acknowledgment would be tantamount to a legitimization of the Reform movement. The photos he would publish, showing Rabbi Eliyahu honoring a Reform rabbi with a personal visit, would surely result in a huge disgrace of Orthodox Jewry and Rabbi Eliyahu personally, as well as a public outcry.

Rabbi Eliyahu reassured them with a smile. "We're doing this for the sake of a commandment, for the sake of the purity of the Jewish nation, and those involved in carrying out a commandment are protected from harm."

The next day, Rabbi Eliyahu went to the Reform rabbi's house, and sure enough, beside the entrance stood a photographer from Canada's most widely read newspaper. He had three cameras dangling from his neck, and he made sure to photograph Rabbi Eliyahu from every possible angle together with the Reform rabbi. Rabbi Eliyahu received the keys and handed them over to the Orthodox community to be used for the sake of their purity.

Later that day, Rabbi Eliyahu instructed Rabbi David Sabbah, the chief rabbi of the Sephardic community in Quebec, to go to the photographer and buy all the photographs he had taken. He said that Rabbi Sabbah should make the purchase even at an exorbitant price, if necessary, to avoid the desecration of G-d's

Name that would surely occur if people would see Rabbi Eliyahu at a Reform rabbi's home.

Rabbi Sabbah indeed approached the photographer about making the purchase. But the photographer said all the photographs technically belonged to the Reform rabbi. Nevertheless, he was prepared to sell them to Rabbi Sabbah at a higher price when they were ready.

The next day, when Rabbi Sabbah returned to the photographer to buy the pictures, he found the man boiling with rage. "Your rabbi is a magician! All the pictures I took on all three cameras are ruined! I've never experienced such a thing in my entire career. I lost everything I wanted to earn from both of you!"

When Rabbi Sabbah related the story to Rabbi Eliyahu, Rabbi Eliyahu smiled and said, "From here you can see how important the commandment of purity is before the Holy One blessed is He."

Rabbi Eliyahu opening a *mikvah* at a Gush Katif hotel (credit: harav.org)

Ayatollah Khomeini's *Mikvah*

When Ayatollah Khomeini took over Iran in 1979, many Jews had already fled the country. Some had managed to bring a little of their property with them, but most had to leave empty-handed. During the reign of the Shah,[2] most Persian Jews felt confident that their lives and livelihoods were safe, mainly due to the close connections the Shah had with the State of Israel. But in almost no time at all, everything collapsed.[3]

Ayatollah Khomeini's[4] rise to power triggered a massive wave of anti-Israel sentiment and general anti-Semitism. Many Persian Jews, mostly wealthy ones, were tried in kangaroo courts of the revolution, where they were sentenced to death by hanging, and their property was confiscated and given to Khomeini's people.

The lives of Jews in Iran turned upside down in this anarchic atmosphere. And *mikvah*-goers suffered in particular, as non-Jews would harass and bother them whenever they tried to fulfill the mitzvah of immersing in the *mikvah*.

The situation came to the attention of Rabbi Eliyahu, who turned to Ayatollah Khomeini directly by way of a formal letter from the State of Israel. The rabbi wrote to the ayatollah, saying that he was sure the ayatollah wouldn't do anything against a person's faith or against the word of G-d. He wrote that he was certain that Khomeini would agree that it wasn't right or fair that a person should face persecution when going to immerse in a *mikvah*, and he was convinced that such things had been done without his authority, as he was an honest, decent man, and so on.

Khomeini's officers were rather suspicious of the letter, but the

---

2. Mohammad Reza Pahlavi, also known as Mohammad Reza Shah, was the last shah of Iran. He ruled from 1941 to 1979.

3. The Shah fled the country on January 16, 1979. By February 11, 1979, his monarchy had been completely overthrown.

4. Ayatollah Khomeini was the founder of the Islamic Republic of Iran. He led the Iranian Revolution that ultimately overthrew the last shah and ended 2,500 years of Persian monarchy.

ayatollah nevertheless wanted to see what else Rabbi Eliyahu had written. He read about the problems that the Muslims were causing the Jews, and immediately he ordered that a new *mikvah* be built for them. In addition, he even placed guards on site to prevent the Muslims from bothering those Jews who were simply trying to keep the halachah properly.[5]

WORKING WITH THE DEAD

A Story Forbidden to Tell

A certain G-d-fearing individual had still not been blessed with children after many years of marriage. He loved his wife very much, but he desperately wanted children, and after ten years had passed without his wife conceiving, he decided to divorce her in order to marry someone else.

Precisely the week that the *get* (divorce document) was to be handed to his wife, the man's father passed away. It was Motzae Shabbat, and there was no one who could do the *taharah* (purification before burial) for the deceased. Rabbi Eliyahu rolled up his sleeves and started to perform the *taharah* himself, so that the burial could take place the same night and the deceased's body wouldn't have to be left waiting until the next day when the burial society would arrive.

During the *taharah*, someone who was helping Rabbi Eliyahu with the process told him that the son of the deceased was about

---

5. As heard from Effi Cohen Tzemah, deputy mayor of Bet She'an.

to divorce his wife right after the seven days of mourning, because they had not had children after more than ten years of marriage.

The rabbi took a note and put it between the burial shrouds, underneath the head of the deceased. After that, he said to the deceased, "When you reach Heaven and arrive at the Heavenly courtroom, demand that your son be blessed with children."

The rabbi went out of the purification room and told the deceased's son, "Don't get divorced — within a year you'll have children."

Later, the rabbi said to the man who had helped him with the *taharah*, "Don't tell anyone what you've seen here until after I'm no longer in this world."

And, indeed, this story remained untold until the twenty-fifth of Sivan 2010, when the rabbi returned his soul to his Creator. After the *shivah*, the man who had been with the rabbi in the purification room came to Rabbi Eliyahu's family and shared this amazing story.

Just as the rabbi had said, the couple's first son was born within the same year that the man's father had passed away. Afterward, more children were born, year after year, exactly as the rabbi had ordered the deceased.[6]

Lessons from the Dead

Rabbi Naim Eliyahu, one of Hacham Mordechai's brothers, recalled how much Hacham Mordechai yearned to hear *mussar* (ethical advice). Once, Hacham Mordechai personally performed the ritual purification on an individual who had recently passed away. Hacham Mordechai didn't know the man at all — and he was at that time the chief rabbi of Israel.

---

6. As heard from Rabbi Haim Suissa, one of the rabbi's assistants and the CEO of the Darche Horaah Institutions.

His brother Rabbi Naim went to him and said, "I'm your older brother — if there's no one available to do a *taharah*, call me and I'll do it."

But Rabbi Mordechai answered, "All day long I'm giving *mussar* to other people, but there's no one to give *mussar* to me. When I'm purifying the dead, I learn a big ethical lesson from it."

Secret Missions

Every Friday afternoon, Rabbi Eliyahu would leave his home for some unknown reason, headed to some unknown destination. No one in the house knew why he went out or to where, and the matter aroused a lot of curiosity in his children. When his son Shmuel was about seven years old, he decided that the next Friday he would surreptitiously follow his father to uncover the reason for his father's Friday afternoon outings, and indeed, that's what he did.

The next Friday afternoon, the young Shmuel kept a close watch on his father when he left, as usual, before Shabbat. Furtively following from behind, Shmuel kept pace as his father walked through the streets of Jerusalem, crossed Jaffa Road, and entered a building. The young Shmuel also went into the building, walking after him, and continued the mission he'd set for himself.

"This is what I saw," he later related. "My father pulled on white clothes and put on boots and went into a room. I followed him into the room, and saw nothing but a bed, which was covered in a white sheet." Of course, the young Shmuel was caught immediately.

"What are you doing here?" Rabbi Eliyahu asked his son, sending him out of the room.

The young Shmuel waited until his father emerged. "I dared ask him what he'd been doing there. He explained that many people pass away close to the beginning of Shabbat and that there's no one to perform the ritual purification, so that's what he went there to do."

Only later, as he got older, did Rabbi Shmuel understand that his father was doing the purifications so that people could be buried on the same day, before Shabbat.

⚊⚊

PURITY OF SOUL

Infusion in Doses

Rabbi Shlomo Ben Eliyahu, the rabbi of the Mateh Asher regional council,[7] frequently accompanied Rabbi Eliyahu when he would visit the sick in the hospital. On one occasion, one of the patients asked Rabbi Eliyahu if it was permissible for him to receive sustenance via an intravenous tube on Yom Kippur.

Before the rabbi replied, he raised his arms to the heavens and cried, "Master of the Universe! See what a Jew lying in his sickbed thinks of! They love You and Your commandments. Have mercy on us and send us a speedy recovery!"

In the Merit of Holiness

A case was brought before a group that works to rescue young Jews from spiritually dangerous situations. In this particular case, a young Jewish girl had been entrapped by a vile, impure cult, and the organization wanted to help her escape. Although they had succeeded in making contact with her, she was so deeply entrenched in the impurity, and so trapped within a fog of powerful spiritual

---

7. In the western Galilee area of northern Israel.

confusion, that she refused to leave. She was essentially a spiritual prisoner there.

The caseworkers approached Rabbi Eliyahu, hoping that his deep love of the Jewish people and purity of heart would hold sway against the potent forces of impurity controlling the girl. They sought his advice on how to release the girl from the influence of this vile cult.

"Tell her to ritually wash her hands according to the advice of our great master the Ben Ish Hai," he advised them. He then elaborated. "When a man can't go to the *mikvah* to purify himself for whatever reason, he can also purify himself by ritually washing his hands forty times. Tell the girl to do this ritual washing and then she'll agree to leave the cult."

The rabbi then explained exactly how to do it. "First of all, wash the right hand ten times, and then the left hand ten times. With each pouring of water, concentrate on one of the letters of G-d's Name — *yud, heh, vav, heh*. For example, when doing the right hand — *yud*, when washing the left hand — *vav*, and so on. Then, wash the right hand ten times consecutively and then the left hand ten times, and again with each wash, concentrate on one of the letters of G-d's Name."

The rabbi explained that this method relies on deep spiritual secrets that can raise a person out of the depths of impurity. "Although this method isn't really for women, who do need to go to a *mikvah* to purify themselves, and ritual handwashing doesn't help them, do it for this girl anyway," he said, "and then you will be able to get her out of the impurity into which she has descended."

Indeed, she performed the specific ritual handwashing that Rabbi Eliyahu had prescribed. She began to understand the danger she was in, and the rabbis successfully managed to get her out of the terrible cult and back to the safety of her own home.

After she was out of harm's way, she assisted another girl from the same cult who was similarly entrenched in the depths of impurity. And everything was in the merit of the rabbi's holiness that pulled them up and out of there.[8]

Bar Kochba's *Tefillin*

Rabbi Eliyahu once met Professor Yigael Yadin,[9] the archeologist who excavated some of the most historically significant sites in Israel.[10] When he worked on the Masada site, in the region of the Dead Sea, he uncovered a number of *mikvaot*, as well as *tefillin* and many other holy items.

"At that time there was no access to Masada via the Dead Sea, only via Be'er Sheva," Rabbi Eliyahu later recalled. "As I was then serving as a rabbinical judge in Be'er Sheva, the professor called me to come and view the discoveries.

"When I arrived there, he showed me the *mikvaot* he had uncovered from that period. I measured the *mikvaot* and found that they met the measurements required by Jewish law. I noticed a slot cast into the side of one of the walls of the *mikvah*, and when I asked Professor Yadin if he knew what it was, he admitted that he did not.

"I explained that it was a mark to show that the water had reached forty *se'ah* (a halachic measurement),[11] and that they had

---

8. This story was heard from Harel Hatzroni, of OU Israel.

9. 1917–1984. He was also an IDF soldier and politician.

10. His excavation sites included the Qumran Caves (where the Dead Sea scrolls were discovered), Masada, Hazor, Tel Megiddo, and caves in the Judean Desert, where artifacts from the Bar Kochba revolt were found.

11. This is the minimum amount of water needed to fill a *mikvah*, as mandated by Jewish law.

placed it there to ensure that the water didn't fall below that level. He was delighted with the discovery.

"Afterward, the professor brought me a pair of *tefillin* that he had found during the dig. I told him that I wanted to see if they were *tefillin shel Rashi* or *shel Rabbenu Tam.*[12] The professor was very polite as he said, 'Honored rabbi, you may be an expert in Jewish law but perhaps not such an expert in history. Rashi[13] and Rabbenu Tam[14] lived around eight hundred years ago in France, but this site at Masada is from almost two thousand years ago in the land of Israel. It's not possible that these *tefillin* could follow the opinion of Rashi or Rabbenu Tam!'

"I gently explained that *tefillin shel Rashi* and *tefillin shel Rabbenu Tam* were the names of different halachic methods for preparing the *tefillin*. Although they were identified by the names of more recent rabbis, they were in use for many, many years before those rabbis lived."

Rabbi Eliyahu explained that after they had opened the *tefillin*, they found that they were written according to Rashi's ruling. The writing was extremely clear, despite the two thousand years they had been buried in the ground.

When Rabbi Eliyahu shared this story with some of his students, they asked how it was possible that Professor Yadin didn't start donning *tefillin* right away, after seeing that the fighters of the Bar Kochba revolt had made such an effort to do so. Wasn't he

---

12. These are two types of *tefillin*, prepared according to two different halachic approaches and understandings.

13. Rashi is an acronym for Rabbi Shlomo Yitzhaki. He lived from 1040 to 1105, in France. He was the author of comprehensive commentaries on the Talmud and Tanach, both of which remain a centerpiece of Jewish Torah study today.

14. Rabbi Yaakov ben Meir, 1100–1171, best known as Rabbenu Tam, was one of the most renowned Ashkenazi rabbis and leading French Tosafists. He was one of the most prominent halachic authorities of his generation, and was a grandson of Rashi.

inspired by seeing their example and witnessing how they kept that commandment even under such difficult conditions?[15]

Rabbi Eliyahu's students were stunned that Professor Yadin hadn't been inspired by the *tefillin* as a link between the generations. They were sure he must have seen the appeal of continuing the same path, using *tefillin* and *mikvaot* and inheriting the land of Israel.

Rabbi Eliyahu explained that Professor Yadin looked at the *tefillin* as a professor of archeology, and not as observant Jews would see them. He cited an example from the Talmud, saying that if we would meet Abaye[16] today, we would be interested in his spirit, his opinions, and his words. But an archeology professor would be interested in what Abaye was wearing, what he ate, and other such material things. "We are trying to continue the path, walking it in reality, traveling it in our own lives," he said, "not just looking at that path as an interesting trail from the past."[17]

A Desert Rectification

Rabbi Eliyahu once traveled through the Mojave Desert, which is situated between Los Angeles and the desert resort town of Palm Springs. The area was completely desolate, with no signs of life. In the middle of the journey, Rabbi Eliyahu suddenly instructed his driver to stop.

They pulled over on the side of the road, in the middle of this desert. There they noticed the remains of some food. Rabbi

---

15. They were besieged by the Roman army, which had surrounded Masada. They eventually committed mass suicide rather than surrender to the Romans.

16. A famous rabbi from Talmudic times, Abaye lived in Babylonia. He was born near the close of the third century, and passed away in 339 CE.

17. This story was related by Eitan Melamed, one of the congregants at the Hechal Yaakov synagogue.

Eliyahu said, "A Jew ate here once and didn't make a blessing over the food. His act needs to be rectified."

They ate there and made blessings over their own food with deep and careful concentration such as they'd never done before.[18] The rectification was complete.

---

18. This story was shared by Rabbi Yigal Kutai of Hevron.

Chapter Seven

Piety

The Holy One blessed is He only loves those who love Israel. According to the measure that a person increases his love for Israel, so too the Holy One blessed is He increases His love for him.

This is true regarding the shepherds of Israel, who the Holy One blessed is He desires very much. They give themselves for their flock, seeking to help and safeguard them, and to improve their lot in their every way. They are ever ready to stand in the breach to pray for them, beseeching G-d to cancel harsh decrees against them and open the gates of blessing…

In honor
of
**Dr. James V.
and
Catherine C. Benedict**

A LOVE OF THE LAND

Fighting with Fire and Fortitude

Rabbi Eliyahu was known for receiving everyone with great warmth. Even when he was a member of the Rabbinical High Court, petitioners would find in him a listening ear, a soft reply, and a warm response. This unique trait of his always stood out. But whenever he taught Torah and gave halachic opinions, he was firm in his beliefs. And when it came to questions about the land of Israel, he was known for being particularly unyielding. This came, of course, from a deep love of the Holy Land, and not from any political opinions or affiliations. When Israel's fate was on the line, he fought with fire and fortitude. His attitude toward the Gush Katif[1] expulsion was one of the most prominent examples of this trait.

Rabbi Mordechai Eliyahu beside the sea at Gush Katif (credit: harav.org)

---

1. Gush Katif was a bloc of seventeen Israeli settlements in the southern Gaza Strip. The IDF evacuated the region in August 2005, forcibly removing the 8,600 residents of Gush Katif from their homes. The communities were completely dismantled and demolished under Israel's unilateral disengagement from the Gaza Strip.

During the period when Gush Katif was being evacuated, he shouted, cried, and even attacked — contrary to his usual practice. Of course, this was done alongside fervent prayers and out of his great love for Torah, the land of Israel, and the Jews who settled the land. When Rabbi Eliyahu saw the danger facing these Jews, he cried out with all his heart, both as an individual and as part of the communal prayer gatherings he arranged. He traveled to the Tomb of the Patriarchs in Hevron, pouring out his heart for the sake of the Jewish people. Rabbi Shlomo Moshe Amar, the former chief rabbi of Israel,[2] recalled that Rabbi Mordechai's efforts for the sake of the Jewish people were truly extraordinary.

Rabbi Eliyahu arranged communal prayers for the sake of the Jewish nation on many occasions. When he would become aware of some decree hanging over the Jewish people, he would immediately organize a public prayer rally and call on the people to entreat G-d. He often cited the words of the Rambam,[3] who wrote that whoever does not cry out to G-d when there is a decree is cruel.[4] Sometimes the purpose of the Jewish people's troubles is to inspire repentance among the people; not reacting, or treating these troubles with indifference, only leads to greater difficulties.

"And so we must cry out today," Rabbi Eliyahu would say, referencing the Rambam. "When people want to hand over parts of the Land to non-Jews, we must pray and cry out to G-d."

Sometimes Rabbi Eliyahu would meet with the heads of

---

2. Rabbi Amar is the current Sephardic chief rabbi of Jerusalem. He was the Sephardic chief rabbi of Israel, the *Rishon LeZion*, from 2003 to 2013.

3. Rabbi Moses ben Maimon, often called Maimonides, was born in Cordoba, modern-day Spain, in 1135 or 1138. He served as a rabbi, doctor, and philosopher in Morocco and Egypt, becoming a most influential and prolific Torah scholar. His work, particularly the *Mishnah Torah*, remains a cornerstone of Torah study today.

4. *Mishnah Torah, Hilchot Ta'aniyot* 3.

government and Cabinet ministers to warn them about returning the territories of Israel. He would grasp the hand of the senior officers who would come to him, beseeching them to guard the lives of the Jewish people without fear. When there were disturbances on the Temple Mount and a number of Arab troublemakers were killed by fire from the Israeli security forces, the local press and international media whipped up quite a storm. But Rabbi Eliyahu phoned the officer in charge of the Temple Mount security forces, reassuring, encouraging, and blessing him to continue on the same path and not be afraid. He knew when to be forthcoming and friendly and when to use fortitude and fire.

Son of Fatima

After the Six-Day War, Israel's soldiers reached the Cave of the Patriarchs in Hevron. Although the Patriarchs and Matriarchs are entombed there, the Arabs did not permit entry to the Jews, claiming that Avraham, Yitzhak, and Yaakov belonged only to them. They gave permission for Jews to climb only until the seventh step leading up to the tomb, and no further.

When Israeli forces liberated Hevron, Jerusalem, and other sites in the Six-Day War, Chief Rabbi Yitzhak Nissim sent Rabbi Eliyahu to visit and inspect the Cave of the Patriarchs, the Kotel, and Rachel's Tomb. When they were at the cave, a number of soldiers entered. This was the first time anyone had been inside after the battles.

There were many high-ranking army commanders and numerous soldiers there, among them Yitzhak Rabin,[5] Haim Bar-Lev,[6] and

---

5. Rabin was IDF chief of staff during the Six-Day War.

6. 1924–1994. He was a military officer in pre-state Israel and during the early years of statehood. He was deputy chief of staff during the Six-Day War. He later served as a government minister and ambassador.

Uzi Narkiss.[7] A number of prominent rabbis were also present. Some of the soldiers were injured, some were hungry, and most of them were exhausted after days of fighting. They saw the rugs in the cave and lay down, soon falling asleep. Suddenly, the sheik in charge of the cave, a man named Jibri, came out and started shouting at the commanders and soldiers.

"Get out of this cave!" he yelled. "You have no respect for it! We Muslims wash our hands five times when we come here. We take off our shoes and honor this place. But you show no respect whatsoever. Your soldiers are eating here, sleeping here, walking on the rugs with their dirty boots. You have no respect for this holy place — leave!"

Apparently, he was right.

Everyone was silent — except one.

Rabbi Eliyahu, who understood Arabic, as did most of the senior commanders, responded, "Listen to me, sheik. You know that if a servant comes before the king in soiled clothes, or serves him food on a filthy tray in front of all the king's ministers and servants, he will surely be put to death.

"But if the king's son was absent from his mother and father's home for many years, and his father spent many nights worrying about him and his mother crying for him, if that son was to return home after many years, how do you think the king would receive him? What if he simply wandered in without making an appointment? What if he showed up with torn, dusty clothes, and interrupted the king's conference with his ministers, crying, 'Father, I came home!'?

"What if he approaches his mother, the queen, calling, 'Mother,

---

7. Uzi Narkiss, 1925–1997, was a general in the IDF, commanding the units in the Central Region during the Six-Day War.

I'm here'? His mother and father would surely hug him, loving him, and thanking G-d with all their hearts for his homecoming, even with his ripped, dirty clothes — because he is their son."

Rabbi Eliyahu looked at the sheik and said, "Avraham was our father. Sarah was our mother. We behave here as though in our own home. You, however, are the 'sons of Fatima,' the children of the maidservant Hagar. You behave as is appropriate for a servant to behave, and we behave as is appropriate for children to behave!"

The sheik turned red with shame. Not only did he have no rejoinder for the rabbi, he had been called a "son of Fatima," son of the maidservant. He was insulted. He turned on the spot and stormed back into his room in a great rage.

The senior commanders there immediately turned to Rabbi Eliyahu, asking in dismay, "Why did you do that?

"We want to live in peaceful coexistence with the Arabs," they said. "Why did you have to upset him?"

Rabbi Eliyahu replied, "You have to tell them the truth. That's the only thing they understand."

The argument continued for a few minutes, until the door of the sheik's room suddenly opened. The sheik exited his room with his head down, approaching Rabbi Eliyahu in deference. "Oh Wise One, oh Master, please forgive me!" he cried.

Rabbi Eliyahu didn't turn to him or even respond. He simply looked at the commanders and said, "You see what language they understand? I grew up among the Arabs from when I was a young child in the Old City of Jerusalem. Tell them the truth and they will understand!"

Shop during the Three Weeks!

A group of South African Jewish tourists came to visit Israel, but they arrived during the Three Weeks (a period of mourning for the Temple). According to halachah, this is not normally a time when pleasure shopping is usually permitted. They asked their tour guide about that, and about touring in general. Although he told them the halachah — that these activities were forbidden — he decided to ask Rabbi Eliyahu about the issue. The tourists had very little time in Israel and would surely want to purchase all kinds of souvenirs and mementos.

Rabbi Eliyahu answered that not only was it permitted, it was actually a commandment. "It's a mitzvah for them to tour the country during the Three Weeks, a mitzvah for them to purchase souvenirs, and definitely a mitzvah for them to shop and travel as much as possible."

The guide sought clarification as to why this was permitted. Rabbi Eliyahu explained that the Three Weeks are connected to the sin of the spies who came to check out the land of Israel but didn't understand its value or importance and brought back negative reports.[8]

"Tourists from abroad need to learn to love Israel and fix that sin," Rabbi Eliyahu said. "If they don't go touring, how will they acquire a love of the land? And if they don't go shopping, how can they take home the story of our beautiful land to their families?"

Praying against Predictions

According to Rabbi Eliyahu, Rabbi Baruch Shapira,[9] an elderly rabbi in Maale Adumim, was one of the thirty-six hidden righteous

---

8. The sin of the spies, known as the *het hameraglim*, is discussed in *Bamidbar* 13:1–33.

9. Born in Russia in 1903/4, Rabbi Shapira moved to Israel around 1932, where he studied Torah in depth, distinguishing himself with profound insights into matters of revealed and hidden Torah, as well as with his broad knowledge in areas of archeology, botany, mathematics, physics, and medicine. He was the rabbi of Mitzpe Ramon and spent his later years in Maale Adumim. He passed away in 1995.

men of the world.[10] Rabbi Eliyahu related that Rabbi Shapira had written him a letter that discussed the expulsion of Gush Katif — about ten years before the issue of Gush Katif ever arose for public discussion and political discourse.

But even though Rabbi Eliyahu had seen the letter and believed that Rabbi Shapira had Divine inspiration, he repeatedly told everyone that the expulsion would not happen. He repeated this sentiment many times, adding that people needed to pray and fight about it and not allow it to happen. He gave instructions about what should be done[11] should the expulsion take place; nevertheless, he constantly urged both the politicians and the settlers to stay strong. He told the settlers not to desert their homes, not to pack, and not to participate in any part of the expulsion.

Rabbi Eliyahu was asked how he could say that it wouldn't happen when he knew from Rabbi Baruch Shapira that it *would* indeed come to pass. "Our job is not to know what will happen, but rather to pray that the decrees will be canceled," Rabbi Eliyahu explained. "That's what the Baba Sali did. That's what Rabbi Ephraim Hakohen[12] did. That's what Rabbi Menahem Menashe,

---

10. Rabbi Eliyahu made this statement in his eulogy for Rabbi Shapira at the rabbi's funeral.

11. In a filmed interview on Israel's Channel 2 news directly prior to the Disengagement, Rabbi Eliyahu said that soldiers and police officers must carry out their assignments, but that they should do so with tears. Regarding the residents of Gush Katif, Rabbi Eliyahu said they should stay put and remain in their homes, but that if the soldiers and police officers came to take them away, they should go with them, without resistance. That way, there would at least be peace between Jews, even if the government was making a terrible mistake.

12. Hacham Ephraim Hakohen, 1885–1956, was a student of the Ben Ish Hai. This erudite kabbalist and scholar knew most of the kabbalistic literature by heart. He headed Oz V'Hadar, the kabbalist yeshivah housed in Porat Yosef.

the Tinsmith, did. And the same goes for Rabbi Yehudah Fetaya[13] and Rabbi Yitzhak Alfia."[14]

He continued, "They would sacrifice themselves to cancel the decrees against Israel. We need to do that, too."

In the days leading up to the Gush Katif expulsion, a group of kabbalists sat down together at the home of Rabbi Haim Cohen,[15] the "Milkman," asking him, "Why is Rabbi Eliyahu saying, 'It will never happen'? We can see [through deep spiritual insight] that it's going to happen. With the same sacred foresight that Rabbi Baruch Shapira envisioned it, Rabbi Eliyahu certainly sees it, too. In fact, he sees more than we all do, and he knows that it's happening. So why does he endanger his credibility by announcing to everyone that it will not happen?"

The Milkman answered, "Why does the Holy One, blessed is He, show us the future? To foretell it to people so that they will see how wise we are? Or so that they will say we have Divine inspiration? G-d forbid! Everything that is shown to us is for the express purpose of inspiring us to pray. We must pray for the cancellation of the decrees, whether we see them from Heaven or we don't."

That was Rabbi Eliyahu's approach. The verse says, *Upon your walls, O Jerusalem, I have posted guardians all day and night, continually; they will never be silent. You who call upon Hashem, do not be silent! Do*

---

13. Rabbi Yehudah Fetaya, 1859–1942, was an Iraqi-born scholar who was recognized for his piety and Torah knowledge at an early age. He ultimately moved to the land of Israel. He is particularly renowned for kabbalistic knowledge, writings, and practices.

14. Rabbi Yitzhak Alfia, 1878–1955, was a Syrian-born scholar and *dayan*, as well as a respected kabbalist. Rabbi Mordechai Eliyahu is said to have also referred to him as one of the thirty-six hidden righteous men of the world.

15. Known as the Halban, Milkman, in Hebrew, Rabbi Haim Cohen lived from 1935 to 2019.

not give Him silence until He establishes and makes Jerusalem a source of praise in the earth.[16] Rabbi Eliyahu embodied the Talmudic precept that even when a sharp sword is hovering on a man's neck, it is forbidden to give up hope of mercy.[17]

It is forbidden for the Jewish people to cease praying. As discussed in *Megillat Esther*, even when Mordechai Hatzaddik saw that the decree against the Jewish people was already "signed" in Heaven, he wasn't deterred from praying. He spurred Esther and the entire Jewish community in Shushan to pray with all their might to rescind the decree. That was Rabbi Eliyahu's modus operandi: that we shouldn't be impressed by what we see from Above, but rather strengthen ourselves in prayer and faith and not let go.[18]

Joy in the Morning

One of Rabbi Eliyahu's grandsons recalled that his grandfather didn't get involved in elections. He would usually say that everyone from all the various parties had something good to offer, and if he could, he would vote for everyone. To those who asked him directly and personally, he would tell them to vote for a religious party.

After the assassination of Yitzhak Rabin,[19] there was a great deal of incitement from the political left against the rabbis and the religious public. During the 1996 prime ministerial elections, Rabbi Eliyahu got publicly involved in the political scene for the first time, praying with all his heart for the success of Binyamin

---

16. *Yeshayahu* 62:6–7.

17. *Berachot* 10a.

18. Rabbi Shmuel Moreno, *rosh yeshivah* of the Maayane Yeshuah yeshivah, related the incidents discussed here.

19. He was assassinated by rightist activist Yigal Amir on November 4, 1995, at the end of a Tel Aviv rally in support of the Oslo Accords.

Netanyahu,[20] who was running in the elections directly against Shimon Peres, the left's candidate.

In those days and in that atmosphere, it seemed clear to everyone that Shimon Peres was going to win. All the polls showed an obvious victory for him against Binyamin Netanyahu, whom the media blamed for the incitement that had led to Rabin's death. In fact, even the election-day exit polls at the balloting centers showed Peres scoring a decisive victory. Nevertheless, during the entire election period, Rabbi Eliyahu encouraged Netanyahu, and on May 29, 1996, the day of the elections, he fasted and prayed all day. Netanyahu won by a margin of 29,457 votes — less than 1 percent of the total votes cast that day.

Rabbi Eliyahu's grandson Amihai later related, "He sent us to help at the election headquarters, so we went. That night, the media was already reporting that Shimon Peres had won, basing their announcements on the exit polls. I went to my grandfather's house and told him what was going on. But he said, 'They're wrong — Netanyahu has won!'"

The idea seemed farfetched, as the left was already holding celebratory speeches and such. Yossi Sarid,[21] a leftist politician and news commentator in the leftist media, was even moved to remark, "There is a G-d!"

Upon hearing this, Rabbi Eliyahu retorted, "He doesn't even realize yet just how much there is a G-d!"

At some point during that long night, some of Netanyahu's aides

---

20. The first Israeli prime minister to be born in Israel after the establishment of the state. He was born in 1949, and has served in many government roles, including his first stint as prime minister from 1996 to 1999, and again from 2009 to the present. He is Israel's longest serving prime minister.

21. 1940–2015. Sarid served as minister of the environment and minister of education during his long political career and was a member of the Meretz party. He also wrote a weekly column for the *Haaretz* newspaper.

called Rabbi Eliyahu. Rabbi Eliyahu comforted them, quoting the verse, *"One goes to sleep weeping at night but in the morning, there is a song of joy!"*[22]

Upon hearing that, Amihai returned home relaxed and at ease. He was certain that if his grandfather had said this, it would come to pass.

Early the next morning, Rabbi Shmuel Eliyahu woke Amihai before the sunrise prayers. "There's been a turnaround," he said. "Netanyahu has won!"

"Abba, I know," Amihai answered. "Saba already told me that last night."

"Well, you see, it happened!" he said.[23]

A LOVE OF THE JEWISH PEOPLE

Crying Over the Attack – Before It Happened

One of the *roshe yeshivah* of Ohr Somayach invited Rabbi Eliyahu to the dedication of a new Torah scroll. He called a week before the terrorist attack at the Mercaz HaRav Yeshivah, where eight students were massacred.[24] He later related, "The moment the rabbi heard the invitation, he burst into tears, weeping aloud. I was astonished by his reaction, and asked him what was the matter.

"The rabbi answered, 'If only snow will fall that night!' That response was a mystery in my eyes — for a week."

---

22. *Tehillim* 30:6.

23. Rabbi Amihai Eliyahu, Rabbi Mordechai's grandson, shared these recollections.

24. The attack took place on March 6, 2008.

At Mercaz HaRav Yeshivah

The day of the attack, Rabbi Eliyahu called for a public prayer rally at the Kotel. It was ostensibly a prayer gathering for Jonathan Pollard,[25] but no one understood why this assembly was so critical or so immediately necessary, specifically on that day. Many students from the Mercaz HaRav Yeshivah showed up for the public prayers.[26]

Rabbi Eliyahu joined the public at the Kotel and requested that the prayers be extended a little more, and then more. And still, no one understood the urgency.

The prayers finally ended. Just at the time when the boys from the

Rabbi Mordechai Eliyahu with Rabbi Efraim Rosenfeld
of Mercaz HaRav (credit: Mercaz HaRav)

---

25. Pollard, born in 1954, was a former intelligence analyst for the U.S. government. In 1987, as part of a plea agreement, Pollard pleaded guilty to spying for and providing top-secret classified information to Israel. He was sentenced to life in a U.S. federal prison for violations of the Espionage Act. Pollard is the only American to have received a life sentence for passing classified information to a U.S. ally. He was released in 2015.

26. This rally, and its timing, are discussed in an editorial in the English *Hamodia*, "The ABCs of *Simhah*." Rebibo, Joel. Israel edition. March 7, 2019, p. 23.

yeshivah were traveling back from the Kotel, the terrorist entered Mercaz HaRav, massacring eight boys. The victims were among the younger students who had stayed in the yeshivah's library to study Torah. The buses returning the older students from the Kotel were blocked on their return by police barriers. The barricades had been set up to close off the road near the yeshivah after the attack.

In the Mossad

There was a man from Safed who was born in that holy northern city around the time the State of Israel was founded.[27] His family was religious, with many rabbis counted among them and their ancestors. It was a time when the security of the state was constantly under threat, and the man, who was just a boy at the time, grew up on tales of Arab uprisings and massacres. It was quite clear to him what would happen to the State of Israel if the Arabs were to win, G-d forbid.

The older members of the family frequently recounted stories of Arab abuse of both the living and the dead. It didn't matter how friendly their Arab neighbors were. With the cries of fallen Jews ringing in his ears and painful images of Jewish victims assailing his nightmares, the boy grew up with a strong message that one must fight to survive.

He joined the Mossad, pursuing evildoers across the globe. With excellent intelligence, the officers routed out terrorists and warmongers in Europe, South America, Egypt, Sudan, Iran, and even Antarctica. There was no terrorist who could hide from them. The Mossad men would arrive quietly, in small groups, locate the terrorist, and dilute some "sugar" in his coffee. He would go to sleep and never wake up. Sometimes they would stage

---

27. This story was related by this man.

an "accident." And sometimes there was no choice and they had to resort to traditional methods and shoot him.

The bodies were not always found. And the Mossad men were never found. They would vanish just as they had appeared, without ever being seen or heard. That was their job, and they never revealed more than that. Even in the State of Israel, they were unknown. Apart from their immediate commanders, even their own families didn't know what they did. Secrecy was their daily bread; in fact, it was their life, and they guarded it with great zealousness.

But there are mishaps in life, and an accident occurred on European soil. The team had been tasked with liquidating a terrorist with a great deal of Jewish blood on his hands, and unfortunately, it appeared that they'd made a mistake in identification. While the man they killed wasn't exactly a righteous individual, their mistake cost them dearly. The country in which it happened wasn't prepared to let it go.

The agents were told, "If you had killed a murderer, they would make a show of investigating and then the case would be closed. But to kill an innocent man?" That was a problem. That country's intelligence organizations began to close in on the Mossad team. Two operatives were caught, and only the man who related this story — and his partner — escaped.

It seemed that the entire Interpol was in pursuit of them, but the international police agency didn't know who they were looking for, what the agents looked like, or any other information. There were no witnesses, and there was no one who could describe or name them, not even their own friends or family.

The man and his fellow officer immediately flew back to Israel to report on the catastrophe that had occurred. They left the rescue of their Mossad colleagues up to the government. Presumably, the State of Israel would pay something and the officers would be freed. As soon as the two men landed in Israel, they were rushed to the prime minister's office to report on the embarrassing incident, sharing all the details of what had taken place, who had been killed, and what had caused the slip-up. They were immediately ushered into the office, where all the higher-ups waited to hear every detail so no more mistakes would be made.

Rabbi Mordechai Eliyahu was waiting at the prime minister's office that day, and even the Mossad officials involved did not know how he knew or what he was doing there. Only ten people in the entire world knew about this incident, and he was among them. The Mossad men were not the sentimental type; they were exceptionally well trained and trustworthy. Israel's security was of the utmost importance to them and they had endangered their lives for the country's citizens more than once. It was a team comprised of the elite of the elite.

At the prime minister's office, there was a great deal of tension. But Rabbi Eliyahu was standing right by the building's entrance and he immediately signaled to one of the two agents to come over to him. Without even understanding what he was doing, the man went. He immediately noticed the great light in Rabbi Eliyahu's eyes, and a wordless exchange of understanding took place between them. Somehow, Rabbi Eliyahu knew. He gave the agent a blessing and told him that nothing bad would happen to his friends; they would simply have to stay in detention in Europe for a while.

His words gave a lot of encouragement and support to the agent, who was, as expected, in a low state. His blessing was that the agent should continue, he should be strengthened, and he shouldn't break down, but should be able to carry on performing the holy task he was involved in.

The Mossad officer didn't ask Rabbi Eliyahu who he was, and he had no idea how Rabbi Eliyahu knew any of his story. What he saw was a holy man, and he knew that there was such a thing in the world. In Safed, where he was born, he had met such people in his childhood. He understood that Rabbi Eliyahu had been sent from Above.

Of course, the Mossad is not the kind of organization that relies on miracles, not by any stretch of the imagination. They prepare every mission down to the smallest detail, checking into every potential scenario, scrutinizing all the details of every possibility at every level. But even with everything being so well prepared, many of their agents recognize how much G-d helps them. They often felt they had seen Him "face to face" in their missions and felt like G-d was with their team, so to speak, helping out in times of need.

At the inquiry, the two agents went over every single aspect of the botched mission with their commanders and operators. The information would later be used in future missions. They gave every possible detail to the prime minister and Cabinet ministers, hoping that some of this information could free their colleagues. When the agent from Safed finally left, he began searching the Mossad files to find out who that rabbi was. He didn't have to search long. It was Rabbi Mordechai Eliyahu.

He kept this story in his heart, not sharing it with his wife, children, or friends. After all, it was a state secret. Many years passed. Although he didn't know if Rabbi Eliyahu remembered him, he certainly remembered the rabbi. When he was older and could no longer perform the kind of jobs he had once done, the man eventually moved back to Safed. Other operatives took over his job, and he was just called in to advise and support the new, younger team.

One day, the man heard that Rabbi Mordechai Eliyahu was coming to Safed for the bar mitzvah of his grandson. It was just a year before his passing, and Rabbi Eliyahu was by then wheelchair-bound and very weak. He had already suffered a heart attack and stroke by that point.

The public really wanted to see him, so the family held prayers in Kikar Hameginim, the central square in Safed's Old City. The former Mossad agent joined the great crowd filling the square, coming to pray along with everyone. Rabbi Eliyahu was so weak, he could barely lift his head. But when the agent arrived in the square, Rabbi Eliyahu raised his eyes, as though he was looking for him. He signaled to the agent from afar, motioning for him to come close. He gave the man a firm greeting, clearly recognizing and remembering him decades later — and after having had only one meeting. Rabbi Eliyahu clearly knew who he was.

Rabbi Eliyahu pointed to the walking stick in the former agent's hands. "What is that?" he asked.

"It's for my back," the man answered. "I'm having back pain."

"Throw it away!" Rabbi Eliyahu said. "You need to be healthy."

There were many people standing in line to receive a blessing, but Rabbi Eliyahu didn't let the former agent go until he had blessed him from the depth of his heart. The man never saw Rabbi Eliyahu again. But right before the operation he had on his back shortly thereafter, the man saw Rabbi Eliyahu in his mind's eye. Moments before the surgery, he clearly envisioned Rabbi Eliyahu blessing him in Kikar Hameginim, waving his hand with a dismissive gesture.

The agent knew the procedure would be successful and felt that Rabbi Eliyahu was truly with him. Later on, when the man finally shared his story, he said, "That's my story. It's just a part of the rabbi's story. We're not talking about his Divine inspiration here, just about his caring for all of Israel. Caring about the people's success, the success of those fighting for the nation, those anonymous fighters whom I was once privileged to be a part of. Where are there other people like that man?"

Rahel Protects Her Sons

The story about Rahel Imenu is one of the most unique stories told about Rabbi Eliyahu...

When Rabbi Eliyahu was initially released from the hospital at the end of 2008, it was only a partial release. He was allowed to leave the hospital grounds for a few hours each day, returning each night to continue treatment, until he was finally fully discharged. The initial release took place toward the end of Hanukah, and when he would leave the hospital for the day, he would ask to be taken to Rahel's Tomb in Bet Lehem, where he would pray. When he finished, he would return to the hospital. That's what he wanted each day, so his assistants complied, even though they didn't know his reasons or understand why he wanted this.

Operation Cast Lead[28] began at that time. Throughout the operation, and until its end twenty-two days later, stories and rumors began to circulate about the soldiers seeing a woman who guided them in Gaza, preventing them from entering booby-trapped buildings. When they inquired about her identity, she apparently answered, "Your mother, Rahel." The stories sounded like works of fantasy, with Rahel Imenu, who passed away thousands of years ago, suddenly appearing in Gaza, of all places.

---

28. The IDF launched Operation Cast Lead in Gaza on the seventh day of Hanukah, December 27, 2008. The government began the operation following persistent terrorist activities and a constant missile threat directed at Israeli civilians from the Gaza Strip. The military's aim was to take down terrorist infrastructure in the Strip. It ended just over three weeks later, on January 18, 2009, following a ceasefire.

But when Rabbi Eliyahu's assistants began looking into these fanciful tales, they learned that there wasn't just one person behind them, or even two. And they discovered that the talebearers were not dreamers and fantasists. The people telling these stories were commanding officers, combat soldiers, and many others who could clearly discern the difference between reality and imagination.

One of the stories, related by David Ezra, father of a soldier in the IDF Paratroopers' Brigade,[29] is as follows:

> The commander ordered us to enter one of the buildings to clean and scope it out. We knew terrorists were very likely holed up in the buildings. They had been preparing for our arrival for a long time and had set up ambushes. Their main goal was to capture a soldier alive and turn him into a second Gilad Shalit.[30]
>
> We were very cautious about entering places where potential ambushes could be lying in wait, but one can't stay still — he must continue advancing. We would enter a building under heavy protection, clean it out, and move on.
>
> One day we received an order to enter one of the deserted buildings. We followed the usual procedure, knocking on the door and preparing to break in. Suddenly, a woman appeared behind us, saying in Hebrew, "Don't go in — it's a trap!"
>
> We had no idea who she was, but we had a good

---

29. An elite infantry brigade under the Central Command.

30. Shalit was an IDF soldier who was captured by Hamas terrorists on June 25, 2006, when they kidnapped him through a cross-border tunnel near the Israeli border. Shalit was held hostage for five years, until his eventual release on October 18, 2011, as part of a prisoner exchange deal.

feeling about her. "Don't go in from here," she said, pointing to the entrance we were about to use. "Enter from the other side."

I don't know why we listened to her; maybe it was because we sensed that she was speaking out of love and compassion. But we did as she advised. The house was empty but, indeed, it was rigged with explosives. If we had entered from the door where we had intended, we would almost certainly have been injured or even killed.

Who was she?

In the storm of war, we didn't have time to ask any extra questions. Who was that woman? Maybe she was Jewish and married to an Arab? Maybe she was married to a collaborator? We carried on with the surveillance, house after house, and suddenly we saw her again, signaling to us, "Don't enter from here; go in from there!"

This time we knew with certainty to listen and do exactly as she had advised, and we asked her, "Who are you?"

"Rahel, your mother," she replied with a radiant smile. "Don't worry, I'm always with you," she said. And with that, she turned and vanished.

When Rabbi Eliyahu's followers asked him if such a story was possible, he replied, "Of course!"

And he told the story of Rabbi Yehudah Fetaya, who prayed at Rahel's Tomb with a quorum of kabbalists in order to stop Rommel's armies. Erwin Rommel was a general of the Nazi German army. Known as the Desert Fox, he had already conquered several countries in North Africa by late 1941 and early 1942, and was advancing toward Egypt. It seemed there was no one who could stop him.

In those days, the British army was forced into retreat after retreat. Rommel was clearly eyeing an entrance into the land of Israel, where he could conquer the land and give its inhabitants up into the hands of Hitler. While all this was going on, Rabbi Yehudah Fetaya was praying fervently at Rahel's Tomb, and there were public prayers held in Damanhur, Egypt,[31] as well, at the tomb of Rabbi Yaakov Abuhatzera, a leading Moroccan rabbi of the nineteenth century.[32] Rabbi Fetaya reported that he saw Rahel Imenu actually praying alongside them.

"I see our mother Rahel praying together with us, facing the Tomb of the Patriarchs," he reportedly told the others. Although he could perceive her, the rest of the men could not, though they reported that they felt her presence.

Rabbi Eliyahu finished the tale by saying, "I was at Rahel's Tomb just a few days ago, and I told her, 'Your sons are going to war now. Go and help them! They are your children.'"

People wanted to know how it was even conceivable that Rahel could just suddenly materialize in modern times. They wanted to know how she possibly could have been seen by so many soldiers at once. And they wanted to know why so many years had passed

---

31. These prayers were led by Rabbi Yitzhak Alfia. He traveled to Egypt to pray after Rabbi Abuhatzera visited him in a dream and told him to come and offer supplications at his grave. The story of this trip and the public prayers in Egypt is recounted in Rabbi Dovid Hoffman's "Rabbenu Yitzhak Alfia" in *Heroes of the Spirit: 100 Rabbinic Tales of the Holocaust* (Lakewood, New Jersey: Israel Bookshop, 2009).

32. Also known as the Abir Yaakov and Abu Hasira, Rabbi Yaakov Abuhatzera (1806–1880) died en route to the Holy Land from Morocco. He was buried in Egypt, and his tomb became known as a holy site to which people make prayer pilgrimages. He was the grandfather of Rabbi Yisrael Abuhatzera, the Baba Sali.

without her making any other appearances, from her days to recent times.

The body is just a garment for the soul. The soul is the essence and it does not die. There are those who live only in the garment, the body, while others connect to the soul and live through that. Rahel Imenu lived through both. She was a real person, a mother of sons, on one hand. And on the other, she was a mother of the entire Jewish people.

Yirmiyahu saw Rahel at the moment of the Exile after the First Temple was destroyed. Two thousand years after her death, he saw her crying for her children. *Thus said G-d: A voice is heard on high, wailing, bitter weeping. Rahel weeps for her children — she refuses to be consoled for her children, for they are gone.*[33]

What Yirmiyahu saw was no illusion. He saw the real prayers of Rahel — a prayer that G-d heard. *And He said, "Restrain your voice from weeping and your eyes from tears, for there is reward for your work," says the L-rd, "and they will return from the enemy's land. And there is hope for your future," says the L-rd, "and your children will return to their border."*[34]

That promise still exists in our days. It exists and manifests in our times through these soldiers, Rabbi Eliyahu explained. "How could she *not* be there?"

The soldiers who saw Rahel experienced something real, Rabbi Eliyahu said. In a situation in which soldiers are sacrificing themselves for the Jewish people, such a thing can happen. At a moment of self-sacrifice, a moment when a person is totally at one with the Jewish people, it happens. It would have been a miracle if Rahel hadn't been there, to help her children.[35]

---

33. *Yirmiyahu* 31:14.

34. Ibid., vv. 15–16.

35. Rabbi Shmuel Eliyahu, the rabbi's son, related these events.

A Blessing for the Arabs

Once, during a period when there were many shootings and terror attacks on the roads, Rabbi Eliyahu needed to travel to the Cave of the Patriarchs. But, as usual, he refused to ride in a bulletproof car, saying he would travel only in the same cars that residents living in Judea and Samaria regularly used. Rabbi Eliyahu and those accompanying him traveled in a convoy, so that the vehicles both in front of and behind the rabbi's car served as security vehicles.

At one of the first bends in the road during their journey, an Arab-driven taxi pushed into the middle of the convoy, coming quite close to the rabbi's car, literally driving right behind it, riding its tail. All those in the security vehicles were tense, fearing a possible terrorist attack, and they tried to overtake the Arab's taxi in every possible way, but they met with no success. The taxi stuck to the back of the rabbi's car like a leech, and nothing they tried could change the situation.

Though they made many attempts, the security officers couldn't get in between the rabbi's car and the Arab's taxi to separate them. Anxiety was high and nerves were tense, so much so that the convoy drivers almost got into an accident. But then Rabbi Eliyahu himself solved the problem by asking to pull over at the side of the road. All the cars in the convoy pulled over, too, with everyone on edge and full of apprehension. The Arab taxi also pulled over. Three men wearing kaffiyehs[36] and a woman in a jilbab[37] stepped out of the car.

Rabbi Eliyahu's assistants gathered around him to protect him

---

36. A traditional Middle Eastern headdress, and in relation to the Israeli-Palestinian conflict, a symbol of Palestinian nationalism and solidarity.

37. A long and loose-fitting coat or outer garment.

from the taxi's Arab passengers. But Rabbi Eliyahu just smiled widely and said, "Call them over so they can get a blessing!"

Rabbi Eliyahu's assistants were shocked. A *blessing* for these *Arabs*? Weren't they in enough danger already? But they didn't dare go against the rabbi's instructions, so they called the Arabs over. To everyone's great surprise, they came.

As they approached the rabbi, they removed their kaffiyehs, revealing the white yarmulkes they were wearing underneath. To the even greater surprise of Rabbi Eliyahu's assistants, the "Arabs" revealed that they were a group of undercover agents on a mission to protect the rabbi on the roads in those dangerous times.

A LOVE OF FELLOW MAN

The Power of a Prayer

"Everyone knew the power of the prayers and blessings of my brother, Rabbi Mordechai Eliyahu, both when he was the chief rabbi and even before that," Rabbi Shimon Eliyahu, one of Rabbi Mordechai's brothers, recalled.

Rabbi Eliyahu in prayer

"I want to tell you about the power of his prayers when he was a boy not yet thirteen years old — a young boy before his bar mitzvah," he said. "I was eleven then, and it was before the War of Independence. We both learned at Yeshivat Porat Yosef in Jerusalem's Old City, where there were also elementary school classes. One day I went with all the students in my grade to pray for the recovery of Guy Shama, the custodian of the yeshivah. His family had asked that the yeshivah students go after school to pray for him at Rahel's Tomb, and that's what we did."

In those days, the roads to Bet Lehem and Rahel's Tomb were open, so the class went to pray there, with the teacher accompanying all the students back to Jaffa Gate afterward. He gave each boy a *grush*[38] so they would have money to travel home by bus. Rabbi Shimon recalled, "In our house you wouldn't have even found a penny, and because our home was close by, I decided to walk there. When I crossed the road, I was hit by an Arab bus and knocked down, left critically injured. I had no form of identification on me. I was covered in blood, and they took me to an Arab hospital, where I lay in bed.

"The doctors couldn't get a drop of information out of me," he continued. "I had forgotten everything. My head was swollen to twice its size, and even if someone had known me, he wouldn't have recognized me with my injuries."

Meanwhile, Shimon's mother was waiting for him at home. When the hour grew late, she began to worry. She asked Shimon's yeshivah friends if they had seen him, and they told her that they had left him with everyone at Jaffa Gate. Right away, she started making the rounds to the local hospitals together with the young Mordechai, who was two years older than Shimon.

---

38. At the time of this story, *grush* referred to a coin with a hole in it and was valued at 1/100th of a pound. Named after an Ottoman coin, the *grush* was replaced by the lira when Israel became a state in 1948. At that time, coins worth 1/100th of a lira were called *grushim*. The name persisted until the lira was replaced by the shekel in 1980. *Grush* today is slang for a very small value.

They went from hospital to hospital, one after the other, but didn't find him. From there they went to what was then called "Moscow Square," today known as the Russian Compound.[39] The police station was located there and the officers told Mrs. Eliyahu and the young Mordechai that there had been an accident and that indeed there was a young, injured, unidentified boy at one of the Arab hospitals.

Mrs. Eliyahu and Mordechai rushed to the hospital. There they found Shimon lying on one of the beds, his head swollen and his memory gone. The doctors told the two, "This child is gone — he has maybe one more day to live and no more."

"My mother burst into tears," Shimon later recalled. "But Mordechai, who was with her, said, 'Where was Shimon before he was injured? At Rahel's Tomb. Let's go to our mother Rahel and pray to her to heal him.'"

And so the two of them went to pray at Rahel's Tomb. There, the young Mordechai turned to Rahel Imenu, saying, "My brother Shimon was here earlier and prayed for someone's recovery. On his return, he got run over and now he's in the hospital. Pray for him, pray that he should recover!"

By the time they finished praying, it was too late to return to the hospital, as the facility didn't permit family visits at those hours. Mrs. Eliyahu and the young Mordechai returned home, planning to return to the hospital early the following morning. When they got there, they found Shimon still alive — despite the doctors' dire predictions that he wouldn't last the day. Much to the surprise of the department's physicians, Shimon had outlasted the twenty-four-hour period they had given him to live. Not only that, he

---

39. A district in central Jerusalem, it was among the first neighborhoods built outside the Old City walls. The area covers roughly seventeen acres between Jaffa Road, Shivte Yisrael Street, and Haneviim Street.

had regained consciousness and was starting to recognize people. The improvement was so dramatic that the doctors released him the very next day.

After he was given a clean bill of health, Shimon returned home and began the long process of recovery and recuperation. Later, his mother told him about their special prayers at Rahel's Tomb, especially the prayer of a boy not yet thirteen years old for his younger brother.

Taking on Another's Suffering

As related by Jonathan Pollard's wife, Esther, she went to visit Rabbi Eliyahu and told him about Jonathan's worsening medical situation.[40] She feared for his life. "Jonathan is like one of your family," she said to the rabbi, "and you are like 'one of the family' with the Holy One blessed is He. You have to do something for him, something out of the ordinary. Make the most of the fact that you're one of the family up Above! I'm worried that he's going to die," she pleaded.

Rabbi Eliyahu heard her entreaties, telling her he would do something. "We told Jonathan, and we were sure that his difficult medical situation was already behind him," Mrs. Pollard recalled. "We thought the rabbi would make a special petition of prayer for Jonathan's recovery; after all, he was one of the greatest kabbalists in Israel. It turned out we were wrong."

Two weeks after that, Mrs. Pollard attempted to visit the rabbi but was turned away by his assistants, who told her he wasn't well. "That was very rare," she said. "He would always receive me almost immediately. Yet, day after day, his office staff informed me that he was ill. He was apparently suffering from terrible back

---

40. This was probably in 2006.

pain that was so excruciating that he had to get a new car so that he wouldn't have to bend down."

Finally, after about two months had elapsed, Mrs. Pollard was summoned to see the rabbi. She went into his room and saw that he was suffering almost intolerably. The pain was so sharp that he was having difficulty speaking. "I understood then that he had taken Jonathan's illness upon himself," Mrs. Pollard recounted. "I told him that I had a message from Jonathan, who asked me to make it clear that he wasn't prepared to let the rabbi suffer on his behalf."

The rabbi smiled at her with the grin of a father whose son has caught him in the process of planning or preparing some special surprise for him. She tried to persuade Rabbi Eliyahu otherwise, but his eyes told her to stop. He had decided to take the sickness upon himself, and from then on, he didn't have a single day of good health. His medical situation just progressively deteriorated. He suffered for four years. "I am positive that he did it for Jonathan," she said.

An Open-Door Policy

"Why don't you close the door of your home?" Rabbanit Eliyahu's neighbor once asked her, when she observed the almost constant stream of visitors and supplicants coming and going from the rabbi's home on a daily basis. Sometimes it appeared that half the Jewish nation was going in and out every day, seeking advice and blessings, or simply going to gaze at the radiant face of the rabbi.

Because he was dealing with his beloved Jewish people, it was simply impossible for Rabbi Eliyahu to refuse or turn away any of those who had sought him out.

He was never heard saying, "not now," or "I'm in a hurry," or "time is of the essence," or "I can't," or "it's not possible..." He was always sacrificing himself, his time, and his energy for the Jewish people. And, indeed, people could always visit him and find solace and salvation in his presence.

One night, at two o'clock in the morning, there was a knock at the rabbi's door. "Should I open it?" asked the *rabbanit*.

"Of course you should!" answered the rabbi.

They opened the door and a woman entered, crying bitterly, and laid her request before the rabbi: "I'm undergoing an important operation tomorrow, and I refuse to have the surgery without the rabbi's blessing."

The rabbi encouraged her and blessed her. When she left, Rabbi Mordechai turned to his wife, saying, "You see? How could we possibly close the door?"

In Pain and Gratitude

One day, during the time when Rabbi Eliyahu was hospitalized, he had to undergo an extremely painful procedure. Usually such a treatment would be carried out under a general anesthetic to reduce the pain, but as the rabbi's state of health was quite delicate at that time, his doctors decided not to administer the sedative. Instead, they would perform the procedure while Rabbi Eliyahu was conscious, alert, and able to fully feel. His assistant Reb Asaf Aharoni was with him throughout.

When the procedure was complete, Rabbi Eliyahu asked where the administering doctor was. The doctor, who was right behind Reb Asaf, first turned to the attending nurse, saying that of course the rabbi would be asking for pain reducers and she should prepare the medication. But Rabbi Eliyahu didn't ask for medication at all, nor did he mention the pain. Rather, he wanted to say to the doctor, "Thank you so much."[41]

A Synagogue Is Formed

A unique synagogue was founded in Afula: a Moroccan Carlebach-style place. The synagogue followed the Moroccan tradition and customs, and once a month integrated the tunes of Rabbi Shlomo Carlebach.[42] This is how it came about:

One of the synagogue's founders, Mr. Haim Elbaz,[43] was in Tiberius with his wife and suggested that they go to pray at the tomb of Rabbi Meir Baal Hanes.[44]

When they arrived at the tomb complex, they saw Rabbi Mordechai Eliyahu, without his official rabbinical robe and without a huge crowd surrounding him. Mr. Elbaz jumped at the opportunity to speak with him. He approached him and said, "Honored Rabbi, we're about to found a new synagogue."

Rabbi Eliyahu gazed at Mr. Elbaz for a moment and said, "It will go speedily and easily!"

Mr. Elbaz thanked Rabbi Eliyahu, but didn't understand what the rabbi had meant about "speedily and easily." He then returned to Afula and began the lengthy process of getting the synagogue off the ground. The first step was drafting a letter to the city's mayor to request a meeting with him. At that meeting, the founders

---

41. Reb Asaf Aharoni related this story.

42. Known as Reb Shlomo by his followers, Rabbi Carlebach was a singer and rabbi. He lived from 1925 to 1994.

43. Mr. Elbaz is today the president of the synagogue.

44. Rabbi Meir was one of the greatest *Tanna'im* of the fourth generation. He lived during Mishnaic times and is one of the most frequently cited Sages in the Mishnah.

would be able to appeal for a building to use and seek approval for their plans.

Within two days, Mr. Elbaz had succeeded in reaching the mayor.

"Listen," the mayor said, "you guys are really blessed! Come down to my office right away with all the members of the synagogue committee."

Mr. Elbaz and the others were in complete shock. The rabbi's blessing seemed to be working really quickly. They went to the mayor's office and were received immediately. After they had all sat down, the mayor turned to Mr. Elbaz and said, "I'm surprised at you. Why don't you dream bigger? Why are you dreaming so small? Dream big!"

Mr. Elbaz had no idea what the mayor wanted or meant. He had just been hoping for a building to start with.

"Listen!" the mayor continued. "You already got the basic building a few days ago. Now, imagine a big synagogue, and that will happen with great ease, too!"

Before the rabbi's blessing, the founders had tried turning to the mayor and every other possible contact in the municipality. They had exerted every kind of effort and left no stone unturned. Of course, they had prayed extensively as well. But there had been no response. Yet from the moment the rabbi gave his blessing — that it would go speedily and easily — they had sat down with the mayor and been given a promise that they would see their dreams fulfilled. All that occurred within two days — speedily and easily. The synagogue, called Meorot Nissim, was indeed built, and today continues to host regular prayer services.[45] It's a

---

45. Meorot Nissim is located at 10 Batzir Street in Afula.

physical manifestation of Rabbi Eliyahu's blessing — and a source of merit for his memory.

King David Will Decide...

Rabbi Eliyahu would greatly encourage everyone who wanted to build in the land of Israel or who was involved in settling the land. There was a building contractor who would come to see Rabbi Eliyahu every Friday with maps and plans for all kinds of plots, in order to decide whether he should buy or invest in them or not.

The deals often involved astronomical sums of money. The contractor would lay the maps and plans in front of Rabbi Eliyahu, placing a book of *Tehillim* beside him. Rabbi Eliyahu would take the book of *Tehillim*, open it at random, read a verse, and give the contractor his answer, according to what he had just read.

Sometimes the rabbi would show the contractor the verse to which the book had opened. "See what's written here?" he would ask, and the contractor would understand on his own.

Once, the contractor went to visit Rabbi Eliyahu and, rubbing his hands together, he told the rabbi about a real estate proposition that had potential for a tremendous profit. The rabbi opened the *Tehillim* and answered, "Don't take it; it's no good."

"What?" the contractor asked in total shock. It was very difficult for the man to accept such a verdict, especially as it was one of the most lucrative — and certain — deals that had ever fallen into his hands.

"But..." he tried to argue.

Rabbi Eliyahu was unmoved.

Ultimately, the contractor followed Rabbi Eliyahu's advice, continuing to visit in the weeks that followed. During one of those visits, the contractor couldn't hide his smile. He related to Rabbi

Eliyahu how it had already become clear that the plots in that "done deal" were all part of a massive scam. Everyone who had invested in that particular real estate had lost all his money.

Rabbi Eliyahu wasn't surprised, of course. In fact, from his point of view, it wasn't news at all; he had seen it in advance. However, in his humility he didn't say, "I told you so," or "Aren't you glad you listened to me?" or anything like that. He simply moved on to the next matter at hand.

The Miraculous Bottle of Alcohol

The Eliyahus celebrated the bar mitzvahs of their sons in their home at 2 Ben Zion Street in Jerusalem's Kiryat Moshe neighborhood. By the time their third son, Yosef, reached bar mitzvah age, Rabbi Eliyahu was already the chief rabbi of Israel. There were many guests, but the rabbi and *rabbanit* decided not to discriminate between the boys and held Yosef's bar mitzvah at home, as they had done with the others.

In honor of the bar mitzvah, the Lubavitcher Rebbe sent a small bottle of alcohol, which Rabbi Eliyahu decided to split among all the guests. The *rabbanit* heard this and wondered, "How can one possibly divide such a small bottle between the hundreds of guests here?"

But Rabbi Eliyahu calmed her down, saying that he would portion it out with a teaspoon. *It still won't be enough*, the *rabbanit* thought. But she didn't say a word.

At the end of the bar mitzvah the rabbi came up to her and told her that the tiny bottle had been enough for everyone...and there was still some left.

Chapter Eight

Humility

And Rabbi Yehoshua ben Levi[5] said, *How great are the humble-spirited that, in the time of the Temple, a person would sacrifice a burnt offering, and the merit of the burnt offering would be his; he would sacrifice a grain offering, and the merit for the grain offering would be his. But he whose character is humble, it is written that he is considered as if he brought all the sacrifices.*[6]

As it is said, *True sacrifice to G-d is a contrite spirit.*[7] And this is praise of the humble-spirited, who are humble in their hearts and their thoughts. And it is written further, *And the Holy One blessed is He said to them, "My children, I long for you, that even though I bestow greatness upon you, you make yourselves small before Me."*[8]

---

1. An *Amora* and scholar of the Talmud, Rabbi Yehoshua ben Levi lived in the land of Israel in the first half of the third century.
2. Talmud, *Sotah* 5b.
3. *Tehillim* 51:19.
4. Talmud, *Hullin* 89a.

In loving memory of
Albert Allen *a"h*

אברהם בן סלחא ע"ה

Mr. Albert Allen was born in Cairo, Egypt, and was involved for many years in supporting and furthering various causes. A founding member and *gabbai* of the Sephardic Minyan of Englewood, NJ, he was also involved in many other Jewish organizations including Yeshiva University, Yeshiva of North Jersey, Congregation Ahavath Torah of Englewood, NJ, and the Jewish Outreach Network. His endeavors were conducted with warmth, wisdom, and generosity, and he is greatly missed by his family and all who came in contact with him.

Dedicated by
The Allen Family

THE MAKINGS OF TRUE ROYALTY

That's Why There's Laundry

Rabbi Shmuel Eliyahu would relate that his father was accustomed to speaking to children as if they were the same age as him, as equals. In fact, he would speak to everyone like that. Once, during a visit to one of the prisons in Ramle,[5] Rabbi Mordechai saw some teenagers behind the fence, and asked the prison warden who they were.

"That's the youth wing of the prison," the warden replied. "And those are juvenile detainees."

"I would like to go over there to speak with them," Rabbi Eliyahu said.

"It can't be done," the warden replied. "They'll go wild and make trouble and throw eggs on your official rabbinical robe."

But Rabbi Eliyahu replied, "If they throw eggs, there are laundries for that! I'm not leaving the prison without speaking to the young inmates."

The moment that the young prisoners were told that Rabbi Eliyahu was coming to visit them, their leaders and "counselors" organized among themselves, breaking into the storeroom where the eggs and tomatoes were kept, so that everyone would have some projectile to throw at the rabbi.

The rabbi arrived at the prison's youth wing, and all the teens made a huge ruckus. The rabbi gazed at them and saw a youth of about fourteen, who Rabbi Eliyahu quickly identified as their leader.

The rabbi asked him, "When will it be quiet here?"

---

5. There are today five prisons in Ramle. The prison Rabbi Eliyahu visited was most likely Maasiyahu, a minimum-security facility.

"In three minutes," promised the boy.

And, indeed, in exactly three minutes, the boy raised his hand and total silence reigned. Then Rabbi Eliyahu began to speak with them from his heart, with great love, for a full hour. He told them, "You are not delinquents. All your life is before you. You can return to a healthy, normal, full life. Get out of here and come to me!"

In the meantime, Rabbi Eliyahu had sent his assistant out of the prison to purchase candies and all kinds of things that they couldn't get inside the facility.

When the storeowner heard who the candies were for, he wanted to pay for them out of his own pocket, but the rabbi's assistant wouldn't let him. He told him, "Next time you can pay, but this time it's the rabbi's good deed!"

When Rabbi Eliyahu finished speaking, all the young inmates came up and stood in an orderly line to receive a blessing from the rabbi. Sure enough, he blessed each and every one of them, with tears in his eyes as if he was their father.

At the end of all the blessings, the leader of the young prisoners, who had organized both the ruckus and the silence, stood and said to the rabbi, "We have eggs and tomatoes in our pockets, and we want to throw them at our 'counselors,' who encouraged us to throw them at you. Rabbi, can we?"

Rabbi Eliyahu answered, "Under no circumstances are you to throw anything at anyone. They're Jews, too, and they need to be drawn close as well. They also need to repent." He then distributed treats and goodies to all the youngsters.

Rabbi Eliyahu had the ability to speak to each person on his level — whether he was a settler, a child receiving his first Humash, or a tomato-wielding, disgruntled young prison inmate.[6]

---

6. As heard from Rabbi Shmuel Eliyahu.

Throwing Tomatoes

Every day the rabbi's family would meet people who would emotionally share stories and miracles related to Rabbi Mordechai. Of course, it was not just the miracles that were sensational, but also the wondrousness of the man himself. And the greatest wonder of all is that because of his tremendous humility and his straightforwardness, most people never knew how great he really was.

Many years ago, when Rabbi Eliyahu was serving as a rabbinical judge in Be'er Sheva, a respected member of the community appeared before him, presenting a divorce claim against his wife. Rabbi Eliyahu spoke with him, seeking to clarify the situation and the details involved.

The man claimed that he was blessed with great wealth, but his wife was extremely thrifty. She bought cheap clothes and food and lived so simply that he felt uncomfortable living with her and being married to her, and he wanted a divorce. The situation was rather unusual, as divorce claims generally had the exact opposite profile.

Rabbi Eliyahu told him to return at nine o'clock the next morning with his wife. When Rabbi Eliyahu finished hearing all the cases in the rabbinical court for the day, he went to the Be'er Sheva market and bought the worst fruits and vegetables he could find. The produce was the sort that usually isn't even sold because of its old, wrinkly, squishy, rotten appearance.

The next day he returned to the rabbinical court with his purchases. At the court, he summoned one of the secretaries who he thought was suitable for the job, and asked her to wear a headscarf, posing as though she was a married woman, and throw the rotten tomatoes at him when the divorce-seeking couple arrived.

And so, when the couple went in to see the rabbi, a woman with a basket in her arms came into the courtroom, and asked in her shrillest voice, "What did you buy? You couldn't find any other garbage to purchase that you want to bring all the rubbish from the market home with you?"

The woman didn't calm down until she had taken the fruits and vegetables from the basket and thrown them at the rabbi. She left the courtroom in a huff.

"Don't pay it any mind," Rabbi Eliyahu said to the stunned couple. "She's a little upset, and rightly so. Tell me your complaints," he said, while cleaning his robe from the remains of the rotten produce.

The husband, who wanted to present the divorce claim, tried to voice his complaints, but the words stuck in his throat. Only inarticulate thoughts came out.

"Go home now," Rabbi Eliyahu said. "And come back another time if you want."

That particular couple never did return for another divorce inquiry.

When the couple left, Rabbi Eliyahu removed a clean suit from a bag he had brought with him from home. The secretary who had dressed up as his wife took off the headscarf and went into the rabbi's room to seek forgiveness for playing her role to perfection.

"Don't worry!" Rabbi Eliyahu told her. "You merited being part of saving someone's marriage. May it be G-d's will that you should merit to build a loyal house (*bayit ne'eman*) in Israel," he blessed her. And of course, his blessing came to pass.[7]

---

7. The people involved related this incident to Rabbi Eliyahu's family after his passing.

The Rabbi Serves Breakfast

When Rabbi David Lahiani[8] was serving as the rabbi of Safsufa,[9] he once traveled early in the morning to Jerusalem with Rabbi Shmuel Eliyahu, one of Hacham Mordechai's sons, on rabbinate business. After their early morning prayers, Rabbi Shmuel went to his parents' home to fulfill the commandment of *kibbud av va'em* (honoring one's parents) and Rabbi Lahiani accompanied him.

Rabbi Shmuel Eliyahu at a Kol Tzofecha Torah class

When they came in, Rabbi Eliyahu glanced at the clock and remarked, "It seems like you've already prayed, but you haven't yet eaten breakfast. Come, let's go into the kitchen."

Rabbi Shmuel did as his father said, telling Rabbi Lahiani to join them. Although he would have preferred to stay in the living

---

8. Rabbi Lahiani, who recounted this incident, later became the rabbi of Ziv Hospital in Safed.

9. Safsufa is a moshav in northern Israel, located near Meron.

room, Rabbi Lahiani saw that Rabbi Shmuel wouldn't have that and wanted him to come with them to the kitchen for breakfast. Rabbi Lahiani obeyed, following them into the kitchen, sitting next to Rabbi Shmuel. Hacham Mordechai, meanwhile, proceeded to serve them bread, cheese, and vegetables. He outdid himself when he asked, "Can I make you an omelet?"

Rabbi Lahiani was utterly embarrassed. He whispered to Rabbi Shmuel that he didn't feel comfortable with Hacham Mordechai standing there, cooking for him and serving him. But Rabbi Shmuel replied, "You see I'm a guest here myself and I do what the host tells me — you just do the same!"

Rabbi Lahiani thought that was the end of it, but after the bread, cheese, vegetables, omelet, and drinks, Rabbi Eliyahu pulled some cakes from the fridge, warmed them in the oven, and gave several slices to his son and Rabbi Lahiani. Not only that, he placed several pieces in a bag and said to Rabbi Lahiani, "Bring these home for your wife and tell her they're from my house."

When he later recalled this incident, Rabbi Lahiani remarked, "I saw with my own eyes how to truly fulfill what is written about the patriarch Avraham, *And he stood over them beneath the tree and they ate.*"[10]

Honor for Great Rabbis

A group of friends was waiting at the bus stop to travel to the *sheloshim*[11] speeches for Rabbi Eliyahu. A woman at the bus stop who was standing near the group asked where they were from. They responded that they were from Nazareth Illit,[12] and that they

---

10. *Bereshit* 18:8.

11. The *sheloshim* marks the end of the initial thirty-day mourning period for someone who has passed away.

12. Nazareth Illit was renamed Nof Hagalil in 2019.

were on their way to the *sheloshim* ceremonies for Rabbi Mordechai Eliyahu, to show their respect for him. When she heard his name, she exclaimed, "The Jewish people have lost a great leader!"

Her reaction revealed that she must have had some personal connection to the rabbi, so the men standing there asked her if she had a story about him. Indeed she did. This is her account:

> A few years ago, one of our close relatives, from a respected Jerusalem family, got married. My husband was standing at the entrance to the wedding hall when the rabbi arrived, dressed in the official garb of the *Rishon LeZion*. All the guests gathered around him, kissing his hand and asking for a blessing.
>
> One of those present told the rabbi that Rabbi Ovadia Yosef was already in the hall. Rabbi Eliyahu immediately removed his official robe and entered the hall in a regular rabbinical coat, saying, "One *Rishon LeZion* here is enough. If I go in dressed like this, everyone will come up to me and perhaps it will lessen the honor due to Hacham Ovadia."[13]

If the *Rabbanit* Says So...

For many, many years, Shalom Konaniyan Cohen would transport the rabbi every morning in a very simple car. He would take him to prayers at sunrise and then drive him back home. On many occasions, people offered to transport the rabbi in more luxurious vehicles, but the rabbi always refused — just Shalom Konaniyan Cohen drove him.

Reb Shalom saw many things when he was with the rabbi, listened to many questions, heard many answers, and witnessed

---

13. As heard from Yosef Nahum of Nazareth Illit.

many wonders. But the rabbi would always warn him, "Whatever you see, don't tell." And thus he never did reveal them.

But there were things that were permissible to share, things that were connected to the rabbi's behavior, his modesty, and his humility. Reb Shalom related that when Rabbi Eliyahu was chosen to be chief rabbi of Israel, he bought the rabbi a *tallit* with an ornate silver border. At that time, such prayer shawls were made with four rows of silver, and very few people had one — just hassidic rebbes and other very prominent people.

"When I brought the rabbi the *tallit*, he didn't want to wear it," Reb Shalom recalled. "'What am I, a rebbe?' he asked, and refused to accept the *tallit*."

It was the *rabbanit* who finally won him over. She told him, "You can't do anything about it! You've been chosen to be *Rishon LeZion*, and wearing a fancy *tallit* is all part of it."

The rabbi looked at the new *tallit* and sighed. "Okay, if you say so, I suppose there's nothing I can do."

SLOW TO ANGER

I Don't Know How

Everyone who knew the rabbi also knew that he didn't get angry. Shalom Cohen[14] once related that his friend came to ask for advice and a blessing from the rabbi regarding a certain matter. In the end, he didn't follow what the rabbi had advised. Reb Shalom

---

14. Shalom Cohen was another close student of Rabbi Eliyahu, not to be confused with Shalom Konaniyan Cohen, his early-morning driver.

felt uncomfortable about it and begged the rabbi not to get angry that his friend hadn't followed his counsel.

The rabbi replied, "Never in my life have I gotten angry, and never in my life have I been strict with someone. I still haven't learned how to get mad."

Once, the rabbi did speak of anger, as Yisrael Tawil, one of the cantors in the Hechal Yaakov synagogue, related. "My brother had a heart attack, tearing the main arteries. They raced him to the Shaare Zedek Hospital, where he was told that he needed an emergency operation. My brother told me, 'I'm not having any operation without the rabbi's blessing.'

"It was already after midnight. The doctor told us to hurry, saying it had nothing to do with a rabbi but with the doctors. But my brother refused to move without the rabbi's blessing.

"I dialed the rabbi's number and begged him to forgive me for calling at such a late hour. The rabbi answered, 'I would have been angry if you hadn't called me! He should have the operation. It's good you phoned. Now I can do a *pidyon nefesh* (special prayers for the redemption of the soul) for him!'"

In Honor of Hillel

A certain Jew who wasn't so strict in his observance of Torah and mitzvot heard the story of Hillel,[15] in which someone bet his friend that he would succeed in making Hillel angry.

He went to Hillel on the eve of Shabbat, when Hillel was bathing, and bothered him with all kinds of ridiculous questions. Nevertheless, despite all that, Hillel didn't even get ruffled. The Jew who heard the story wondered if today's rabbis have the same

---

15. Renowned sage and scholar, circa 100 BCE–10 CE. He was a teacher of the *Tanna'im*.

level of patience. He said to himself, "Of course they all know the story, and probably even use it in their lectures. I want to see for myself if they really practice what they preach."

He prepared a list of various well-known rabbis' phone numbers. At two o'clock in the morning, he called one of the rabbis, and asked him innocently, "What blessing do I make on a sugar-coated apple?"

The rabbi's reaction was immediate. "Couldn't you call at a normal hour to ask such questions?" and slammed down the receiver.

The man carried on calling rabbi after rabbi. Everyone had the same response — indignation at being woken in the middle of the night for such an inane question.

At three in the morning, he dialed Rabbi Mordechai Eliyahu. When the rabbi picked up the receiver, the Jew said, "Can I ask you a question?"

"Of course!" answered the rabbi. "Just tell me, can the question wait one moment while I wash my hands?"

The Jew agreed, and a few moments later the rabbi's voice could be heard over the phone, friendly, patient, and warm: "Yes, I'm ready to listen!"

When the Jew presented his question about the sugar-coated apple, the rabbi gave him a detailed answer. At the end of the call he said, "You can call me and ask me whatever you want, whenever you want!"[16]

Humility Instead of Greatness

When he was learning at Porat Yosef, Hacham Mordechai was a very diligent student. He studied page after page after page of

---

16. As related by Rabbi Tuvia Weizman in his book, *Stories I Loved to Read.*

Talmud, absorbing it quickly and deeply. But when the head of the yeshivah, Hacham Ezra Attiya, would pass by, Hacham Mordechai would immediately turn back many pages, as though he was still at the beginning of the Gemara.

There was a man who would occasionally come to argue with the yeshivah boys about things he knew nothing about. He had no shame, and everyone who knew anything about Talmudical topics realized that he was talking complete nonsense, but he just carried on nonetheless.

One day, the students lost their patience and started arguing with him, showing him all his mistakes in such a way that he was ultimately embarrassed and proven to be a real fool. He was offended and hurt, so he went to the head of the yeshivah, complaining that the students had treated him so disrespectfully.

Rabbi Mordechai Eliyahu as a young yeshivah student
(credit: Rabbi Shmuel Zafrani)

As Hacham Ezra arrived to rebuke the students, everyone managed to disappear, and the only one left was the young Rabbi Eliyahu, who had paid no attention to what was going on around him, had no idea what had happened, and had simply carried on studying. Hacham Ezra called the young Mordechai to his office and began to rebuke him.

During all this time, the young Mordechai never uttered a word.

Eventually, the mistake was revealed: he was not at all involved in the incident, and Hacham Ezra came to ask him for forgiveness.

"Why didn't you tell me that you weren't involved?" asked Hacham Ezra.

"Hearing rebuke is always good," Rabbi Eliyahu replied.[17]

The Appliance Repairman

Once, after Hacham Mordechai had been appointed chief rabbi of Israel, a certain woman called the rabbi's house, looking for a washing-machine technician. It was a mistake; the name of the repairman was printed next to Rabbi Eliyahu's in the phone book.

When she asked for the technician, Rabbi Eliyahu replied that she had called the wrong number. A few minutes later, she called back, and the rabbi again explained that it was the wrong number. Later, she repeated the same mistake, and yet again, the rabbi repeated that he wasn't the repairman.

She told the rabbi how upset she was that she wasn't managing to reach the technician, as she had guests arriving the next day and couldn't possibly manage without her washing machine. The rabbi asked her what the repairman's name was, but she didn't remember exactly. The rabbi asked her to wait a moment, got a phone book, and went through the names with her one by one, until he reached one whom she said was her regular repair person.

"Write down the number," the rabbi told her. But she didn't have a pen. She went to find one — and it didn't work. She brought a pencil — and the point broke.

"It's okay," the rabbi told her. "I can wait until you find something to write with."

---

17. Rabbi Haim Ben Shushan related this incident. Rabbi Haim Ben Shushan, the son of Rabbi Yeshuah Ben Shushan (mentioned in an earlier story), was a very close student of Rabbi Eliyahu.

Eventually she found a pen that worked, and slowly, slowly, she took down the number.

When she had written down the number, she calmed down and asked the rabbi, "So if you're not the repairman, then who are you?"

"Mordechai Eliyahu," the rabbi told her.

The woman was shocked. "You're the rabbi? Oy, forgive me, please!" And so she kept the rabbi on the line for another quarter of an hour begging forgiveness.

In the afternoon, her son came home from *kollel* and she told him the tale and related how embarrassed she was. And he told Rabbi Yaakov Cohen, who shared this story with the family.[18]

A Private Class

In 1984, Rabbi Shlomo Ben Eliyahu, the rabbi of the Mateh Asher regional council, accompanied Rabbi Eliyahu on a trip around southern Israel to strengthen people in their Judaism and observance. They, along with Hacham Mordechai's driver and his assistant, Rabbi Yehudah Mutzafi, went to Netivot, Sderot, and Ofakim. The trip had been arranged well in advance, coordinated with the chief rabbinate's office and other organizers. Posters had been hung in the streets of those cities, inviting the public to come hear the rabbi's lectures.

They arrived in Netivot at the arranged time, but to their great surprise, the hall was closed and locked. While they were busy looking if there was perhaps another entrance, their eyes fell on an enormous sign announcing that the lecture had been canceled. The rabbi returned to the car, while the others tried to find someone

---

18. Rabbi Yaakov Cohen was the head of the Jerusalem-based Siah Israel organization, which publishes holy books. Rabbi Cohen passed away in December 2018.

who could explain the matter. There was no limit to their shock when they discovered that people with no authority to do so had printed notices that the rabbi was sick and couldn't attend.

The rabbi's escorts were filled with anger, but it was the rabbi who calmed them down. "I see in this an act of Heaven, not of man," he said.

They continued to Sderot, where they made the same discovery. The rabbi wouldn't give up and said that they must continue on to Ofakim. Perhaps this hand of evil hadn't reached there, and people were waiting to hear Torah? Maybe they had taken time off from their affairs to attend the lecture.

"How can I renege on my mission?" the rabbi asked. Rabbi Shlomo heard him muttering to himself, "Let my soul be as

dust to everyone,[19] and after Your commandments my soul will follow."[20]

When they arrived in Ofakim, the same sight awaited them: a locked and empty hall. At the entrance, the guard greeted them in astonishment. "But they told us the lecture was canceled!"

While they were still talking to the guard, one solitary woman rushed up to the hall. She wanted to learn Torah. Rabbi Eliyahu immediately told the guard, "Open the gates.

Rabbi Eliyahu giving a lecture

We'll teach this woman Torah!"

The huge hall was empty. Only the one woman from the town

---

19. From the verse at the end of the *Shemoneh Esreh*.

20. Perhaps referring to *Tehillim* 119:32.

sat there. They invited the guard to join in, too. The rabbi spoke with great enthusiasm and delivered the lecture from beginning to end, exactly as he had prepared, just as he would have done in front of a crowd of hundreds. Rabbi Shlomo was amazed and astonished by Rabbi Eliyahu's noble behavior.

Many years later, Rabbi Shlomo's brother-in-law, Rabbi Ron Ben Moshe, told him how he had met someone who had returned to Torah observance. That man emotionally shared that the motivation for him to come back to Torah observance had been the rabbi's behavior that night in Ofakim. *If the rabbi was prepared to speak for the sake of just one woman, apparently there really was something to the Torah,* that security guard thought — *some truth.*[21]

━╫━

HIDDEN GREATNESS

Why the Rain Falls

One particularly stormy, wintry Shabbat evening, Rabbi Eliyahu went to a *shalom zachor*[22] at the home of one of the families in Jerusalem's Kiryat Moshe neighborhood. After he had blessed the family, the rabbi continued on his way to the synagogue for the special *bakashot*[23] prayers, according to the Sephardic custom on winter Shabbat evenings.

That Shabbat was extremely rainy. Several people had

---

21. Rabbi Shlomo Ben Eliyahu told this story.

22. A festive gathering held on the Friday night immediately following the birth of a baby boy, according to Ashkenazi custom.

23. A specific set of liturgical hymns composed by Sephardic scholar-poets and sung using the traditional Sephardic musical system known as *maqam*.

accompanied Rabbi Eliyahu, and they noticed that rain was constantly falling, except when Rabbi Eliyahu was walking through the streets. During the short time that the rabbi was walking from place to place, the rain would completely stop, and the moment that he entered a building, the deluge began again.

When they left the synagogue after the *bakashot* prayers, they saw, as they had anticipated, that the rain stopped. One of the men accompanying him couldn't restrain himself and asked Rabbi Eliyahu, "Rabbi, it seems that every time you step outside, the rain stops, and as soon as you go back indoors, it starts raining again."

Hacham Mordechai was shocked, and immediately responded, "Not at all! The rain stops for me? It doesn't depend on me. I decree that it should rain now!"

The minute that Rabbi Eliyahu finished speaking, an amazing thing happened: Torrential rain, the likes of which wasn't usually seen in that area, began to pour down. Rabbi Eliyahu, who wasn't wearing a coat, was soaked to the bone. And the man who had asked him about the whole matter was terribly sorry that he had caused a righteous man such distress, partly because Rabbi Eliyahu got soaked because of his curiosity, and partly because he'd uncovered the rabbi's secret.[24]

Half a Minute

After one of the members of Rabbi Eliyahu's congregation celebrated the birth of a grandchild, he was honored with an *aliyah* to the Torah during the sunrise prayers, and everyone sang for him.[25] At the end of the prayers, just before Rabbi Eliyahu began his well-attended weekly class on the Ben Ish Hai, the new

---

24. As heard from the one who questioned Rabbi Eliyahu about the rain, Rabbi Moshe Harari, author of the *Mikra'e Kodesh* series on the festivals.

25. This man was a Professor Elya — first name unknown.

grandfather said to the rabbi, "Did you see how, within half a minute…" But the rabbi interrupted him and wouldn't let him speak.

Rabbi Eliyahu giving a lecture at Hechal Yaakov

After the class, one of the congregants approached the new grandfather and asked him what he had been planning to say. He related that he had accompanied his daughter-in-law to the hospital, where the doctors told them that the baby wasn't lying in a good position and they would thus have to perform a Caesarean section. The grandfather-to-be raced from the room to the public telephone in the department (as this took place before cell phones were common), and called Rabbi Eliyahu to get his blessing.

The rabbi gave his blessing, and by the time he returned to where his daughter-in-law was — no more than half a minute later — the doctors told him that at that very moment the baby had turned around, and his daughter-in-law could give birth naturally.

He wanted to tell this to the rabbi, but Rabbi Eliyahu, in his humility, stopped him from sharing it.[26]

---

26. As heard from Moshe Shammai, a congregant at Hechal Yaakov.

Mordechai Eliyahu, the Printer

On the day that Rabbi Mordechai finished his tenure as chief rabbi of Israel, he made a thanksgiving celebration, like the *kohen gadol*, the High Priest, would do when he would safely emerge from the Holy of Holies following Yom Kippur. *And he made a feast for his loved ones when he left the holy place in peace.*[27]

At the celebration, many praises were related about Rabbi Eliyahu, and all the time he sat with a smile on his face. After all the blessings had been made, Rabbi Eliyahu told a story:

> You know that there are those who call me "Mordechai Eliyahu" and others who call me "Mordechai Ben Eliyahu." In the telephone book, I appear as the latter,[28] but day to day, everyone calls me the former.
>
> There's a Jew who works at a printing press in Jerusalem — and his name is Mordechai Eliyahu. When people open the telephone book, they find his name instead of mine. I met him once, and he told me what a hard life he had. People call him and ask him questions, and he tells them, "I'm not a rabbi. I'm just a simple person."
>
> But they insist, "Yes, yes, we know the rabbi is very humble, but please could you answer the question?" And this printer has to again explain that he's not a rabbi, and not the Rabbi Mordechai Eliyahu, and it takes them a while to realize he means it.

---

27. *Mishnah Yoma* 70a.

28. Although the rabbi referred to himself and his family as "Eliyahu," the name "Ben Eliyahu" was on some government records. Today some of Rabbi Eliyahu's descendants use the family name Eliyahu, while others go by Ben Eliyahu.

I asked him, "If that's the problem, why don't you get an unlisted number?"

"G-d forbid!" the printer responded. "In the end I give everyone your phone number, and that's a great honor for me, to be able to help people find the proper answers to their questions."

The rabbi then concluded, "When you were saying all those praises, I said to myself, 'I know that all those praises are exaggerated.' I then thought, 'Why tell them? Of course they must be referring to the other Mordechai Eliyahu!'"

The Rabbi's Neighbor

A number of years ago, a young man traveled to Israel from France for a visit. Fate intervened and on that same visit, he found his soul mate and got married. He ended up staying in Israel with his wife. Right after the wedding, his sister let the young couple use an apartment she owned in Jerusalem's Kiryat Moshe neighborhood.

They were energetic and youthful, and it didn't matter to the young couple that their new home didn't have much: just two mattresses and a few pieces of old furniture. A few days after they had moved in, they heard a knock on the door. When the groom opened it, he saw a man with a pleasant face, wearing a white shirt, with a big black yarmulke on his head, holding two cups of tea and a plate of cookies. "I'm your neighbor, Mordechai," the man said. "I came to meet you and drink some tea with you."

The groom brought the nice neighbor inside. Before "Mordechai" left the house, the groom suggested that they dance, in honor of his recent marriage. The neighbor answered the invitation with a radiant expression, and together they jumped up and danced together in the living room.

One day, when this young man was wandering around the Mahane Yehudah market,[29] he saw a picture of Rabbi Mordechai Eliyahu on display at one of the stalls. He thought to himself, *That rabbi looks so alike to my neighbor. I wonder if he knows him…*

The next time he bumped into his neighbor, the young man asked him if he knew Rabbi Mordechai Eliyahu. The neighbor smiled and said, "Yes, I know him."

The young man then said, "Rabbi Mordechai Eliyahu looks so similar to you." The neighbor just smiled.

Some time passed, and the young man was in need of a certain book. He knocked on his neighbor's door, asking if he by any chance had the book. The neighbor smiled and said that he should feel free to go into his library and take the book. The young man was astonished by the size of his neighbor's library, and there, on the wall, he saw a picture of Rabbi Mordechai Eliyahu. He gazed

(Credit: Eliyahu Family)

29. Often referred to as "the *Shuk*," this famous Jerusalem market is located between Jaffa Road and Agrippas Street.

at the picture and at his neighbor's face, again noticing how close the resemblance was between them.

Another two months passed, and then, late at night, the young man heard people's voices in the stairwell. He went out to see what was going on, and suddenly he saw his neighbor in front of him — but this time he was wearing the robe of the *Rishon LeZion*. Only then did he finally realize that the "neighbor" *was* Rabbi Mordechai Eliyahu.[30]

Tear Up the Photo

After Rabbi Eliyahu was appointed chief rabbi of Israel, he went to various rabbis to get their blessings — among them the Gerrer Rebbe, Rabbi Elazar Menahem Mann Shach,[31] Rabbi Yosef Shalom Elyashiv, Rabbi Yitzhak Kaduri, Rabbi Yehudah Tzadkah, and the Baba Sali.

When Rabbi Eliyahu arrived at the Baba Sali's house, he took the Baba Sali's hand and kissed it. A photographer there snapped the picture of the chief rabbi of Israel, wearing his famous robe, kissing the hand of the Baba Sali. That photo was widely publicized. But what was not revealed was the photo that was taken immediately afterward, of the Baba Sali taking Rabbi Eliyahu's hand and kissing it.

There were many people there, and everyone who witnessed the interaction was amazed.

The photographer who took the first, famous photo of course caught the second shot, too. But immediately after the visit with

---

30. As heard from Shlomo, the former neighbor of Rabbi Eliyahu.

31. 1899–2001. Rabbi Shach was a leading Lithuanian *haredi* rabbi in Bnei Brak, Israel, and a *rosh yeshivah* of the Ponevezh yeshivah.

the Baba Sali, Rabbi Eliyahu called the photographer and said, "You must tear up the photo! I forbid you to publish it." The shocked photographer immediately agreed not to publish the photo until after the rabbi's death. He saved the negative and developed it after Rabbi Eliyahu passed away.[32]

The Rabbi's "Perfume"

Shalom Konaniyan Cohen, who served as Rabbi Eliyahu's early morning driver for many years, was privileged to accompany the rabbi to many places around the country. Every time they arrived somewhere, everyone would accord them great honor.

---

32. As heard from Rabbi Shmuel Eliyahu. Although some people have said that they've had the privilege of seeing the photo, Rabbi Eliyahu's sons still have not.

"It wasn't hard to understand that all that honor wasn't for me, but for the rabbi," Shalom recalled. "And so every time when 'we' were being honored, I would remind myself of a story that I heard from Rabbi Eliyahu one Shabbat, in the name of the Ben Ish Hai." This is the story:

There were two donkeys walking together. One of them was loaded with fine perfumes that needed to be transported from place to place. Later, when this particular donkey was returned to his stable, he boasted to his friend, "Today everyone loved me so much. Everywhere I went, people tried to get close to me, to smell me and to honor me."

The second donkey replied, "You dumb donkey! Let's see you tomorrow when you're carrying refuse like you usually do, and then we'll see if everyone honors you!"

The next time the donkey was loaded with refuse and led through the streets, everyone fled from him. The donkey thought they were fleeing from him because he was strong like a lion. When he went back to his stable, he started boasting to his friend again, that everyone was scared of him because he was so strong.

"You dumb donkey!" the other donkey said. "Yesterday you were loaded with fine-smelling perfumes, so everyone came close to you. Today you were carrying a load that smelled terrible, so everyone ran from you. So you should know that it's not you that determines whether you get respect but what you're carrying!"

"So," continued Shalom, "every time I went somewhere with the rabbi, I would remember and review this story and remind myself of its message. But once, I was shocked to hear the rabbi telling this story in reference to himself. 'You think all this honor is for me?' he asked me. 'Not at all! It's only because of the Torah that I teach and share with people. See what respect there is for the Torah!'"

Students crowding around Rabbi Eliyahu after his Torah class

Chapter Nine

Fear of Sin

And there is no way to learn awe other than great diligence in Torah and all her ways.

And the person who reflects upon and occupies himself with this matter always, when he's resting, when he's moving, when he's sleeping, and when he's rising, until the truth is set in his heart — that is, the truth that the Shechinah exists everywhere, and we stand before it at every moment — then that person will truly fear Him. And that is what King David would pray for, as is said, *Teach me, O L-rd, Your way, that I may travel in Your truth; unite my heart to fear Your Name.*[1]

---

1. *Tehillim* 86:11.

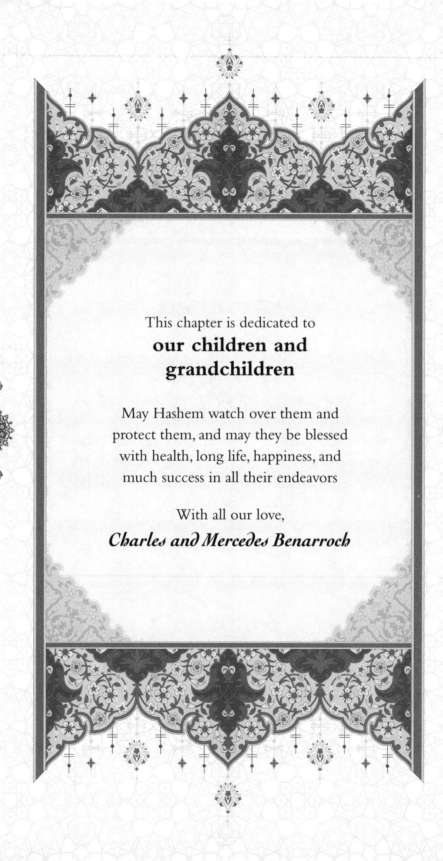

This chapter is dedicated to
our children and grandchildren

May Hashem watch over them and
protect them, and may they be blessed
with health, long life, happiness, and
much success in all their endeavors

With all our love,
Charles and Mercedes Benarroch

FEAR OF HEAVEN FIRST

Esteem It and It Will Exalt You

A row of stony, expressionless soldiers faced the approaching Israeli delegation. The luggage and belongings of each member of the delegation were checked thoroughly, and the tension was palpable.

It wasn't every day that people like this entered the palace of this South American president. This dictator was renowned for his great despotism toward his citizens, which he also expressed in his hostile attitude toward the Jews. Every day, people were thrown into jail through no fault of their own, and every week, innocent citizens disappeared, never to return.

If someone so much as dared show even the slightest sign or indication that could be interpreted as disrespect for the president and his rule — and certainly if a person even thought of harming him — there was only one fate for him: death. Fear and terror ruled in the state, and the palace's ostentatious façade clearly broadcast the president's powerful grip on the nation.

During the visit, Rabbi Eliyahu appeared before the president with dignitaries of the community, accompanied by the Israeli ambassador and the president's translator. After the rabbi had spoken, he presented his gift to the president: *Ethics of the Fathers*, translated into Spanish. The president briefly leafed through the book, thanked the rabbi politely, and laid it on the table.

During the conversation, the president took out a cigar and began to smoke. He pulled out an ashtray and placed it on top of the book the rabbi had just given to him. Rabbi Eliyahu saw the ashtray sitting on top of a holy book, and instinctively put out his hand, moving the ashtray from on top of the book to the table.

Everyone sitting in the room froze for a moment, in shock at the rabbi's "chutzpah." The ambassador turned white as a sheet, the members of the delegation clasped their hands in fear, and the president's guards were standing ready to carry out expulsion orders on the guests. The president said nothing. He just moved the ashtray back to its previous place on top of the book.

"Tell the president to please move the ashtray. We don't put ashtrays on holy books," Rabbi Eliyahu whispered to the ambassador, who was sitting beside him.

"It...it...it's not possible," stammered the ambassador. "It's not appropriate to give him instructions like that... He really doesn't like it when you give him any kind of instructions..."

"Even so — tell him not to put the ashtray on the book. It's a holy book!" Rabbi Eliyahu insisted.

The president noticed the whispering and demanded that the ambassador tell him what the rabbi had said. The ambassador muttered something, but didn't give a clear answer, so the president told the translator to explain what had been said. Under great duress, the translator repeated word for word what the rabbi had said. Meanwhile, Rabbi Eliyahu explained to the translator that it wasn't acceptable to place ashtrays on holy books, all the while removing the ashtray from the book again and placing it on the table.

After this explanation, the president didn't dare return the ashtray to the book, but the story didn't end there. At the end of the meeting, the president got up from his seat, took Rabbi Eliyahu by the hand and began to escort him outside.

No one understood the meaning of what they were seeing, nor did they know what would happen next. Some thought the dictator might be intending to personally drag Rabbi Eliyahu to prison. Others thought he was simply handing Rabbi Eliyahu over to the ever-ready soldiers waiting just beyond the palace gates.

But instead, they walked outside to a red carpet and an honor guard. Everyone was in shock. Could all that respect and glory really be intended for Rabbi Eliyahu? It quickly became clear that it was indeed for him — and not only that, the president had given very last-minute instructions to arrange it. Usually that red carpet and honor guard were reserved solely for heads of state and the most important, honored individuals...

The president himself accompanied Rabbi Eliyahu to his car, actually opened the car door for him, and parted from him with a brief bow. Before they separated, he asked the rabbi to come and visit him again before he returned to Israel.

The second meeting took place several days later. This time, the president requested that the meeting be private, just between the two of them. The president's men and the Israeli representatives were not invited. Even the translator remained outside, and the president and Rabbi Eliyahu had to somehow manage by themselves.

The two were closeted in the room at length, until finally they exited, their faces expressionless. Neither the president nor the rabbi agreed to reveal what they had spoken about, nor how they had conducted a conversation in two different languages, and they parted cordially and went their separate ways. It was only many years later that Rabbi Eliyahu finally agreed to divulge to his family what had actually taken place during that secret meeting. And it was to Rabbi Eliyahu's grandchildren's credit that the full story finally came out, with their persistent questions of "Saba, what happened there?"

This is what he said:

> The moment the door closed behind us, while I was still standing there, frozen and utterly confused about the purpose of the visit and the reason we had been left alone, the president surprised me. This powerful president, before whom the entire country

quaked in fear and utter terror, got down on all fours before me and kissed my knee.

He didn't stop there, but bent his head and asked me to bless him. But before I did so, I asked him how he could help the Jewish people. He thought a little and then replied that he could sell oil cheaply to Israel.

I asked him for more help, and he promised that he would behave decently toward his Jewish citizens, respecting them, their religion, and their way of life. As soon as I heard this, I laid my hand on his head and blessed him that he would merit to be good and bring benefit to the Jewish people. The president was very moved by the blessing, and we parted in peace.

After the meeting, the ambassador asked Rabbi Eliyahu how he had merited receiving such a great honor from this dictator, who was known to be callous and uncaring when it came to giving honor and respect to others. Rabbi Eliyahu didn't get excited. He answered quite simply, "Here, it's written in the verse, *Esteem it and it will exalt you.*[2] That is to say, if you respect the Torah, people will respect you."

He continued, "I didn't receive all that honor as an individual, but because I worried about the honor of the Torah. And the man who stood in front of me knew how to appreciate that, and he honored both the Torah and his own presidency."[3]

Buying Napoleon's Throne

While Rabbi Eliyahu was the chief rabbi of Israel, he visited

2. *Mishle* 4:8.

3. As heard from Rabbi Shmuel Eliyahu.

France as part of a delegation for an official state visit. During that period, France was pressuring Israel to make a "goodwill gesture"

Rabbi Eliyahu giving a speech on a state visit to
France (credit: Government Press Office)

and give parts of Jerusalem and other areas of the country to the Palestinians as part of the peace process. So the Foreign Office requested that Rabbi Eliyahu avoid speaking about Jerusalem or the land of Israel, and just focus on issues dealing with Judaism. They were worried about making a diplomatic faux pas and were concerned about maintaining cordial relations between France and Israel, especially considering how fragile the relationship was at that point.

The visit included a formal state reception, with many invitees, including then-Prime Minister Jacques Chirac,[4] and numerous other dignitaries, among them leaders in the French government, senior rabbis of the country, and more. Before the state reception, Rabbi Eliyahu had to go on an official visitors' circuit and tour

---

4. Jacques Chirac, born in 1932, was prime minister of France from 1974 to 1976 and from 1986 to 1988. He served as president of the country from 1995 to 2007.

for guests of the state. One of the stops on this tour was at a state museum where many French cultural and historical treasures are housed.

During the tour of the museum, the visitors were shown the royal throne on which Napoleon sat. "When did Napoleon live?" Rabbi Eliyahu asked the guides.

Although they were a little taken aback by his "uneducated" question, the escorts answered it, "explaining" all the details of when Napoleon had lived. They understandably thought that Rabbi Eliyahu must not be aware of this information. Then Rabbi Eliyahu asked another "ignorant" question: "Is Napoleon's throne for sale?"

An awkward, uncomfortable silence ensued. Some of the Israeli embassy staff members, who were standing behind Rabbi Eliyahu, began whispering to each other. "What kind of rabbi is this? He's embarrassing us! What sort of questions are these?"

But even with all their hushed murmuring, they didn't manage to make the rabbi cease and desist from his inappropriate questions...

Finally, the hosts replied, "No, Napoleon's throne is not for sale. It's a very important item, and a historical one. We don't sell such national treasures."

They continued along the tour, arriving at a display about the kings who had ruled France. The rabbi was shown some of Louis XIV's furniture. Louis XIV was known for his extravagance and wealth, and the luxury of his lifestyle was quite evident from the artifacts Rabbi Eliyahu was seeing. "Who was Louis XIV?" Rabbi Eliyahu asked. "And how long ago did he live?"

The hosts dutifully answered.

The *rabbanit*, noticing the confusion and surprise on the faces of the museum directors, tried to hint to her husband to stop with his "tasteless" questions. But the rabbi just winked and carried on.

"What did Louis XIV contribute to the world?" he asked. "Was he a moral king?"

"No," the hosts replied candidly. "None of the French monarchs were exactly ethical or just. But that's our history, and we're proud of it and respect it nonetheless."

The museum tour finally came to an end, and with it, Rabbi Eliyahu's exasperating questions. The next stop was the official reception with the French prime minister. At the event, the French prime minister spoke and gave a blessing to Rabbi Eliyahu. Rabbi Eliyahu, in turn, stood up and began to speak, with an embassy employee translating for him.

Rabbi Eliyahu began by discussing his visit to the museum. Everyone who had accompanied him on that tour began getting tense, remembering his bizarre questions. He described how his hosts seemed so puzzled. Could it really be that the chief rabbi of Israel didn't know who Louis XIV was? Was it possible that he didn't know when Napoleon had lived? These were famous historical figures, after all.

The rabbi continued, relating how he had asked the museum directors if these historical figures were moral people. Although they stammered a bit when answering, they told the truth — yet asserted that they were still proud of them. "And so," Rabbi Eliyahu said, "you expect me to know about and honor the history of France, even though I live in Israel. And I accept that. But tell me, don't we need to know about and honor our history, too? Shouldn't you honor it as well?"

He explained: "Moses told us to never give the land of Israel to strangers. Shouldn't we respect that? Why should we respect your kings, who lived two or three hundred years ago, and not respect the kings of Israel — King David and King Solomon — who lived three thousand years ago, and honor their tradition?"

The *rabbanit* was listening carefully. Being fluent in several languages, including French, she heard what the rabbi was saying — and she heard the words of the embassy translator. She soon became aware that the translator was censoring the rabbi's words, changing them as he saw fit. The *rabbanit's* loyalty was only to her husband, of course. She wasn't impressed or intimidated by the importance of those present, and she signaled to the rabbi that the translator was "editing" his words.

Rabbi Eliyahu also wasn't cowed by kings and presidents. He stopped in the middle of his speech and announced over the microphone, right in front of all those assembled, "I became aware that the translator doesn't really understand the speaking style of rabbis. It's important to me that the prime minister hears me and understands what I'm saying. I ask that the chief rabbi of France translate for me instead."

Left with no choice, the translator was replaced in the middle of the speech. This time, the translator gave over the rabbi's speech word for word. Rabbi Eliyahu related how he had asked whether Napoleon's throne was for sale and how much it was worth.

"I asked to buy it," he said, "and everyone there burst out laughing!" He went on to tell them how they had "explained" to him at the museum, in all seriousness, that the items that had belonged to Napoleon were of great national importance and were not for sale. The directors said, "They are historical items, and we don't sell history."

"Napoleon lived two hundred years ago, and you give him so much honor that you won't even sell his throne," Rabbi Eliyahu said. "And I ask, should we sell Jerusalem, the city that has belonged to the Jewish people for two thousand eight hundred years?"

The entire audience, in a show of tremendous emotion and inspiration, got up and gave him a standing ovation. Even the

French premier got up, approached the rabbi, shook his hand warmly, and said, "I have never heard such things in my life!"

He stayed there, still holding the rabbi's hand, apparently particularly moved. He asked Rabbi Eliyahu to stay a little longer than the time that had originally been scheduled.

Meanwhile, the embassy staff urged Rabbi Eliyahu to leave. They had no idea what else the rabbi had in mind and they wanted to get him out of there as fast as possible. They knew that he didn't — and wouldn't — listen to their advice or bow to their whims. And he could — and would — say whatever he wanted, now that he had detached himself from the embassy translator who had been carefully censoring his words.

But the rabbi wasn't in any hurry to leave, of course. His staff informed the embassy clerks that the rabbi was staying at the direct personal request of the prime minister.

After a short time, the prime minister once more called the audience to attention and announced, "I know that this is not part of the official program, but we have deviated from the written agenda because we have a very special and important event for which we didn't prepare.

"We have an extremely valuable gold medallion that is awarded only to presidents of the country. When we organized this reception, we weren't thinking of presenting anyone with such a medallion and it was not here in the hall. But Rabbi Mordechai Eliyahu's enlightening words were a once-in-a-lifetime experience, and we very much want to honor him for his special speech."

He then asked everyone to remain awhile until the presidential medallion could be brought to the hall and presented to Rabbi Eliyahu as a special form of recognition for his unique words.

One of Rabbi Eliyahu's grandsons, Rabbi Elad Eliyahu, who is a rabbi in Gedera,[5] once related that his grandfather showed him this special medallion. He brought it out in relation to a certain court case concerning idol worship. "He showed me the medallion with a cross, and the cross had been all scraped off and worn down," Rabbi Elad related. Then Rabbi Eliyahu told the story of what happened on that state visit to France, recounting how, as soon as he returned home, he took a file and scraped the cross until it was erased.

Rabbi Elad told his grandfather that the medal had certainly been of great artistic and historical value but was now ruined. "But Saba smiled that gentle smile of his, as if to say, 'What does all that matter to me compared to the *Shulhan Aruch?*'"

Do Not Sit on the Chairs

Rabbi Eliyahu once told an amazing story about *shatnez* (a forbidden mixture of wool and linen) in one of his classes. On one of his trips to Russia, during which Rabbi Eliyahu was to participate in an important conference, he entered the event hall only after everyone had already taken their places and sat down. There were many rabbis there, and everyone was waiting until Rabbi Eliyahu entered.

When the hall's employees saw him come in, they brought him a large, padded chair, but he remained standing and refused to sit down. He remembered that many years earlier he had read in a book of halachic questions and answers that the rabbis in Russia were careful not to travel in the gentiles' wagons, as it was then common practice in Russia to make cushions and quilts from *shatnez*.

Similarly, when they would travel by train, the religiously

---

5. He is the rabbi of the Ohr Hahaim Hakadosh synagogue.

observant wouldn't sit in the first-class cars, where the seats were upholstered. Instead, they traveled in the crowded third-class section, where there were bare, solid wooden seats. Thus, Rabbi Eliyahu was wary of sitting on an upholstered chair that had been manufactured in Russia.

The man running the conference noticed that Rabbi Eliyahu had remained standing, and he figured that Rabbi Eliyahu might be worried that the chair wasn't strong enough. This Russian official approached Rabbi Eliyahu, trying to persuade him to sit down. "Honored rabbi," he said, "don't worry! Our chairs are known for their quality and strength. We reinforce the edges of the padding with linen and wool, which provides stability to the entire chair." His translator quickly relayed his words.

The moment Rabbi Eliyahu heard what the official had said, he ordered all the rabbis present to stand up and wait until regular, unpadded chairs were brought in for everyone.

Concerning Costly Dinnerware

When Rabbi Eliyahu was visiting Los Angeles, he paid a call to the home of one of the richest and most influential members of the Jewish community. This man supported many Jewish schools and other Jewish organizations, and he had invited Rabbi Eliyahu, together with various important members of the community, to come have lunch at his vacation home. The luxurious estate was built on the edge of a cliff overlooking the ocean, and was only accessible by helicopter.

Rabbi Eliyahu felt that attending the lunch was a priority, as he wanted to support this generous donor. Rabbi Yigal Kutai,[6] one of the *roshe yeshivah* of Yeshivat Hameiri, was with him. He

---

6. He is also the head of the Hevron Heritage Center.

recalled, "We arrived at the wealthy man's home. I remember the rabbi's expression in the guest room, a room made entirely of glass, which looked out from the heights of the cliff onto the wide, open expanse of the Pacific Ocean. It was truly a stunning view. The rabbi gazed out at the ocean for several minutes, with an interesting expression on his face. He didn't say much. He just murmured, 'Beautiful, beautiful.'"

As they stood there, the host opened a curtain, revealing another huge lounge. In the middle of that room was a magnificent table, all set for the meal. On the table were some of the most expensive, stylish place settings on the market. The wealthy man had purchased this costly dinnerware especially in honor of the rabbi's visit to his palatial home.

"See what plates I've bought in your honor!" the rich man enthused.

The rabbi looked at the dishes and asked, "Did you immerse them in the *mikvah*?"[7]

The rich man shook his head. "What? Can't we still use them?" he worried. "After all the trouble I went to, we'll have to eat off disposable dishes?"

Thankfully, Rabbi Eliyahu immediately thought of a solution: immersing the plates in the ocean. He asked if there was a way to access the ocean from there, and the host nodded. "There's a rope ladder that runs from the lounge, down the cliff, to the ocean," he said.

There were many place settings and all the accompanying dishes, and the worried host suggested that his staff immerse them. He had no idea, of course, that only Jews can immerse dishes in a *mikvah*.

---

7. According to Jewish law, new dishes and cutlery must be immersed in a *mikvah* before use.

Rabbi Eliyahu didn't tell him that such a thing was forbidden. Instead, he turned to Rabbi Gavriel Cohen,[8] who was with them, and said, "You go down first and immerse the dishes." Then he motioned to the waiters, who were dressed in expensive uniforms. "All the waiters can carry the dishes down the rope ladder and hand them to Rabbi Cohen."

A small smile began to spread over the host's face. He knew he was having a unique experience, and that nowhere else in the world would such a story take place. He gave the order right away, and soon his expensive dishes were packed into cartons and lowered down the rope ladder to the sea below. Rabbi Cohen made a blessing and immersed them, and they were hauled back up to the man's home.

Everyone was moved to see how only one thing impressed Rabbi Eliyahu: Jewish law, and not all the silver and gold — and fancy dishes — in the world.

Rabbi Cohen finally finished the job. The ocean had been very rough that day, and he was completely soaked from the waves that had swept over him as he worked. "I'm so sorry," he apologized to the host as he came back up, sopping wet and dripping all over the lounge. "Some of the plates got swept out to sea. The water was so rough…"

"Don't worry about the dishes!" the host generously replied. "But look at you — all your clothes are soaked. I'll give you a new, dry suit to wear."

"Check that it doesn't have any *shatnez* in it," the rabbi whispered to Rabbi Cohen.

And so, they finally sat down to the sumptuous meal their

---

8. Rabbi Cohen is the head of the West Coast Rabbinical Court in Los Angeles, California.

wealthy host had had prepared for them. They all ate, while the rabbi added to the pleasure of the meal with words of Torah. It was a lavish meal like nothing they'd ever seen before, with the very highest standard of kashrut.

Every one of the guests was completely bedazzled by the truly remarkable hospitality and the out-of-this-world meal, enjoying pampering and tastes the likes of which they'd never experienced. Nobody noticed that the rabbi didn't eat a thing.[9]

HEAVEN HELPS

A Divine Delay

A *mashgiah* from Jerusalem's Caesar Premier Hotel came to ask forgiveness for a grievance that he had had against Rabbi Mordechai Eliyahu, after which he had gotten a glimpse of the depth of the rabbi's Divine inspiration.

He related that during the period when Rabbi Eliyahu was serving as the chief rabbi of Israel, Rabbi Eliyahu signed on the kashrut certificates of imported meat to authorize them. The Caesar Hotel required many different beef cuts, and they would use special cuts for their important guests. These were the kind of delicacies that can't always be found on the general market.

On one occasion they had been waiting a long time for a

---

9. This story was recounted by Rabbi Yigal Kutai. Rabbi Eliyahu likely didn't eat there because he was extremely stringent in his observance of kashrut and rarely ate in other people's homes. According to Rabbi Ya'aqob Menashe, founder and spiritual leader of Midrash Ben Ish Hai in Queens, New York, as quoted in an article in the *Jewish Star*, July 16, 2010, "Remembering Rabbi Mordechai Eliyahu *zt"l*," Rabbi Eliyahu consumed only bread and water when traveling.

particular meat to arrive, and the importer gave them the date on which the meat was expected to arrive at the port by boat. The hotel staff was sure that shortly after the meat was delivered there, it would be brought to the hotel. After all, it was in the best interests of both the importer and the hotel owners to get it there as quickly as possible.

But, to their great distress, the staff received the message that after the meat had arrived safely at the port, Rabbi Eliyahu had refused to sign the kashrut certificate for it. This was especially frustrating to the hotel employees, as the meat had been slaughtered by a team of *shohtim* (ritual slaughterers) who the chief rabbinate of Israel had sent abroad. Thus, the chief rabbinate should have had no problem issuing their kashrut seal after the meat had made its long journey and finally arrived in Israel. The situation baffled the hotel staff.

Everyone involved in the affair was angry or resentful, and words were uttered that shouldn't have been. This went on for about two days. And then a message was received from the meatpacking facility: the factory had accidentally shipped non-kosher meat to Israel, sending the kosher meat to another country. Those frustrating days saved many Jews from eating non-kosher meat, both in the hotel and in other places. Although the hotel staff didn't understand Rabbi Eliyahu's behavior at first, they were later stunned and astonished by his Divine inspiration.[10]

Hametz on **Pesah**

A few months before Pesah, the *rabbanit* would begin cleaning their house thoroughly, so there wouldn't be a crumb of *hametz* (leavened bread) left in it. Rabbi Eliyahu himself would also check the house during *bedikat hametz*,[11] taking hours to inspect every

---

10. The head *mashgiah* at Jerusalem's Caesar Hotel related this story.

11. A thorough examination of the entire house that takes place the night before Pesah.

corner to make sure that not even a hint of *hametz* remained to be found.

One year, on the night of the Seder, Rabbi Eliyahu couldn't sleep. He said to his wife, "I dreamt that there is *hametz* in the house!"

"If so," she answered, "I'm not staying in this house for even a moment. But it's not possible — I cleaned the entire house, and there isn't a corner that you haven't checked yourself."

She asked her husband to tell her exactly where the *hametz* was, but he said, "We have to look."

She checked the entire house again, but still didn't find anything. She went back to Rabbi Eliyahu and asked him to do a *she'elat halom* (a method used to interpret dreams).

"Open the book," he told her, handing her a Tanach. He then told her to count a certain number of pages. She counted and turned the pages, and then Rabbi Eliyahu told her to count a certain number of lines. She counted. Then he told her to count a certain number of words. "What word is there?" he asked.

"Healing," she answered.

"Go to the medicine cabinet," he instructed.

She went to the medicine cabinet, and there it was: wheat-germ oil, which the doctor had prescribed right before Pesah as a treatment for one of the children.

The doctor had given it to her after *bedikat hametz*, without realizing there was a *hametz* problem with it, and she had stored it in the medicine cabinet.

"If it hadn't been for the rabbi's dream, I would never have known that there was *hametz* in my house on Pesah," the *rabbanit* said.[12]

---

12. Rabbanit Tzviyah Hana Eliyahu, the rabbi's wife, related this story.

Beware of *Hametz*

Rabbi Binyamin Aviad[13] was the supervising rabbi of the Shafir region.[14] His responsibilities included overseeing the kashrut of the Sugat factory. At the time, the factory was importing a product called Minute Rice from abroad. This rice had undergone all the necessary checks and received the required permits before being brought into the country and the factory.

Rabbi Aviad was in the habit of consulting with Rabbi Mordechai Eliyahu about the factory's products. But when he mentioned this particular one, he was surprised to hear Rabbi Eliyahu rule that the rice was not permitted for Pesah. (Rice is usually permitted for consumption during Pesah for Sephardic Jews.)

The factory had all kinds of kashrut permits for the rice for Pesah, which Rabbi Aviad told Rabbi Eliyahu about, but he remained firm and refused to permit the rice for Pesah at all. The factory had no choice, so they left the rice sitting in sacks outside the factory.

After a few weeks of the rice lying outdoors in the sun, it began to emit a strong, rotten odor. It then turned yellow. All of this was very unusual for uncooked rice. The factory sent it to a laboratory for examination, and they discovered that the rice had been coated in wheat-germ oil, which is pure *hametz*.[15] Rabbi Eliyahu had somehow known that…

Don't Eat the Salad

One Shabbat, the *rabbanit* noticed that her husband wasn't eating

---

13. 1930–2004. He was also a member of the council of the chief rabbinate of Israel under Rabbi Ovadia Yosef and Rabbi Shlomo Goren.

14. The Shafir regional council is in southern Israel near the city of Kiryat Gat.

15. Rabbi Shlomo Ben Eliyahu, the rabbi of the Mateh Asher regional council and a son-in-law of Rabbi Aviad, shared this story.

the salad she had prepared and served. He usually *did* eat it, so when the *rabbanit* saw this, she didn't eat it either. That Motzae Shabbat,[16] she asked him why he hadn't touched the salad.

"Did you buy the vegetables from the same store you always buy them from?" he asked.

"No," she answered. "I bought them from a shop in the Geulah neighborhood that had a kashrut certificate."

"The vegetables in that shop haven't been tithed,"[17] Rabbi Eliyahu announced. "Don't buy from there anymore."

Miraculous NYC Shortcut

Rabbi Eliyahu was an authority in the laws of circumcision. More than once, when people came to ask him questions about circumcision, he would end up correcting the baby's circumcision himself.

On one occasion, Rabbi Eliyahu asked one of his contacts to arrange a meeting for him in New York with a well-known *mohel*. This man was known as *"the* rabbi who does circumcisions." After the meeting, Rabbi Eliyahu was scheduled to travel to Manhattan, where he had been engaged to give a Torah talk in one of the synagogues.

Rabbi Eliyahu's conversation with the *mohel* was apparently very important; they discussed the circumcision methods employed in the States among various *mohelim*, and the rabbi guided the *mohel* on different areas that required improvement regarding circumcisions, explaining how they were performed in Israel. It was important for

---

16. Rabbi Eliyahu was accustomed to speak only *divre Torah*, words of Torah, on Shabbat, so his wife likely waited until after Shabbat to discuss this issue, as it was not Torah-related.

17. Any produce grown in the land of Israel may not be eaten until tithes have been separated in accordance with Jewish law.

Rabbi Eliyahu that the circumcisions in the States be performed in complete accordance with Jewish law.

During this meeting, Rabbi Mutzafi, Rabbi Eliyahu's assistant, called Yitzhak Ovadia, who was with Rabbi Eliyahu at the time, and told him to notify Rabbi Eliyahu that it was time to leave. If he wanted to arrive in time for his speech in Manhattan, he would need to depart right away, as the journey could take up to an hour. Yitzhak relayed this information to Rabbi Eliyahu, but he simply waved his hand, gesturing that there was still time. Apparently, his conversation with the *mohel* was of great significance, and he put off the journey to Manhattan, although there was a huge audience waiting for him there.

Rabbi Mutzafi called again a short time later. He was very surprised that they hadn't left yet. Yitzhak told him that Rabbi Eliyahu was still speaking with the *mohel* and that he was aware they needed to leave. Twenty minutes later Yitzhak approached Rabbi Eliyahu to explain that they really needed to leave.

He asked how long it would take to travel to Manhattan, and Yitzhak replied, "When there are no traffic delays — thirty minutes. If there are tie-ups — forty-five minutes."

"There's still time," Rabbi Eliyahu declared, and carried on his conversation with the *mohel*. A short time later, the rabbi got up and asked again how long it would take to get to Manhattan.

"We don't have enough time," Yitzhak answered. "Even if there is no traffic, and there are no delays, we won't make it on time."

The rabbi said they would leave, so they finally departed. When they reached the highway, Yitzhak saw how heavy the traffic was and suspected that the entire journey would be in vain. But then they experienced a miracle. Heavy traffic clogged the two right lanes, but the left lane was completely empty.

Yitzhak couldn't understand why no one was traveling in the

left lane. He thought that perhaps the police had closed the lane further ahead, but he decided to take a chance and drive in that lane anyway. They were in such a rush that he prayed they wouldn't run into any police. Soon it became clear that there were no police around at all — and the left lane was clear for no apparent reason.

"I have lived in New York for many years," Yitzhak later recalled, "and I have never seen such a thing, not before that event and not after."

For the entire journey to Manhattan, every road was clear for the rabbi, even though everyone else was stuck in traffic tie-ups alongside them. "I will never forget it, nor will I ever understand why no one else drove on the empty roads like us. When we got off the highway, all the traffic lights were green, all the way to the synagogue in Manhattan," Yitzhak said.

The people at the synagogue knew what time Rabbi Eliyahu and Yitzhak had left Brooklyn and asked Yitzhak how they could have possibly arrived so quickly. "I told them that I simply didn't know — the road had somehow been empty," Yitzhak said. They made a forty-five-minute trip in just ten minutes. "Who knows if it was something to do with that important conversation the rabbi had with the *mohel*?" Yitzhak wondered.[18]

Seeing the *Mezuzot*

Someone who was experiencing a great number of difficulties phoned Reb Asaf Aharoni, one of Rabbi Eliyahu's assistants. Several people had suggested to this man that he get advice and help from Rabbi Eliyahu, who could sort out his problems.

The man asked Reb Asaf to approach Rabbi Eliyahu on his behalf. Rabbi Eliyahu, in turn, instructed Reb Asaf to ask this man about his *mezuzot* and see if he had checked them in recent

---

18. Mr. Yitzhak Ovadia of New York shared this recollection.

times.[19] The man replied that all the *mezuzot* in his home were new, good ones, but he said that since Rabbi Eliyahu told him to check them, he would.

The man took the *mezuzot* to be checked, and the scribe told him that they were kosher to the highest standard. He came back to Reb Asaf with the answer and asked what he should do next. Reb Asaf turned to Rabbi Eliyahu, only to hear him repeat that there was a problem with the *mezuzot*.

When Rabbi Eliyahu would check *mezuzot* himself, sometimes he would say, "This was written by a G-d-fearing scribe," and sometimes he wouldn't say anything at all. When questioned as to how he knew who was G-d-fearing and who wasn't, he replied, "I hold the parchment and I can feel it."

Yet, these *mezuzot* were being checked by someone else, so Reb Asaf thought that perhaps the first scribe hadn't been enough of an expert. He sent the man to a scribe he knew and trusted, and the man paid to have his *mezuzot* checked for the second time.

The second scribe attested that the *mezuzot* were kosher to the highest standard. He also investigated who had written the *mezuzot* and found that the scribe from whom the man had purchased the *mezuzot* was a G-d-fearing Jew.

When the man came back to Reb Asaf, he was understandably upset. He had now paid twice to have his *mezuzot* checked and each time he heard that they were fine. He felt that he had been fooled by those who called Rabbi Eliyahu a kabbalist. The man wasn't someone who was accustomed to going to rabbis for advice, and had only come to Rabbi Eliyahu because he had a number of problems. He then launched into a diatribe against rabbis...

Reb Asaf began to worry that this whole incident could lead

---

19. *Mezuzot* must be checked periodically to ensure that no damage has occurred to the parchment due to weather, age, or other conditions.

to a desecration of G-d's Name. He approached Rabbi Eliyahu to discuss it with him again.

Rabbi Eliyahu smiled. "Is it my fault that he hangs his *mezuzot* upside down?"

Reb Asaf returned to the man and asked him to describe how he had hung the *mezuzot*. From his description, it immediately became clear that the man was indeed inserting them in their cases upside down, just as Rabbi Eliyahu had said.

Reb Asaf explained how to properly hang the *mezuzot*, and the man thanked him profusely. But before he hung up, he inquired how Reb Asaf had known he was hanging the *mezuzot* upside down. He answered that Rabbi Eliyahu had told him so.

The man was astonished. "How on earth did he know that my *mezuzot* were upside down?" he asked.

Reb Asaf had no answer.[20]

---

20. Reb Asaf Aharoni, the rabbi's assistant, related this story.

Chapter Ten

Holiness

Only one who is holy always cleaves to G-d. His soul resides among the truly enlightened ones, with love and fear of his Creator.

He is considered as if he walks before G-d while still here in this world. And a person such as this is considered like a Tabernacle, like a Temple, and like an altar. As recorded in the writings of our blessed Sages, *Then G-d ascended from upon him —* the Patriarchs are the chariot of G-d.[1]

---

1. *Bereshit Rabbah* 69.

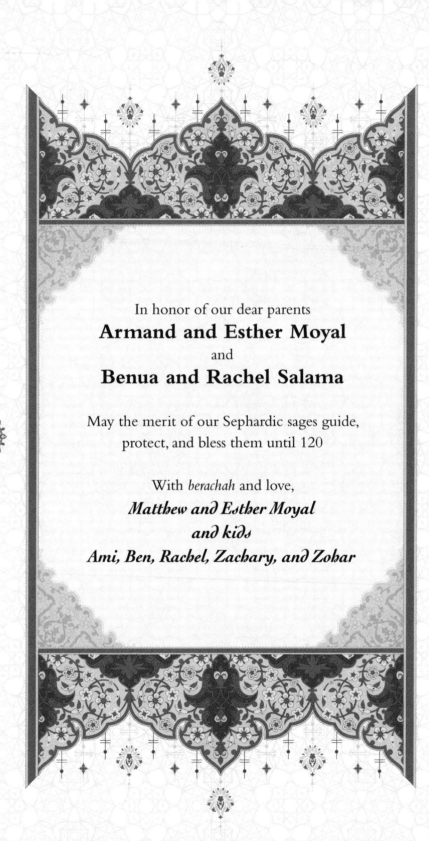

In honor of our dear parents
Armand and Esther Moyal
and
Benua and Rachel Salama

May the merit of our Sephardic sages guide,
protect, and bless them until 120

With *berachah* and love,
*Matthew and Esther Moyal
and kids
Ami, Ben, Rachel, Zachary, and Zohar*

GREATNESS OF SOUL

Tangible Holiness

Rabbi Yisrael Abuhatzera, the Baba Sali, was known to tell people that he bore witness that Rabbi Mordechai Eliyahu was a *tzaddik yesod olam* — a righteous man on whom the world is founded — an extremely high, unique level.

When Rabbi Eliyahu would come to visit the home of the Baba Sali, the Baba Sali would invite Rabbi Eliyahu to sit beside him on the couch, a liberty he didn't permit to anyone else. Once, the Baba Sali grasped Hacham Mordechai's holy hands and tried to kiss them forcibly, asking the rabbi to bless him. Rabbi Eliyahu attempted to avoid this honor and pull his hands away. But the Baba Sali rebuked him, saying, "I know who you are and what your soul is, and you will bless me!"

The Baba Sali would consult Hacham Mordechai in halachic matters and act according to his opinion, and so he would say, "By us, we rule according to the Ben Ish Hai and the instructions of Rabbi Mordechai Eliyahu."

The Baba Sali even gave Hacham Mordechai a precious Kiddush cup that he had received as an inheritance from his grandfather, the holy Abir Yaakov, Rabbi Yaakov Abuhatzera.

When Rabbi Eliyahu left the Baba Sali's home, the Baba Sali always made sure to accompany him. In his later years, he would ask to be carried out in his chair to accompany the rabbi. Once, at one of the meals at which the rabbi took part, the Baba Sali remarked to him, "Everyone comes here to eat, but you come to hear words of Torah." Just a year before his passing, the Baba Sali told the rabbi, "In Heaven it has been decided that you will be the chief rabbi of Israel. Go submit your application!"[2]

The Light of Holiness

Eliyahu Avniel of Ateret remarked that during his many years as a photographer, he had been privileged to photograph many grooms under the bridal canopy. He noticed that there is often a special kind of light surrounding the grooms at the moment of the wedding ceremony. Sometimes the light was so strong that he didn't even need to use a flash or additional lighting.

Mr. Avniel realized he could even use the light meter on his camera to measure this glow. The special shine reminded him of the verse describing the sun, *like a bridegroom coming out of the bridal canopy.*[3] It was the same light.

Mr. Avniel came to visit Rabbi Eliyahu in the hospital at the same time that Rabbi Yeshuah Ben Shushan[4] was there, praying for the rabbi's recovery. He went to pray with Rabbi Ben Shushan, and took advantage of the opportunity to photograph the people there. He felt it was not an everyday occurrence to be surrounded by such personages, and he wanted to let others share the experience.

Rabbi Eliyahu's son Shmuel was also there, sharing in those special prayers. Mr. Avniel showed him something very unusual on the camera's light meter: Every time he aimed the camera in the direction of the rabbi, a great light appeared and it registered

---

2. From the booklet *"Al Hatzaddikim V'al Hahassidim,"* by Rabbi Haim Ben Shushan, Bet El.

3. *Tehillim* 19:6.

4. 1945–2018. Rabbi Ben Shushan was a highly respected kabbalist, *shohet,* and *mohel.* He was a frequent participant in the prayers at the Kotel and was very close with Rabbi Eliyahu.

on the light meter. When he moved the camera away or pointed it in a different direction, the light disappeared.

And at Rabbi Eliyahu's funeral, Mr. Avniel again saw that light. It was hovering like a kind of halo over the rabbi's body. It was a cloud of light that didn't leave its place through all the eulogies, hovering there until the bier had been carried out, on its final journey, to the cemetery.[5]

The Dancing Chaplain

When Rabbi Eliyahu went to visit someone being held at a penitentiary in Maryland, the prison staff found themselves in a state of utter amazement. Something like this had never happened to them before…

Rabbi Mordechai Eliyahu, the *Rishon LeZion*, had just passed through their security checkpoint, which detected metals using some of the most sophisticated technology in the world at the time, into one of the most heavily guarded U.S. federal prisons. He had a metal zipper on his pocket — and the equipment did not respond to or even detect it.

The gate was supposed to respond to the metal with a series of beeps, but it remained completely silent as he passed through. The officer on duty was so surprised, he called the prison director down to see for himself. After all, day in and day out, without fail, the electric gate had worked, its sensors picking up every bit of metal, and it had suddenly stopped functioning without warning…

In consideration of the rabbi's honor, the security guard had warned the group as they approached, "This is one of the most sensitive gates in the world. With all due respect to the chief rabbi, if someone has anything metallic in his pockets, or if anyone has

---

5. Eliyahu Avniel of Ateret related this story.

had an operation and has metal in his body, he must inform me now, otherwise the gate will sound an alarm." And here the rabbi had passed through, wearing a metal zipper, and no sound had gone off.

"Right before you went through," the officer explained to the group, "a representative from the State Department passed through. Even after he had taken all the metal out of his pockets, the gate sounded the alarm because of the buckles on his shoes."

And when Rabbi Shmuel Zafrani passed through, the alarm sounded because of the metal binder rings in his work diary. But when Rabbi Eliyahu passed through, with his heavily decorated robe and an attached zipper, the gate was silent.

The officer in charge pointed with a shaking hand at Rabbi Eliyahu's zipper.

"What does he want?" Rabbi Eliyahu asked, and Rabbi Zafrani explained all the confusion at the gate.

The rabbi smiled. "That's all that's worrying him?" he asked. He opened the zipper and, in front of the flabbergasted guards, revealed the silver pen that was in his pocket, the watch on his hand, and the cufflinks on his shirt! The gate should have been beeping madly, but instead, it seemed to be struck dumb in the face of the rabbi's holiness.

"It's impossible! The gate must be out of order," the prison director remarked. Never before had such a thing happened. He took the pen from the rabbi's hand, walked through the gate, and the alarm went off. The astonished director handed the pen back to the rabbi, who passed through the gate again, which once more fell silent.

"The prison chaplain, a Christian, was with us," Rabbi Zafrani recalled. "He started singing, laughing, and dancing, and I asked him why."

"You *are* Jewish, right?" the chaplain asked. "Look, when the Splitting of the Sea occurred for the Children of Israel, they sang and danced. And I have worked here for twenty-five years and not once has the gate *not* sounded an alarm. So I have now seen the miracle of the 'splitting of the gate' with my own eyes. Shouldn't I dance?"[6]

Light in the Stairwell

About ten years ago, a man from Mevaseret Zion named Eyal Cohen wanted to buy a motorbike. He was given the name of someone — Dudu — who sold motorbikes for a living and was advised to call him about making a purchase. Cohen phoned Dudu and went to meet him. Dudu was young and had a long ponytail. He didn't appear to be religious at all.

During the course of their conversation, Cohen asked Dudu where he lived. He answered that he resided in Kiryat Moshe, in the same building as Rabbi Mordechai Eliyahu. He mentioned how much he loved the rabbi, and apparently, Cohen's face must have registered a degree of shock, as he went on to say, "Don't look at me like that. I really do love and respect the rabbi very much."

Cohen asked Dudu to share something with him about the rabbi. He thought for a moment and then said, "I'll tell you a story that I told to my friends, and they didn't believe me. But perhaps you, as a religious person, will understand what happened here.

"One night I came home at about four o'clock in the morning, and I wanted to lock my motorbike in the stairwell. It was really dark, and I had trouble finding the hole in the padlock. I had just decided to switch on the light when suddenly I sensed a bright light behind me. It was not the stairwell light but a different light.

---

6. Aharon Granovitch Granot, an Israeli journalist and writer, shared this recollection.

"I turned around, and I saw the rabbi coming down the stairs on his way to prayers, as he did every day in the early hours of the morning. There was a bright light emanating from him that illuminated the entire stairwell, including my motorbike's padlock.

"It was an absolutely amazing sight. I heard once that holy men have a special light, but I never imagined that in my neighborhood there was such a holy person. And especially as the rabbi would always smile at me and greet me whenever we met, even though I don't exactly look religious, I didn't realize what a level he was on. I saw it with my own eyes. Maybe you will believe me!" As he finished his tale, his own light was sparkling in his eyes.[7]

IN THE PRESENCE OF HOLINESS

In the Merit of Minutes

When the Eliyahus were sitting *shivah* for their husband and father, a yeshivah teacher came to console them. He related how he worked with youth who had fallen off the straight and narrow and needed a lot of help and spiritual support to come back.

One of the things he did was bring the yeshivah boys to see

---

7. As related by Eyal Cohen of Mevaseret Tzion.

Rabbi Eliyahu. Visiting the rabbi was an annual event that he tried to do with each group. One year they ran late for the meeting, and Rabbi Eliyahu was in a hurry to leave. Nevertheless, he didn't cancel the meeting, and sat and spoke with the group for a while. He finally left for his lecture, though he was late and people were waiting for him.

Several years later, this teacher met up with one of his former students, and was so happy to learn that this young man was now studying in yeshivah. "Tell me, what was it that turned you around?" he asked his student. "What caused you to drop a life of crime and drugs and return to a normal life?"

The young man answered without hesitation. "The five minutes I spent with Rabbi Mordechai Eliyahu are what turned me around completely. I didn't understand a word he said, but the light on his face — and the love that he showed me — that is what turned me back to the Torah's path."[8]

By the Menorah's Light

Right after the fall of the Iron Curtain, Jews around the world began to renew their connection to their Russian brethren, who had been trapped in the repressive Soviet state. For seventy years, they had been forbidden from praying, studying Torah, or practicing Judaism. During the exciting time of upheaval and renewal when Communism met its bitter end, Rabbi Eliyahu traveled to Russia for a visit, along with top officials from the Ministry of Religious Affairs and the director of the ministry, Zeev Rosenberg.[9]

---

8. As related by Rabbi Yosef Mikor.

9. Rosenberg is also a lawyer and the CEO of the Forum Hevra Kaddisha directors.

Rabbi Avraham Shayevich,[10] Rabbi Pinhas Goldschmidt,[11] and Rabbi Berel Lazar,[12] all part of the rabbinate in Russia, also accompanied him during the visit. They asked Rabbi Eliyahu to visit the archbishop of Russia, who exerted great influence on the masses and could bring the anti-Semitism under control in Russia. This could lead to saving the lives of many Jews.

Rabbi Eliyahu was very sensitive to all matters of Christianity, including the crucifix symbol, which Jews consider a form of idolatry. Nevertheless, for the sake of the Jews of Russia, he agreed to visit the archbishop, instructing his entourage to prepare for the visit. He made the visit conditional on his visiting the archbishop's home and not meeting him in a church.

Ahead of the visit, Rabbi Eliyahu had asked his assistant Rabbi Shmuel Zafrani to buy a pure silver Hanukah menorah, which they would bring along from Israel to Russia. Rabbi Zafrani had asked him why they were doing such a thing, as the visit wasn't coinciding with Hanukah. He replied, "You'll see when we get there."

When they set off for the visit with the archbishop, Rabbi Eliyahu instructed Rabbi Zafrani to bring the Hanukah menorah along. When they arrived, he soon saw why. They were shown into a large room with a long table, at which the archbishop and the rabbi sat at the head, and on the table was a large stone cross.

---

10. Rabbi Avraham (Adolf) Shayevich has been the rabbi of the Moscow Choral Synagogue, Moscow's main synagogue, since 1983. He also represents the Russian Jewish Congress, and is often referred to as the chief rabbi of Russia.

11. Originally from Zurich, Switzerland, Rabbi Pinhas Goldschmidt has been the chief rabbi of Moscow since 1993. He also founded and heads the Moscow Rabbinical Court and serves as president of the Conference of European Rabbis.

12. Rabbi Berel (Shlomo Dovber Pinhas) Lazar is an Italian-born rabbi who has served as the chief rabbi of Russia since 2000. He has been active in Jewish Russian institutions since the early 1990s.

The rabbi explained to the archbishop that it was a Jewish custom to give a valuable gift to a person they were visiting. He told Rabbi Zafrani to remove the Hanukah menorah from its packing, and he placed it on the table beside the cross. The rabbi went on to describe at length the menorah's value and importance as a piece of Judaica, and the archbishop was greatly flattered.

He thanked the rabbi profusely and was clearly very pleased with the gift. The rabbi took advantage of the moment to say that, as they were both men of faith, they should show the politicians how to act.

"Yes, yes," the archbishop agreed.

"We have to tell everyone that religion means peace and love, and that every man should respect his fellow, as we were all created in the image of G-d," said Rabbi Eliyahu.

"Of course," the archbishop said.

"If so, we should guide the politicians and the masses, instructing them to respect believers of all faiths and not oppress them," said the rabbi. The archbishop nodded.

"We'll write an announcement signed by both of us, and publish it across the world; it will be about love, peace, and the prevention of anti-Semitism," the rabbi suggested. Again, the archbishop agreed.

The rabbi removed a notepad from his pocket and began to formulate the text of the declaration. But the ambassador, who was also present, started to protest and suggested that something more formal and professional could be drawn up with the advice of lawyers.

"Now is the right time," insisted the rabbi. "Now or never!"

But the ambassador, who wasn't quite as wise, also insisted, and in the end, the declaration wasn't written at that time.

Later, when the ambassador formulated the text with lawyers, the archbishop didn't want to sign, as his advisers had warned him that it wasn't in their interest to protect the Jews.

Despite that, the rabbi came out of the meeting together with the archbishop, to the waiting reporters, and together they declared that Jews and Christians should not oppress each other. They said there should be mutual respect between believers. The announcement went a long way toward preventing the anti-Semitism that had reared its ugly head in those days.[13]

Removing an Evil Spirit

One day, an eighteen-year-old girl arrived at Rabbi Eliyahu's office, seeking an audience with him. The girl looked terrible. Her father explained that something strange had happened to her a month ago. She had started to exhibit very bizarre behavior, appearing sad and pensive for hours at a time and acting disconnected from and oblivious to whatever was going on around her. During such times, her speech was peculiar as well, sounding disjointed and rambling.

The rabbi asked her father what she had been like beforehand, just a month prior to the beginning of this unusual behavior. He said that she had been a friendly, happy, normal girl, and that they had never seen any dramatic or drastic change in her behavior like they were seeing now.

Rabbi Eliyahu told the father not to be shocked by what he was going to reveal. After a short silence, he said, "She has a dybbuk (evil spirit) inside her."

Her father went completely pale. "What can we do?" he asked in a shaking voice.

"Nothing special," the rabbi said. "The solution is simple." He

---

13. Rabbi Shmuel Zafrani, the head of Rabbi Eliyahu's office, related this story.

instructed the girl's father about what to do. The "cure" involved drinking water that had been poured into the Kiddush cup on Shabbat. She was supposed to follow his instructions for a month, and then the father and daughter were to return to Rabbi Eliyahu.

A month went by, and the father returned with his daughter. Both of them were smiling joyously. The girl was so happy and vibrant, she was barely recognizable. Her father related how he had carefully followed Rabbi Eliyahu's instructions every Shabbat, and his daughter's situation greatly improved. After four Shabbatot, she had completely returned to herself.

After the father and daughter departed, Nissim Lopes, one of the rabbi's assistants, asked how the treatment worked. Rabbi Eliyahu explained that it was a matter of imposing holiness and purity over the impurity of the evil spirit. When there is holiness and impurity together, the holiness pushes the impurity away, he said. After all, just a little light repels a lot of darkness.[14]

We've Arrived

Rabbi Eliyahu once traveled by bus and ended up having to sit beside a woman. Maybe he didn't want to offend her by getting up and moving to a new seat, or perhaps he didn't even notice he was sitting next to her. Either way, he remained sitting there, immersed in his learning.

When the bus arrived at the stop where Rabbi Eliyahu needed to disembark, the woman tapped him lightly on the shoulder, saying, "Mordechai, we've arrived; we have to get off now." Suddenly the rabbi realized that the woman next to him was his wife...

---

14. As related by Nissim Lopes, one of the rabbi's assistants.

HOLY HOMES

The Groom Will Find You

A young woman endured many long years of singlehood while waiting to find her partner. She went to Rabbi Eliyahu, asking for a blessing to find her true partner. She asked him what she needed to do to merit this blessing, but he replied, "You don't need to do anything. Your groom will come to you at home."

Many potential matches were suggested for her during the period following her visit to Rabbi Eliyahu. But for all of them she would need to travel to distant locations from her home in Be'er Sheva. She turned down all those offers, remembering Rabbi Eliyahu's blessing that her groom would come to her at home.

As it turns out, the bridegroom really did come to her at her home. He was there for an entirely different reason, so she got to know him. He turned out to be exactly the kind of man she had been praying and hoping for during all those long years. And so the rabbi's blessing came true down to the exact detail.[15]

A Meeting without Words

There was a young man who suffered as a bachelor for many years while waiting to find his life's partner. Rabbi Eliyahu was well aware of this man's plight, and even suggested a girl for him. She was from a good family and was the daughter of a Torah scholar. But after making many inquiries, this young man decided she wasn't what he was looking for.

But seeing as the rabbi had suggested it, he felt stuck. Finally, he

---

15. Rabbi Binyamin Batzri of Be'er Sheva shared this story. Rabbi Batzri, a descendant of the Ben Ish Hai, was the *rosh yeshivah* of Yeshivat Bet Yosef and rabbi of the Kiryat Ha'avot community in Be'er Sheva. He passed away in 2013.

found a solution: He went to her neighbors, explained the situation, and asked for their help. He sat in their home, pretending to be engrossed in a book. Then he asked them to call her in on some pretext. While she was there, he would be able to get a look at her and her behavior, without going on a formal date. The whole operation was kept secret from the girl, and the young man did not change his mind.

The next time this young man met with the rabbi, he said, "Regarding the girl that the rabbi suggested, I met with her, and I don't think she's for me."

The rabbi raised an eyebrow, looking at the young man with a most penetrating gaze. "You think you can hide the truth from me? You think you met with her? But you never spoke to her!"

The young man was never able to figure out how the rabbi knew.

Good Tidings in Paris

A yeshivah boy had planned to travel to Venezuela with a group of friends on an outreach mission for an Israeli Torah institution. As the date of the trip drew near, the head of the boy's yeshivah summoned him, explaining that he was looking for an emissary from the yeshivah to travel to a suburb on the outskirts of Paris, and he wanted this young man to go.

The boy was deeply disappointed and didn't know what to do. On the one hand, he wanted to travel with his friends to Venezuela, but on the other hand, he had been personally entrusted with this mission by the head of his yeshivah. Although the boy was a new immigrant from France, he didn't want to go back there because of the growing anti-Semitism in the country. He decided to ask Rabbi Eliyahu for advice.

He arrived at Rabbi Eliyahu's house just as his assistants were accompanying him to his car, and they wouldn't let anyone approach. The rabbi had already lifted his foot to enter the car, but he turned to his assistants and instructed them to let the boy ask his question.

So the boy asked his question as quickly as he could, in two brief sentences. Rabbi Eliyahu answered succinctly, "Go to Paris. May you have good tidings!"

So the young man traveled to Paris.

People in Paris's Jewish community quickly saw what a decent young man the boy was and they tried to set him up with the daughters of several prominent rabbis there. But he wasn't ready to get married yet. He was just twenty-two, and his soul was thirsting for Torah. During every spare moment, he sat and devoted himself to Torah study.

Meanwhile, a young woman and a friend had gone on the trip of a lifetime to Europe. But the two girls experienced many delays and ended up departing much later than they had intended. Even though the trip was going to be an abbreviated one, the girls decided not to cancel the Paris leg of their journey.

They had been in Paris for just a few short hours when someone gave them the number of a young man from Israel who they were told could help them if they needed anything. Despite their embarrassment, they called. When one of the girls was talking to him, she felt a deep connection that she could not explain. (She later found out that he had felt the same way.)

Before they got on the plane to return to Israel, the two ended up going out on one date. When that date went very well, they decided to continue seeing each other.

As the young man and young woman got to know each other better, they discovered that they had several mutual acquaintances. But they also realized that if any of their friends had thought of the match, they would have immediately dropped the idea, because neither of them fit the requirements of the other.

They ended up getting engaged. And the boy remembered the rabbi's blessing, "Go to Paris. May you have good tidings!" Within three months, they were married. And within a few short years, their children were happily reading stories about Rabbi Eliyahu.[16]

The *Rabbanit* Forgot, Too

A man once came to Rabbi Eliyahu to complain that his wife hadn't prepared wheat[17] for the Shabbat of the Torah portion of *Beshalah*. In his community, people had a custom to put wheat in the Shabbat *hamin* (cholent) every year for *Parashat Beshalah*, when the Torah portion about the manna is read.[18] The custom relates to the portion's discussion of the manna.[19]

In the *parashah*, Moshe tells the people of Israel that the manna will not fall on Shabbat. Nevertheless, Datan and Aviram go out to search for manna on Shabbat — and of course don't find any. However, the Midrash[20] relates that they had prepared some manna ahead of time, hiding it somewhere so that they could return to the camp and show everyone that Moshe was wrong.

---

16. As heard from Smadar Saban.

17. Some communities have the custom to use buckwheat, or kasha.

18. This custom is actually mentioned by the Bah, Rabbi Yoel ben Shmuel Sirkis (1561–1640), a prominent Ashkenazi European rabbi and *posek*. "According to the custom of eating whole wheat grains on *Shabbat Shirah*, one should be careful…only to eat them during a meal" (*Orah Haim* 208). (*Shabbat Shirah* is the name for the Shabbat that falls out during the week that *Parashat Beshalah* is read.) The custom is found among particular Sephardic and Ashkenazi communities.

19. Some Torah commentators say that the manna resembled kernels of wheat. This reason is mentioned by Rabbi Yisrael Haim Friedman in his *Likutei Mahariah*, *Tevet*.

20. This midrash is cited by Rabbi Avraham Eliezer Hirshowitz, who notes that it's in "the *Yalkut*" on *Shemot* 16:27, and is also mentioned by several other commentators.

So how was it that they didn't find any? Why had their manna disappeared? The birds ate the manna they had hidden.

To this day many Jews have a custom of showing gratitude to the birds on the week of this *parashah* by putting out bird food (such as wheat grains). And, as mentioned, in some communities, this "bird food" is added to the *hamin* as well...

Yet this Jew's wife had neglected to include the wheat in the Shabbat stew, and he was furious. He believed he hadn't fulfilled the "commandment" as required, even though it was just a community custom. It was all her fault...

Rabbi Eliyahu later related that he wanted to appease the man, so he offered him wheat grains from his own *hamin*, which the *rabbanit* had prepared. Rabbi Eliyahu left the room to go get the wheat grains. A few moments later, he returned empty-handed. "My wife forgot to put them in the *hamin*, too! Never mind... We can fix it. They'll prepare it for next Shabbat instead."

The truth was that the *rabbanit hadn't* forgotten to put the wheat in the *hamin*. But Rabbi Eliyahu had no problem "altering" the truth a little for the sake of peace. As he was on his way to get the wheat, the rabbi thought to himself, *If I give him grains from my hamin, he'll be satisfied...but he'll keep being strict with his wife. So what have we gained?*[21]

Whatever My Wife Cooks

Rabbi Zvi Farbstein, the rabbi of Kedumim, once told a colleague that he was in Jerusalem and heard that Rabbi Mordechai Eliyahu was giving a class to laymen on the laws of the festival of Shavuot. He wanted to see how Rabbi Eliyahu was teaching it to them, a lesson in itself.

---

21. Rabbi Mordechai Nagari related this story.

As soon as he entered the synagogue where the class was to be held, he noticed two men arguing about whether one should eat meat or dairy foods on the night of Shavuot. From the looks of it — and the sounds of their raised voices — the argument had already turned into a personal quarrel between the two. Each side was becoming increasingly heated.

The fiery row came to a screeching halt as soon as they heard the sound of Rabbi Eliyahu's car approaching. They figured they would ask Rabbi Eliyahu's opinion on the matter as soon as he entered the synagogue. He came in and began his class. Without any connection to the subject matter, one of the two adversaries asked whether one should eat meat or dairy on the night of Shavuot.

While that man was speaking, his opponent interrupted and had his say. It became immediately clear to all present that there were two antagonists here — and they were staying calm only out of respect for the rabbi.

The rabbi listened to their questions, weighing them with all seriousness, and then he answered that there was a difference of opinion on the subject among the rabbis. On the one hand, he said, there was value in eating meat, as it shows respect for the festival. He mentioned the Talmudic passage that says there is no joy without meat and wine.[22] He then discussed the merits of the other perspective, that eating dairy foods serves a variety of purposes and is in accordance with several customs...

Yet the two men refused to give in, each determined to prove that his side was right. Finally, one of them asked, "What does Rabbi Eliyahu eat on Shavuot night?"

Everyone leaned in to hear his response. Indeed, all in the room were by now quite curious to see how the rabbi would get out

---

22. *Pesahim* 109a.

of the trap that had been laid before him. Rabbi Eliyahu smiled widely. "I eat whatever my wife cooks!" he said.[23]

---

23. Rabbi Yosef Artziel of Kedumim shared this story.

Chapter Eleven

Divine Inspiration

Every wise one from within Israel who has words of Torah for truth; who sighs for the honor of the Holy One blessed is He and for the honor of Israel all his days; and who desires, longs for, and waits for the honor of Jerusalem and for the Temple, and for the redemption that will sprout soon in our days, and for the gathering of the exiles — Divine inspiration rests within him.[1]

---

1. *Tanna Deve Eliyahu Rabbah* 4.

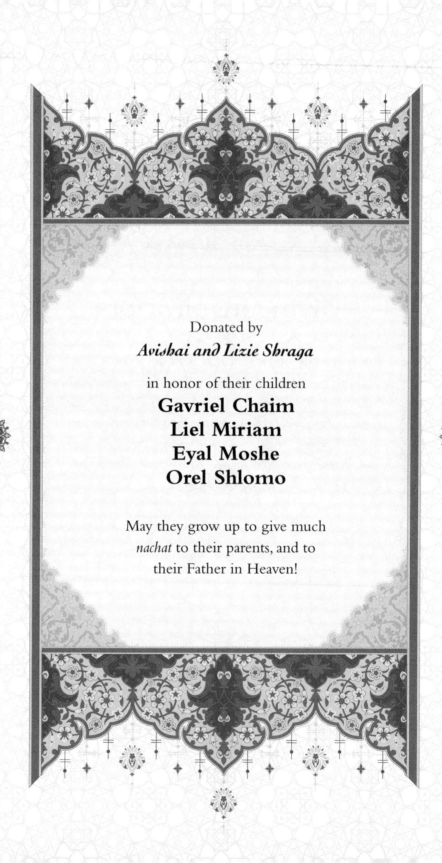

Donated by
Avishai and Lizie Shraga

in honor of their children
Gavriel Chaim
Liel Miriam
Eyal Moshe
Orel Shlomo

May they grow up to give much
nachat to their parents, and to
their Father in Heaven!

DISCREET DISCERNMENT

Everything Becomes Clear

Although Rabbi Eliyahu almost certainly had the ability to see into the future, he concealed this special power, and those who knew him only caught glimpses of it on very rare occasions. Rabbi Yitzhak Elidar[2] experienced one such incident. Rabbi Eliyahu had advised him not to travel outside the land of Israel for any sightseeing, but said that if he needed to go on such a journey for an essential public service, he could — as long as he first sought the advice of a rabbi.

Rabbi Elidar found himself in a situation where he and his wife really needed to travel abroad. One of their children had given birth overseas and he very much wanted to attend the *brit*. Before he purchased plane tickets, he went to speak to Rabbi Eliyahu, asking if he should fly for the circumcision.

"Your wife should go, and you stay in Israel," Rabbi Eliyahu said.

Rabbi Elidar was deeply confused. He didn't understand what the difference was. If it was permitted for his wife, surely it was acceptable for him as well? And if it was forbidden for him, then shouldn't it be forbidden for his wife? But his many years of knowing Rabbi Eliyahu had taught him that sometimes the rabbi knew and saw things that others didn't.

He followed Rabbi Eliyahu's advice, remaining behind as his wife traveled to the *brit*. Rabbi Elidar's heart was with his new grandson and the rest of his family, and it was difficult to not

---

2. Rabbi Elidar was an educator and administrator who was particularly influential in establishing a religious leadership for Ethiopian Jewry in Israel. He worked with the Ministry of Religious Affairs and the Absorption Ministry, and was active in managing Rabbi Eliyahu's office as well. He is in his nineties.

participate in the ceremony, which was on a Thursday. But just two days later, Rabbi Elidar found out exactly why Rabbi Eliyahu had said what he did: Rabbi Elidar's mother passed away on Shabbat.

If he had gone to the circumcision on Thursday, he never would have been back in time to accompany his mother on her journey to the Next World or to be there for her burial. And if his family had postponed her funeral until Rabbi Elidar returned, it would have been a great disrespect to the deceased. Everything became clear.

When Rabbi Eliyahu came to eulogize Rabbi Elidar's mother, he confirmed Rabbi Elidar's thoughts, saying, "Now do you understand?"[3]

Visitor from the Next World

Rabbi Shlomo Ben Eliyahu used to go to the Eliyahus' home on a regular basis, and he would learn and observe there how to teach and serve in the rabbinate. On one of his visits, Rabbi Ben Eliyahu observed something quite strange: A man came in and asked Hacham Mordechai to tell his sons to say Kaddish for him. Seeing as Kaddish is a special prayer recited for the deceased, it seemed rather bizarre that this man was requesting that his sons say it for him while he was alive.

After the man left the room, Hacham Mordechai saw Rabbi Ben Eliyahu's confusion. "That man was not alive," he explained. "He already passed away, but he was given permission to come down from the Next World to arouse his sons to say Kaddish for him. Go follow after him and see..."

Rabbi Ben Eliyahu ran out of the room and saw that the man wasn't in the waiting room, on the stairs, or anywhere at all. He'd simply vanished.

---

3. As heard from Rabbi Yitzhak Elidar.

The Dead Remind Us

For many years, Rabbi[4] Buzaglo served as a rabbinical judge on the *bet din* of Tel Aviv. He customarily prayed at sunrise, so whenever he was in Jerusalem for the night, he would go to pray in Rabbi Eliyahu's synagogue. Whenever Rabbi Buzaglo was there, Rabbi Eliyahu would seat him to his right and instruct the *shamash* to call him up to the Torah. This wasn't a special or particular honor for Rabbi Buzaglo; Hacham Mordechai gave the same privileges to every Torah scholar who visited his synagogue.

One Shabbat, Rabbi Eliyahu directed the *shamash* to call up Rabbi Buzaglo for *Maftir* (a special part of the Torah reading). At first, Rabbi Buzaglo didn't understand why the rabbi had called him up for *Maftir*, and only after he thought for a while did he remember that it was the week in which his mother's *yahrzeit* fell.

Rabbi Buzaglo was shocked that he had forgotten — and that the rabbi had somehow remembered. He wondered how the rabbi had known; after all, there was no way he could have known about his mother's passing and the date on which it had occurred. He went to ask Rabbi Eliyahu about it after the *aliyah*.

Rabbi Eliyahu replied with a smile. "If we don't remember, they remind us. Wait, I'll tell you a story after prayers."

At the end of the prayers, Rabbi Eliyahu told Rabbi Buzaglo a story about a woman named Mrs. Adam. Sadly, she didn't have any sons to say Kaddish for her. So instead of despairing, she bought a burial plot next to the grave of Rabbi Eliyahu's mother, saying to him, "Every time you go to visit your mother's grave, please say Kaddish by my grave, too."

"I can't promise," Rabbi Eliyahu told her.

"Even so," she said, "please try."

---

4. His first name is unknown.

One year, during his tenure as chief rabbi of Israel, Rabbi Eliyahu was rushing to perform the sale of *hametz* for the entire State of Israel on Erev Pesah and didn't have time to visit his mother's grave. When the rabbi arrived home, his young daughter opened the door and said, "Mrs. Adam was here and she asked why you hadn't been to visit her grave this year as usual."

"How did she look?" the rabbi asked his daughter, and she described Mrs. Adam exactly as she had looked when she was alive. The rabbi immediately turned around and went to the cemetery to say Kaddish by Mrs. Adam's grave.

The rabbi shared that story to show people how the dead will remind the living if they forget. But he did not share how Rabbi Buzaglo's mother, who passed away many years ago, reminded him that that week was her *yahrzeit*.[5]

SPIRITUAL VISION

Wake Up

When Rabbi Eliyahu was a young man of just nineteen, the State of Israel celebrated its very first Independence Day. Jerusalem was still being shelled regularly. The young Mordechai and his brother Shimon were sleeping at home, despite the shelling, as there were almost no bomb shelters in those days.

They were sharing one bed, as they didn't have enough beds at home. The young Mordechai would get up early and go to pray in the sunrise *minyan* in the Bet Yisrael neighborhood, and Shimon,

---

5. As heard from Rabbi Buzaglo of Tel Aviv.

who was younger than he was, used to pray in a later *minyan* at the Ohel Rahel synagogue.

One morning, the young Mordechai rose early for prayers, as was his custom, waking Shimon to come join him as well. It was very unusual for him to wake Shimon, and the younger brother remained in bed, saying he couldn't get up yet. But the young Mordechai persisted, refusing to yield and let his brother go back to sleep. The whole incident was very bizarre, as Rabbi Eliyahu never forced people to do anything and always behaved so gently, even as a young man. But for some reason he changed his regular behavior that morning.

When the prayers were over, Shimon realized why his brother had insisted on rousing him so early. They returned home to discover that the bed they had slept on was peppered with holes. The Jordanian legionnaires would fire shells and bullets into the civilian population, and that morning they had fired directly on their house — and bed.[6]

Splinters

The connection between Rabbi Eliyahu and the Lubavitcher Rebbe was unusually strong. Aside from their warm, well-known relationship, there was a special and deep spiritual bond between them, and this tie extended into many hidden and lofty areas.

Rabbi Eliyahu was in New York for the Lubavitcher Rebbe's funeral. Immediately after the rebbe was buried, Rabbi Eliyahu asked his assistants to take him to 770, the building where the rebbe used to pray and give classes,[7] in order to talk with the leaders of

---

6. Rabbi Shimon Eliyahu shared this recollection.

7. 770 Eastern Parkway, also known as 770, is the street address of the world headquarters of the Habad-Lubavitch movement, in the Crown Heights neighborhood of Brooklyn, New York.

the hassidic court and guide them on the future of Habad. The rabbi advised them to gather a group of ten rabbis who would continue the leadership, so that the worldwide Habad community would not become like a flock without a shepherd.

Those ten rabbis would work together to make decisions for and guide the movement. Rabbi Eliyahu requested that the ten rabbis be gathered without delay so that he could speak with and encourage them. While he was waiting for all the rabbis to arrive from their homes, he wandered through the rebbe's *bet midrash* (study hall) without sharing his thoughts or intentions.

At a certain point, he stopped and called over the rebbe's assistants, pointing out some tiny wood slivers lying on the floor. No one could even understand how he had noticed them. Rabbi Eliyahu summoned one of the senior hassidim who was there, asking, "How is it possible that there are wood slivers here that weren't buried together with the rebbe?"

The hassidim didn't understand what Rabbi Eliyahu was asking. He repeated himself, explaining that the wood from the rebbe's *shtender* (a podium-like bookrest) had been used to make the bier on which the rebbe had been carried to the cemetery. Some tiny slivers of wood must have fallen to the floor during that process, and they needed to be carefully swept up and taken to the cemetery, to be placed in the rebbe's grave. Yitzhak Ovadia, one of Rabbi Eliyahu's assistants in America, asked how Rabbi Eliyahu had known where the slivers had come from. He didn't answer.[8]

I Didn't Say I Would Tell

One year, when Rabbi Eliyahu returned from prayers on Rosh Hashanah night, one of the people accompanying him asked,

---

8. Yitzhak Ovadia of New York shared this story.

"Rabbi Eliyahu, it's Rosh Hashanah today, so what's being said about us in Heaven? What kind of new year will we have?"

Rabbi Eliyahu replied, "We'll know when the night has passed."

The next day, on Rosh Hashanah afternoon, when they were walking toward the Bukharan Quarter,[9] where they were going to pray, the same person asked the rabbi again, "So, Rabbi, what's being said in Heaven about the new year heading toward us?"

The rabbi replied evasively, "What's being said is what's being said…"

With a smile, the same man persisted, "But yesterday you said you would tell us what's being said!"

Unmoved, Rabbi Eliyahu replied firmly, but with a smile, "I said that I would know. I didn't say I would tell!"[10]

Graves under the Apartment

A disabled polio survivor wanted to purchase a ground-floor apartment that would be easily accessible for him. He had found one particular place and went to discuss it with Rabbi Eliyahu, but the rabbi advised him against it. "Why not look into something else?" Rabbi Eliyahu asked. He even went so far as to recommend another apartment, in a different building. But it was on a higher floor, and the man kept insisting on the ground-floor apartment.

"It would be so much more convenient for me," he said.

But Rabbi Eliyahu repeatedly advised him against it, saying,

---

9. On Rosh Hashanah, Rabbi Eliyahu typically prayed at the synagogue of Rabbi Shmuel Darzi, a prominent kabbalist.

10. Rabbi Yigal Ibn Denan of Rehovot shared this recollection. Rabbi Ibn Denan established Bet Torah and Hesed Ateret Mordechai Eliyahu, in memory of Rabbi Eliyahu. The Rehovot-based institution runs a *bet midrash*, *kollel*, soup kitchen, and more.

"Don't buy that ground-floor apartment. If you want, buy a ground-floor apartment in a different building, but not there."

The man finally relented and went to look elsewhere. Sometime later, construction work and digging was carried out in that area. It soon became clear that the particular building the man had wanted to buy an apartment in had been situated directly over an ancient cemetery. The apartment the man had wanted to purchase had been built right on top of the graves.[11]

Not Authorized

Rabbi Amram Ederi[12] was responsible for kashrut in the rabbi's office when Rabbi Eliyahu was chief rabbi of Israel. During that period, the signatures of both chief rabbis — Ashkenazi and Sephardic — were required on all the kashrut permits of imported food products before they could be released from customs. Rabbi Amram Ederi would check all the ingredients of the product and review its kashrut permits, and then bring them to the rabbi for his signature.

Rabbi Ederi related that every time he brought these papers to Rabbi Eliyahu, the rabbi would sign the permit on the same day, so as not to delay the importer. Each day of postponement caused the importer great financial loss. Rabbi Ederi had gone through this procedure with Rabbi Eliyahu tens of times, even hundreds, and the rabbi always signed the documents on the same day.

One time, Rabbi Ederi brought some documents for an imported product that needed a permit, but Rabbi Eliyahu didn't endorse it that day, as was his usual custom. Rabbi Ederi waited until the

---

11. Meir Uziel shared this story.

12. Rabbi Ederi was personally appointed to the position by Rabbi Eliyahu. Rabbi Ederi authored *Hakashrut K'halachah*.

next day and went into Rabbi Eliyahu's office to check on the permit, but he still hadn't signed. Meanwhile, the importer began calling to find out what was happening with his product and why it hadn't received the authorization. At first, this importer was very polite, but he began to get quite aggressive — understandably, considering the financial hit he was taking.

Rabbi Ederi didn't have any answer for him except to say that the documents were sitting on Rabbi Eliyahu's desk and he would surely put his signature on them in the next day or so. Although Rabbi Eliyahu was approving other forms, that particular one was just sitting there. Rabbi Ederi was certainly curious about it, but he knew that Rabbi Eliyahu was a man of purpose and felt that it was inappropriate to question his reasons or apply pressure. Instead, Rabbi Ederi would simply inquire after that particular permit and then go on with other business. And Rabbi Eliyahu never answered him.

This went on for two weeks. One day, a prestigious rabbi from Germany called the office, absolutely frantic. He had signed for the kashrut of one of the ingredients in that product whose permit had been sitting on Rabbi Eliyahu's desk. The rabbi explained that there had been a mistake and the kashrut certification was invalid. In fact, the product was completely non-kosher. He begged that the item be taken off the shelves immediately. It was clear that he was terribly distressed over the slip-up, and he asked if Rabbi Eliyahu had already signed the certificate to release the product from customs.

Rabbi Ederi told him that he was very fortunate because the chief rabbi had Divine inspiration. He then shared with him the strange story of the product's permit — something that had never happened before. He explained how Rabbi Eliyahu hadn't signed the document — for no apparent reason — even though it had been sitting on his desk for two weeks already, and even though he had signed hundreds of others on the same day.

Overcome with emotion at seeing this Divine inspiration with his own eyes, and how it had saved so many Jews from eating non-kosher food, Rabbi Ederi went into Rabbi Eliyahu's office to tell him what had happened. Rabbi Eliyahu simply answered, "Okay," moved the permit to the side, and carried on with his work as though nothing had happened.

No Visits

A woman named Leah Bass, from Kiryat Malachi, had vacation from work and decided she would use it to visit her daughters. One of them lived in Yitzhar and the other in Emanuel. Mrs. Bass planned to first head to Emanuel and then, on Friday, to catch a bus from Emanuel to Yitzhar. The bus she was planning to take was the Habad girls' school bus, and she knew that on Fridays there was one free space on it.

On Wednesday morning, she woke up very early, feeling this strong urge to go get a blessing from Rabbi Eliyahu. She had never even met him before, but for some reason she found herself longing to see him and receive his blessing. So she caught the first bus to Jerusalem and arrived at the rabbi's synagogue a little after seven in the morning. There were a number of people already waiting in line to see him.

When it was finally her turn, Mrs. Bass excitedly headed into the room. But before she even managed to open her mouth, Rabbi Eliyahu's face turned red and he began saying, "No! No! No!" He was shaking his head firmly, too, adding to the gravity and severity of the scene.

But Mrs. Bass didn't understand what all this seriousness was about. "No what?" she asked.

"No visiting your girls!" Rabbi Eliyahu announced decisively.

"When?" Mrs. Bass asked, shaken. "Today? Tomorrow? Never?"

"Not before you receive the priestly blessing (*Birkat Kohanim*). Go right now to the Kotel — maybe you'll make it in time."

Mrs. Bass left, feeling utterly confused and in complete turmoil. All her plans had been upended and she had no idea what to do. Nevertheless, she felt like she should go to the Kotel if that was what Rabbi Eliyahu had advised. But because she wasn't from Jerusalem and wasn't familiar with the bus routes and roads, she made it there very late. The morning prayers had already finished, even in the latest *minyanim*.

She decided she would return to Kiryat Malachi, which she did with a heavy heart. Here she had hoped to see her daughters and grandchildren, and spend time visiting with them and enjoying their company, and now she was heading back home to her empty and quiet apartment. Although she intended to hear the priestly blessing as soon as possible, she missed it during the next few days. One morning she woke up early for the morning prayers but felt unwell. When she finally did make it to the synagogue, there weren't any *kohanim* there to give the blessing that day. Friday came and she still hadn't done what the rabbi had instructed.

She prepared for a Shabbat alone. While she was in the middle of cooking and organizing, she heard an announcement on the radio. There had been a terror attack: An Arab car had deliberately plowed into a girls' school bus. It was the very bus that Mrs. Bass had planned to take. She started shaking uncontrollably, realizing that that was what Rabbi Eliyahu had seen with his Divine inspiration.

Mrs. Bass later got the details of the incident. The terrorist had driven into the bus while it was on the way from Emanuel to Yitzhar. Almost everyone on the bus had been injured in some way. Miraculously, the terrorist had hit the bus exactly where the seat behind the driver was located — and that seat had been empty. That was the seat where Mrs. Bass had intended to sit — and had even reserved for herself. That particular spot bore the brunt of the damage and Mrs. Bass shuddered to think of what might have happened to her had she been sitting there.[13]

One Out of Five

When Meir Gradish of Raanana used to visit Rabbi Eliyahu, he would always ask for a blessing for his mother-in-law. His mother-in-law had been born in Poland and she had five names, including Liora, Zina, Lusha, and two others. On one such occasion, Meir asked Rabbi Eliyahu if he could shorten the list of names that he gave him every time.

Rabbi Eliyahu folded up the paper on which Meir had written all the names, stood up, took two steps back, then walked two steps forward, and announced, "Her name is Leah and not any of the names written here."

Meir was very surprised. He went back to his mother-in-law and asked what her real name was. She explained that though she had been named Leah when she was born, she had been living among non-Jews — and they had all called her Lusha. When she moved to Israel, she had been placed on a kibbutz, where they called her Liora. But the name she had been given at birth was indeed Leah.

Empty Cases

A Judaica merchant once came to visit Rabbi Eliyahu, hoping to consult the rabbi about all kinds of problems he was having. He

---

13. Mrs. Leah Bass of Kiryat Malachi later related that she felt she clearly owed her life to Rabbi Eliyahu.

was accompanied by his friend, a scribe who was acquainted with Rabbi Eliyahu. After Rabbi Eliyahu had heard about the various issues this man was facing, he instructed him, "Go check if you have *mezuzot* at home!"

The man was quite confused by Rabbi Eliyahu's instructions. "Of course I have *mezuzot* at home," he declared. "I sell *mezuzot* myself, and I hung all the *mezuzot* in my home on my own."

When they left Rabbi Eliyahu's office, the scribe tried to explain to his friend that Rabbi Eliyahu had just intended for him to check if his *mezuzot* were kosher. When the merchant arrived at home, he went to check his *mezuzot*, and discovered to his absolute astonishment that the *mezuzah* cases were completely empty. There were no parchments inside them.

When Rabbi Eliyahu was later asked how he knew that the *mezuzah* cases were empty, he simply said, "I opened my mouth and the Heavens answered amen…"

IN ANOTHER REALM

I Already Told You

Rabbi Eliyahu's driver, Roni Levi, related that during the rabbi's lifetime, Rabbi Eliyahu had appeared to him in his dreams several times, giving him instructions or telling him what to do. One time Roni had arranged to drive the rabbi somewhere very early in the morning, but he accidentally overslept. Twelve minutes before he was supposed to be at the rabbi's house, Rabbi Eliyahu appeared to him in his dreams.

"Where are you, Roni?" he asked.

Roni jumped out of bed, making it to Rabbi Eliyahu's house at exactly the moment they needed to leave.

Another time, Roni wanted to take his daughter out of her playgroup and switch her to another one. Rabbi Eliyahu wasn't happy about the plan, as it would harm the first playgroup teacher's income, and she was having a hard time making a living. But Mr. Levi wasn't comfortable with this teacher for various reasons and decided to move his daughter to a different playgroup anyway.

That night, Rabbi Eliyahu came to him in a dream and said, "Don't harm the playgroup teacher. She really needs the income, and your daughter won't suffer from it."

Roni was in shock. The next morning he asked Rabbi Eliyahu what he should do. He just looked at Roni and said, "Do what I told you in the dream!"[14]

Forgotten Plans

One year, a woman traveled to Uman, in the Ukraine, with her husband and toddler son. She wanted to give some money to charity, so she made a vow that when she returned to Israel, she would donate thirty shekels. She set the money aside in her purse, with the intention of giving it to someone appropriate when she returned home.

A short time after they returned to Israel, the baby's stroller disappeared from the entrance of their building. The stroller's disappearance was a major red flag, and the woman started thinking that if her property was being targeted, something must have happened. She started reviewing her actions and remembered that she had promised to give that money to charity...but then she forgot about it again.

---

14. As heard from Roni Levi, the rabbi's driver.

Shortly thereafter, their toddler was attacked by an aggressive virus, and he got a terrible eye infection. The virus also affected the young boy's digestive system, and before they knew it, the young family ended up in the hospital with a very sick little boy. They heard that Rabbi Eliyahu was hospitalized in Shaare Zedek as well, and they decided to try to get a blessing from him for their son.

The boy's mother went to Rabbi Eliyahu's room, where she met his assistant, Rabbi Mutzafi, outside the door. Rabbi Mutzafi spoke to Rabbi Eliyahu on their behalf and asked him to give them a blessing. Rabbi Eliyahu told them that they must do a *pidyon* (redemption) over their son's head — in the amount of thirty shekels. He also blessed them with a speedy recovery.

Before Rabbi Mutzafi left the room to relay the rabbi's instructions to the young family, Rabbi Eliyahu said, "And tell her to put the money in a charity box immediately — and not leave it in her purse like last time!"

The toddler's situation improved dramatically, and he was soon released from the hospital. When they arrived home, there was an interesting surprise waiting for them: the stroller. It was sitting right in the entrance as if it had never been missing.[15]

Already Too Late

When Rabbi Eliyahu was hospitalized on the tenth floor of Shaare Zedek, people would come to him to ask him to pray for their loved ones who were also hospitalized. On one occasion, there was a patient on the eighth floor in the same hospital, and his relatives came to ask Rabbi Eliyahu to pray for him. They had gone up just two flights from their relative's room and had headed

---

15. As heard from the baby's mother, Michal Parber of Jerusalem.

directly to Rabbi Eliyahu's room, but the rabbi indicated to them that their relative was already dead.

"How can that be?" they asked. "How can he be dead? Just two minutes ago we saw him alive!" The rabbi was ventilated and thus couldn't speak, but he made motions to indicate that it was too late and nothing could be done.

The relatives raced back down to the eighth floor and saw that indeed, the relative they had left alive just a few minutes before had already returned his soul to his Maker.

A similar story was also related by the *rabbanit*. Her sister Ora was suffering from an illness, but long before the doctors knew about it, Rabbi Eliyahu had already told his wife what her sister was going to be diagnosed with. It later became clear that Rabbi Eliyahu was absolutely right.

Ora was then sent to England for a special surgery that was only performed there at the time. Two days before the operation, however, Rabbi Eliyahu came up to his wife and gently informed her that she should stop working because she was now in mourning.

"But why?" she asked, confused. "The operation isn't even for another two days…"

But Rabbi Eliyahu shook his head, and his wife understood that the Heavenly decree had already been issued. An hour later they received the call that the *rabbanit's* sister's situation had taken a sudden turn for the worse and she had rapidly deteriorated, ultimately returning her soul to the One Who made it.

Uttering His Name

Many years ago, Rabbi Yosef Elnakwa[16] heard a spine-chilling

---

16. Rabbi Elnakwa was the rabbi of Gush Katif. Today he serves as the *rosh kollel* of Yeshivat Hadarom, in Rehovot, and is an author and editor of Torah books. He lives in Yad Binyamin.

story from the *rabbanit*. A Jewish man living abroad was seriously ill. Members of his family who knew Rabbi Eliyahu asked the rabbi to pray for him. Because his situation was so serious, the *rabbanit* asked her husband to make a special trip to the Kotel to pray on his behalf.

The day went by and the rabbi hadn't gone to the Kotel. His wife begged him to go the following day. But the next day passed and when the *rabbanit* asked her husband if he had prayed for the sick man at the Kotel, he replied that there had been a lot of pressure that day at the rabbinical court.

"You must go tomorrow!" the *rabbanit* implored. But the third day passed and the rabbi still hadn't gone.

"Why don't you go?" the *rabbanit* asked him. "His situation is so serious!" she said.

"It's already all over," Rabbi Eliyahu replied.

"Why are you talking like that?" cried the *rabbanit*.

"Do you think I wouldn't pray for someone who I was asked to pray for?" Rabbi Eliyahu asked. "I've been trying to bring his name to my lips for three days already, and for some reason I can't!"

Searching on Shabbat

A number of years ago, there was an incident in which a young child was separated from his parents near the Sea of Galilee. Search parties and rescuers went out to look for him, but Shabbat had almost arrived and they had not found the boy.

People involved with the search operation approached Rabbi Eliyahu, asking if they should continue the search during Shabbat or not. Rabbi Eliyahu replied that of course the search should continue, as it was a matter of life and death.

Afterward, the rescuers asked him, "Where is the child?"

The rabbi answered sorrowfully, "I don't see him. He's not alive. He drowned."

And so the search organizers asked, "If that's the case, should we search for him on Shabbat or not?"

The rabbi replied, "According to Jewish law, you must search for him — so search!" They continued the operation, and a few hours later, the boy's body was found in the water. He had drowned, as the rabbi had said.[17]

Now He's Okay

During the Second Lebanon War,[18] the son of one of the soldiers fighting in it celebrated his bar mitzvah. As his father couldn't take him to see Rabbi Eliyahu and get a blessing, the boy's grandfather — the soldier's father — took him.

They went together to pray at Rabbi Eliyahu's synagogue. Before the prayers began, the boy's grandfather approached Rabbi Eliyahu to ask him to pray for his son who was fighting in Lebanon. The rabbi asked him to write his son's name on a piece of paper, and he placed the note inside his prayer book.

At the end of the prayers, the grandfather approached the rabbi again and asked him a second time to pray for his soldier son.

"Don't worry," the rabbi responded. "He's okay now."

The grandfather was shocked. Did that mean that his son *hadn't* been okay?

When he left the synagogue, the man received a phone call from his son, who told him emotionally, "There was a Katyusha rocket attack on us just moments ago. A rocket fell right beside me, but I was saved. Now I'm okay!"[19]

---

17. As heard from Rabbi Simha Kook, the rabbi of Rehovot.

18. This thirty-four-day military conflict took place in July 2006, affecting northern Israel and the Golan Heights.

19. Rabbi Mordechai Nagari, the chief Sephardic rabbi of Maale Adumim, related this story.

Don't Call Him Yohai

During the *shivah* for Rabbi Eliyahu, one of the popular stories that circulated involved a family that had celebrated the birth of a baby boy. The baby's father had wanted to name him Yohai, but the baby's mother had strongly objected. She had a brother named Yohai, and it wasn't their custom to give a name that was in use by a living relative.

The discussion soon deteriorated into an argument, and the baby's father turned to Rabbi Eliyahu for advice. The rabbi closed his eyes tightly and sat in quiet contemplation for a few moments. Then he suddenly cried out, "Don't dare call him Yohai!"

The baby's father then asked, "So what should we name the baby?"

"Shimon," Rabbi Eliyahu replied firmly.

And so it was.

The day after the circumcision, when the baby received the name Shimon, there was a road accident — and the new mother's brother, Yohai, was killed.

Preparing the Cure First

Rabbi Shai Levy[20] had sought Rabbi Eliyahu's blessing on numerous occasions for a close relative who was in need of a particular deliverance. He would usually write his request to the rabbi, and after Rabbi Eliyahu had given the blessing, he would return the note to Rabbi Levy or put it in his pocket.

One Friday morning, Rabbi Levy again approached Rabbi Eliyahu with the written request for a blessing. As Rabbi Eliyahu read the note, his face grew very serious. He then crumpled

20. Rabbi Shai Levy is the son-in-law of the above-mentioned Rabbi Mordechai Nagari. Rabbi Levy heads the Orot Ha'Ari yeshivah in Safed.

the note in his fist and took it with him. Rabbi Levy was quite surprised by this behavior, which he had never witnessed before.

The next day Rabbi Levy found out that the woman for whom he had been requesting a blessing had been in a serious road accident. Thankfully, she had somehow escaped unscathed. When Rabbi Levy remembered Rabbi Eliyahu's reaction, he understood that the rabbi had seen a decree hanging over her and had wanted to continue praying for her throughout the day.

A Healthy, Holy Boy

When a Jerusalem family was given the news about the wife's pregnancy, the doctors told them they were expecting twins. Her husband immediately went to see Rabbi Eliyahu to get a blessing from him. Usually he would return from such visits happy and uplifted, but this time he came back pensive and serious.

"What happened?" the wife asked her husband. "You didn't manage to get in to see the rabbi?"

"I got in."

"You got a blessing from him?"

"I got a blessing."

"So why are you brooding and down?"

Her husband told her what had taken place. "I told the rabbi that we were expecting twins, and he gave me a blessing, saying, 'You should merit having a healthy, holy boy!' I repeated myself to the rabbi, saying, 'We were told that we are having twins.' And the rabbi again answered, 'A healthy, holy boy!'"

Her husband thought that perhaps the rabbi hadn't heard properly, even with his repetition, so he gestured with his hand, holding up two fingers, meaning twins. The rabbi smiled and repeated firmly, "A healthy, holy boy!"

The first few months passed uneventfully, but then the young couple was informed that there was a problem with the fetuses, and one of them was definitely not going to survive outside the womb. They went back to Rabbi Eliyahu for a blessing, explaining that their unborn babies were in danger.

"As I blessed you before," he said, "don't worry. With the help of G-d, you'll have a healthy, holy boy!"

Indeed, that is what happened. She delivered just one baby boy, but he is truly healthy and holy. And that's what the family continues to pray for, that the rabbi's blessing will always accompany him.[21]

MEDICAL MIRACLES

Only Revealed When Essential...

Mrs. Naomi Knobel worked for many years as the secretary in Rabbi Eliyahu's office (and continues to work there). Rabbi Eliyahu would always show his staff tremendous consideration, but his employees were rarely witness to the rabbi's "supernatural" abilities. Though they had heard numerous stories and could certainly see the rabbi's greatness, the staff usually didn't get to actually observe any of it. On very rare occasions, however, when there was no other option, the rabbi would reveal his unique strengths.

Mrs. Knobel got a personal view of these special abilities when her son came down with terrible stomach pains that had several indications of possible appendicitis. She raced with him to the hospital, calling Rabbi Eliyahu on the way. When they got to the hospital, the doctors wanted to rush the boy to the operating

---

21. As heard from the Matot family of Jerusalem.

theater, telling a frantic Mrs. Knobel that if they waited any longer her son's appendix could burst and the boy could be in a life-threatening situation.

As they were wheeling the boy to the operating room, Mrs. Knobel called Rabbi Eliyahu again. "Your son doesn't need surgery," he said firmly.

Mrs. Knobel was thrown into confusion. On the one hand, her son was being rushed to the operating table and the doctors were in a great hurry to do surgery. And on the other hand, Rabbi Eliyahu was telling her that he didn't need surgery at all.

She called Rabbi Eliyahu back. "Please, the doctors say he urgently needs surgery! Please give him a blessing that the surgery will be successful."

"You have my blessing for your son," Rabbi Eliyahu said gently. "But he doesn't need surgery. It's a mistake," he added with conviction.

Mrs. Knobel felt more distressed and confused at that moment than she had ever felt in her life. Her son's life was in danger, or so the doctors were saying. Yet the rabbi, whom she knew so well, admired so much, and trusted so deeply, was clearly telling her that there was no need for surgery. But the rabbi hadn't actually *seen* her son, she reasoned. He was far away. The doctors were right next to her, pressuring her to let them get started, reasoning that every second counted in this emergency. She was bewildered and distraught.

While all this was going on, the surgeon arrived, having been called in from home to perform the operation. He asked what was going on, and Mrs. Knobel begged him to check her son again. He placed his hand on the boy's stomach, pressing on a few places, and then announced, "Surgery should not be performed under *any* circumstances. This boy doesn't have anything wrong with him — just a bad stomachache. Don't operate!"

Mrs. Knobel and her son were soon leaving the hospital. There was no surgery that day, just as the rabbi had predicted.

Guarding His Bones

Ronit Drazner of Bet Shemesh recalled that her family was very close to the Eliyahus. Her parents had been invited to the Eliyahus' home on many occasions and Ronit's mother was a close friend of the *rabbanit*. They had observed the rabbi's Divine inspiration numerous times over the years. But one incident stood out.

Ronit's husband was in a serious accident — and she witnessed it herself. Her husband had simply crossed the street to get something from a friend who was waiting on the other side. While he was crossing, he was hit by a motorcyclist who was traveling at over 60 mph (100 kmh).

When Ronit saw her husband lying on the road, unconscious and bleeding profusely from a serious head wound, she found herself in terrible shock. She went to call emergency services but accidentally dialed Rabbi Eliyahu's number instead. Fortunately, he answered on the first ring. Ronit told him the story, saying that her husband had just been run over and was lying right there on the road, bleeding from his head and his leg. She asked what she should do.

Rabbi Eliyahu repeated a verse that Ronit didn't catch, and then said, "Don't worry! Even if all his bones are broken, it won't be worse than that. He doesn't have brain damage."

As soon as she hung up, Ronit called the ambulance and her husband was taken to the emergency room. An entire bone was sticking out of his body. It was a hideous and difficult sight. The doctors began x-raying him and then placed a mask over her husband's face as they began wheeling him to the operating room for emergency surgery.

Ronit heard her husband calling something through the mask. "Call Rabbi Eliyahu!" he was saying.

She called Rabbi Eliyahu back right away. He again answered immediately. "Under no circumstances should he undergo surgery. The bone will come out whole; it's not broken," he said. "Operating will only complicate matters more. Insist on another x-ray, and they'll see that the bone is whole and intact."

Now Rabbi Eliyahu was saying all this from his home, while Ronit and the doctors were surrounding her husband in the hospital. Nevertheless, she stood up to the medical team, insisting on another x-ray and demanding that the operation be canceled. They looked at her as if she had lost her mind from the shock of the accident. "That's what Rabbi Eliyahu said," she explained.

The frustrated doctors grumbled, "Who is this rabbi anyway? Can he see what we see? He's not even here!" Seeing as they had no chance of reasoning with the patient's recalcitrant wife, they finally acquiesced, halting the pre-op preps and wheeling her husband back for another x-ray. Indeed, total pandemonium broke out following the x-ray. One doctor called to another who called to another. The bone was whole, as the rabbi had said. There was no need for surgery.

Ronit's husband was taken to one of the recovery wards, where he began the long and difficult healing process. Almost every bone in his body had been broken and needed to be rejoined and casted. But his head was okay. Everything worked out just as the rabbi had said.

Closest Thing to G-d

A young couple was living in Eilat. They had been married for five years, yet they still hadn't had any children. It was a very difficult time for them, enduring uncomfortable and complicated fertility treatments, coping with all the hormones, and facing the constantly dashed hopes, broken dreams, ongoing disappointments, and countless tears. Each time a cycle ended in failure, they felt their hearts break anew. Sometimes the pain was bigger and sometimes smaller. But it was always there, a constant dull ache of longing. They were sinking into depression and despair.

When the husband's father passed away, the young husband started putting on *tefillin*. He wasn't interested in becoming religious, but somehow wearing *tefillin* just felt right to him. While he had the *tefillin* on, he would talk to his father, pray to G-d, and ask for children, happiness, wealth, and so on. Day after day, over and over, he did this, again and again. One day, the young husband took his prayer book and wrote a letter in it to G-d. It was a pain-filled treatise, written in tears. One tear fell on the prayer book, landing right on the word "G-d." He closed the book and put it on the shelf.

G-d heard. A month and a half later, they discovered that the wife was expecting. It wasn't just a regular pregnancy. In fact, she was expecting triplets. And the pregnancy had apparently begun on the day that the young husband had written his angry letter to G-d. After five years of waiting, the feelings the couple experienced were indescribable.

The doctors told them that they were expecting identical twins and another, separate fetus. They were concerned that the pregnancy was dangerous and urged the couple to abort one of them, referring to the procedure as a "reduction." In fact, the medical professionals were even pushing for them to abort the identical twins and leave just the singleton.

The expectant mother was apprehensive and full of anxiety. The doctors had warned her that it was difficult to give birth to and raise three babies, telling her that a triplet pregnancy was extremely high risk and could even end with no live baby. After the years of hope and longing, it was incredibly painful to hear that this pregnancy could end in failure, too. But after years of hope and longing, it was unfathomable to kill the babies. The couple couldn't even bear to hear or contemplate such a thing.

The young couple was under tremendous pressure, and they were deeply concerned about how they could possibly make such a decision. They felt that they had no one to help them, no one to advise them. But the doctors' words had wormed their way into their hearts and one day this couple found themselves on the way to Beilinson Hospital,[22] where a particular doctor would perform the "reduction."

On the way, they stopped at their bank, Discount, in Herzliya. Full of emotion and stress, the wife ended up pouring out her heart to the bank clerk, whom she knew, telling her what they were on their way to do. The clerk knew their story and was shocked. "Maybe you should consult with Rabbi Mordechai Eliyahu?" she suggested. "He's a big rabbi." She explained that one of her close relatives knew Rabbi Eliyahu, and then she jumped up and said, "Give me five minutes. I'll get hold of Rabbi Eliyahu for you."

The couple agreed, and within two minutes, the *rabbanit* was on the line. She begged the young woman not to go ahead with the abortion, and then she passed the phone to her husband. Rabbi Eliyahu spoke with the young woman, asking for her name and her mother's name. He had a few other questions. Then he said, "You have three boys in your womb. Don't do the abortion. I know it will be difficult, but you'll manage to carry the pregnancy almost to the end. It will be worth it…"

---

22. Beilinson Hospital, officially called Rabin Medical Center, is a major hospital and medical center located in Petah Tikvah.

Upon hearing the rabbi's words, the woman burst into tears, sobbing in front of all the bank's staff and customers. They left the bank and did not discuss what had happened. They proceeded to the hospital and signed all the forms. When the young woman was lying on the treatment bed, waiting for the procedure, the husband felt like he'd received some kind of jolt. *What am I doing?* he thought. *I've waited so many years for children and now we're going to kill them?*

"Come on, get up!" he said to his wife. "We're going home!"

There was a lot of shouting and arguing with the staff. The doctors accused them of being reckless, irresponsible, and of endangering the babies. But it was clear to the young couple. They weren't going to do it. And with that, they left the hospital.

On the way home, the young man said to his wife, "We've been through so much. Let's go to one of the doctors in Eilat who has a 3D ultrasound machine. I want to know what gender the fetuses are. If that rabbi, who is hundreds of kilometers away from us, knows what gender they are, then that means he really must know something."

They called the doctor on the way, and he agreed to see them. It was a five-hour drive from the hospital, but they went straight there. The doctor began the ultrasound and after a quick look announced, "I see the first one; it's a boy."

The husband and wife looked at each other, the air full of tension. The doctor, focused on the screen, then said, "The second one is a boy, too."

The couple was on tenterhooks, waiting for the doctor to find the third. "The third one is a boy as well!" he announced.

The husband almost fainted. "I'm not an emotional person," he later related, "but I saw then and there that this rabbi really knew what he was talking about. And if he could identify the genders with no equipment, then he could also know about the babies' chance of survival…"

It was abundantly clear that the couple would not be performing any "reduction" or abortion. The babies were staying.

The new mother managed to carry the pregnancy through the thirty-seventh week, just as Rabbi Eliyahu had said. When the moment of birth arrived, the wife, who had already been hospitalized in Tel Hashomer[23] for several months, entered the delivery room under intense anxiety and nervousness. But an hour later, she had given birth to three sweet little boys. They named them Liam, Liav, and Lior. After so many years of waiting, they had received an indescribable gift, and their appreciation knew no bounds.

The babies had to stay in a special care unit in the hospital for a month. But it was a time of boundless love and gratitude, and the young couple felt wrapped in love and blessings from all their family and friends. During that time, a pregnant woman came into the ward, seeking out the young couple. She explained that she was expecting triplets and the doctors were pressuring her to do a "reduction." She was so uncomfortable with the idea, and she wanted to hear these new parents' thoughts and feelings about it, having heard that they had just delivered triplets.

They shared their miraculous story and showed her the sweet baby boys. Then and there, this expectant woman decided not to do any abortion or "reduction." She was going to carry them to the end. A few months later, she called and informed the couple that she had safely given birth to her triplets. And, not only that, they were all boys. She had given them the same names: Liam, Liav,

---

23. Also known as the Haim Sheba Medical Center at Tel Hashomer, Tel Hashomer Hospital is the largest hospital in Israel, and is ranked as one of the best hospitals in the world.

and Lior, seeing their birth as a continuation of the first couple's miracle.

Rabbi Eliyahu was responsible not just for the birth of those three babies, but for at least six. Why "at least"? The young father in the story ran a newspaper that was published in Eilat and the surrounding areas. When Rabbi Eliyahu passed away, he publicized their amazing story on a full page, along with a photo of the rabbi.

After the story was printed, the newspaper was inundated with replies. So many people were encouraged by the story, inspired to increase their faith and to prevent abortions. Even today, as the story continues to circulate, perhaps there are more babies being saved because of it.

"I won my prize," the triplets' father said. "Not a cash prize — a prize of children. The truth is, I won the prize three times over. We invest everything we have in those children. And every day when I sit and learn or play with them, I just melt. They're growing up, and I thank G-d every minute for giving them to us."

On reflection, he trembles when he thinks about what could have been. If they had listened to the advice of the doctors, he said, he never would have forgiven himself or his wife for the rest of their lives. "I know it's in the merit of the rabbi that we have living children today," he said. He will always remain appreciative to Rabbi Eliyahu — and to the bank clerk who put them in touch with him. "G-d puts angels on earth, special people, people with a touch of the Divine," he said. "We saw one of them. May his memory be for a blessing."[24]

"While They Yet Speak I Will Hear"

Rabbi Moshe Hiyoni, the head of the Ner HaTorah *kollel*[25] and

24. As heard from Eitan Kobi, the editor of the *Hamon B'Eilat* newspaper, Eilat.

25. Located on Bar-Ilan Street in Jerusalem.

principal of the Talmud Torah V'Yomar Yitzhak,[26] recalled that
Rabbi Eliyahu occasionally visited the *kollel* and the Talmud Torah
to give a class and encourage the students. The staff and students
were always thrilled when he came, as they were well aware of the
rabbi's greatness.

On one of Rabbi Eliyahu's visits, a teacher in the Talmud Torah
asked him for a blessing. His wife was expecting, and the baby was
in a horizontal breech position, which was liable to considerably
complicate the birth. The rabbi asked for her name, blessed her,
and then made a motion with his hand, as if turning the baby
around.

The baby must have turned exactly as the rabbi was speaking,
because just moments later, the teacher's wife called. Her labor
had begun and she needed her husband to return home urgently.
The teacher asked permission to leave in the middle of Rabbi

---

26. Talmud Torah V'Yomar Yitzhak is named after Rabbi Yitzhak Ben-Wualid from
    Tetoun, Morocco. The school is located in Jerusalem.

Eliyahu's visit. Rabbi Hiyoni was reminded of the verse, *Before they call, I will answer; while they yet speak, I will hear (Yeshayahu 65:24).* Here Rabbi Eliyahu had just given his blessing, and it was already being fulfilled. Indeed, when the teacher and his wife went to the hospital, they discovered that the baby was positioned properly, and she delivered safely.[27]

---

27. Rabbi Moshe Hiyoni, head of Kollel Ner HaTorah in Jerusalem, related this story.

Chapter Twelve

Resurrection of the Dead

The *Tanna Deve Eliyahu* taught that the righteous ones whom the Holy One, blessed is He, will resurrect, do not return to dust, as is written, *He who remains in Zion and he who remains in Jerusalem shall be called holy, everyone who is inscribed for life in Jerusalem.*[1] *Just as the Holy One exists forever, so too they will exist forever.*[2]

---

1. *Yeshayahu* 4:3.
2. *Sanhedrin* 92a.

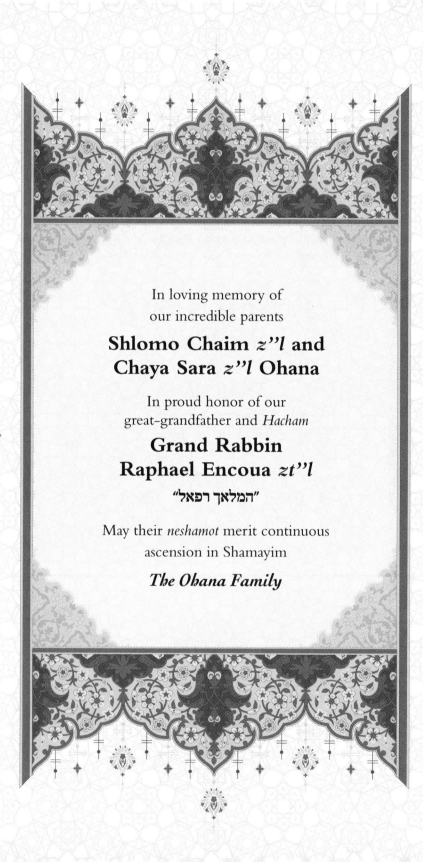

In loving memory of
our incredible parents

Shlomo Chaim *z"l* **and
Chaya Sara** *z"l* **Ohana**

In proud honor of our
great-grandfather and *Hacham*

**Grand Rabbin
Raphael Encoua** *zt"l*

"המלאך רפאל"

May their *neshamot* merit continuous
ascension in Shamayim

The Ohana Family

POWER OF PRAYER

Between Heaven and Earth

Rabbi Eliyahu and his wife were traveling to Los Angeles. In the middle of the flight, Rabbanit Tzviyah noticed that her husband seemed to be in deep, concentrated prayer, but she had no idea why. She found out soon enough, when one of the pilots exited the cockpit with a worried expression on his face. He approached the *rabbanit* and asked her if he could speak with Rabbi Eliyahu, whom he saw was focused on his prayers.

Rabbanit Tzviyah asked what the problem was, and the pilot explained that the plane was leaking fuel, something they were powerless to stop. The *rabbanit* asked if there was somewhere they could make an emergency landing, but the pilot replied that they were now crossing the ocean, somewhere over the middle of the Atlantic.

The *rabbanit* asked if they could possibly reach some island and land there, but the pilot said there wasn't enough fuel remaining to get them anywhere. The *rabbanit* didn't understand how he could be so calm at such a time and why he wasn't waking all the passengers. But she soon realized that creating chaos and mass panic wasn't going to ameliorate the situation.

"So the plane is going to crash into the sea?" she asked the El Al pilot, feeling panicked herself.

"No," he responded firmly. "Not if you ask the rabbi to do something!"

She looked around at all the other passengers and saw that everyone was either sleeping or reading. She turned to her husband, who was still intensely absorbed in his prayers.

"Mordechai, we're in danger," she said.

He didn't respond.

"Mordechai, Mordechai," she urged. But his focus was so powerful he didn't seem to hear her.

The pilot, standing beside the *rabbanit*, saw what was happening and how the rabbi was not responsive. After about ten minutes, Rabbi Eliyahu finally spoke, saying to his wife, "Tell him to keep flying straight to the destination and not to land anywhere on the way. From this moment on, the fuel gauge will not move."

Hearing his words, the pilot returned to the cockpit. The *rabbanit* meanwhile got up and went to where her two children were sitting. They were busy reading and studying, so she didn't interrupt them. No one on the plane knew of the grave danger hovering over all the passengers on that El Al flight. They dozed on, unaware of the immense drama unfolding in the cockpit — and where the Eliyahus were seated.

Rabbanit Tzviyah returned to her seat, where she saw her husband still immersed in quiet prayer. Soon the pilot returned, exclaiming, "The fuel gauges aren't moving! We're at the same exact fuel levels as before; the leak seems to have stopped and the plane doesn't seem to be using additional fuel."

Although the pilot was calm, the *rabbanit* was very tense. Here there was an entire plane, with hundreds of passengers, and they were in danger of death. Yet no one knew except for the Eliyahus and the pilots. The *rabbanit* desperately wanted to do something, but she knew that if the passengers were aware, even for the purpose of praying, they would be overcome with hysteria. She paced the plane, going again to visit her children, who were by now sleeping. The other passengers were mostly asleep, too, blissfully unaware.

Over half an hour had passed since the pilot's initial visit to the Eliyahus. The rabbi was still engrossed in deep prayer. The pilot and copilot took turns coming back to update the *rabbanit*. "The fuel gauge still isn't moving," they would whisper.

The situation continued like this for another two hours. Only as they neared the airport did the plane begin functioning normally again, with no leak but the plane's instruments recording regular fuel use. The pilots and the *rabbanit* breathed a big sigh of relief. After the flight landed, the crew surrounded Rabbi Eliyahu, asking him for blessings. They even requested that he write a special prayer for pilots on their behalf.[3]

Prayer Works

The *B'sha'ar Hamelech*[4] booklet relates the story of a woman who gave birth and sank into a deep depression. From a medical perspective it was classified as a clinical depression, and it included visions and hallucinations. Psychiatrically speaking, it was a real case of postpartum psychosis. Suffering greatly, the new mother somehow made it to Rabbi Eliyahu, albeit in a dazed, confused, and distressed state.

The moment she saw the rabbi, something changed inside. She felt calm and uplifted, as if a beautiful light was hovering in front of her. The rabbi continued to gaze at her, nodding his head. She barely said a thing, and he simply told her, "Prayer and Tehillim!"

From then on, she finished the entire *sefer Tehillim* every single Shabbat. During the week, she completed *sefer Tehillim* by saying the psalms for each day. Gradually, her depression vanished and never returned.

The Key to Recovery

When the Baba Sali was hospitalized in Jerusalem, the doctors told him that he would require surgery. Just then, Rabbi Eliyahu

---

3. Rabbanit Tzviyah Eliyahu related this story.

4. This privately printed booklet was published in 2010.

arrived to visit him. There was a police officer stationed outside the door and he wouldn't let Rabbi Eliyahu in. But the Baba Sali called out, "Let Hacham Mordechai enter!"

As soon as the Baba Sali saw Rabbi Eliyahu, he said, "Bless me that I should be healthy and won't need surgery!" Rabbi Eliyahu blessed him as per his request. Just a day or so later, the Baba Sali was released from the hospital without surgery, continuing to live in good health for many more years.

Rabbi Eliyahu once related that the Baba Sali told him he had received the key to curing the sick and that on his passing he would entrust it to Rabbi Eliyahu.[5]

WORKING MIRACLES

The Water Bottle Went, Too

A seven-year-old boy was afflicted by a strange and mysterious condition: He had suddenly lost his ability to walk. His parents had brought him to hospitals and doctors all over the country, traveling from their home in Eilat, to figure out what was wrong, and how they could cure their son of this bizarre condition.

Even the most expert doctors couldn't find any plausible explanation. They had no idea what had caused the boy to stop walking, and they had no idea how to treat him. In great distress and with no other options, the parents brought their son to Rabbi Eliyahu. He gazed at the boy and said, "He has an evil eye upon him."

---

5. From the *Al Hatzaddikim V'al Hahassidim* booklet.

The rabbi then asked to speak with the boy alone. They talked, and then the rabbi called the parents back in. He removed a large bottle of water from one of his desk drawers and told the parents, "This is water from the Baba Meir, the son of the Baba Sali."

He poured some of the water into a smaller bottle and gave it to them, asking them to make a careful blessing over it with deep concentration and then give it to their son to drink. The parents took the water back to Eilat with them and vigilantly followed the rabbi's instructions. After just a single day of this "treatment," the boy began to walk again. But the bottle of water "walked," too. It simply disappeared and no one knew where it went.[6]

Not a Prophet

One of Rabbi Eliyahu's assistants recalled that at one of the office meetings, he brought a certain case to Rabbi Eliyahu's attention, about a childless couple who had been through many treatments with no success. The assistant then described the medical procedures and the halachic details involved in one of the treatments this couple wanted to do. After the rabbi gave his answers, the assistant added that the couple had begged that the rabbi promise they would have children.

"How can I promise?" Rabbi Eliyahu asked. "I'm not a prophet! It's not possible to promise such a thing."

The assistant then said to the rabbi, "But I know of a case when the rabbi clearly promised, and thank G-d, the pledge was fulfilled..."

The rabbi lowered his eyes, hesitating briefly. Then he said apologetically, "I can't promise. But once, a woman came to me after she had really made every possible effort to pray and plead

---

6. As heard from Rabbi Menahem Burstein, head of the Puah Institute.

to G-d to give her children. She was crying and begged me to promise her that the treatment would succeed.

"It was so hard for me to see her, pleading and broken like that. So I promised..." His voice trailed off. "But as soon as she left the room, I turned to the Master of the Universe and cried out, 'Save me! I promised a woman that she would have children. Now help me so that the promise will be fulfilled!' G-d heard me and performed a miracle for her."

A Supernatural Story

Shmuel Ben Atar, one of the founders of Radio Kol Ha'emet,[7] related that if he hadn't personally witnessed this story, he never would have believed it actually occurred. His father-in-law had suffered a stroke and was completely paralyzed, unable to move any part of his body. All he could do was speak. Ben Atar's mother-in-law had to feed her husband and do everything for him, as he couldn't even pick up a fork or spoon on his own.

She cared for him with tremendous devotion, never leaving his side. But when the experts who were treating him told her that he would never recover from his paralysis, she made the painful decision to place him in an institution, Herzog Hospital,[8] where he could receive the proper care.

Ben Atar had always celebrated the *hillula* (anniversary of death) of the Ben Ish Hai each year, and so did Rabbi Eliyahu. That year, when Rabbi Eliyahu was at the celebration, he inquired after Ben Atar's father-in-law. "He's in Herzog," Ben Atar said, explaining the gravity of the situation.

---

7. This private radio station broadcast to the Orthodox community in Israel from 1995 to 2008.

8. Herzog Hospital is a geriatric facility in Jerusalem that specializes in nursing care for the elderly.

"But that's not possible," Rabbi Eliyahu exclaimed. "He should be healthy!" He arranged with Ben Atar that they would go together to visit him in Herzog Hospital at nine o'clock the next morning.

When Ben Atar arrived at the hospital the following morning, Rabbi Eliyahu was already waiting for him. They entered the facility together and were greeted by a large crowd of people who asked for blessings. As they entered Ben Atar's father-in-law's room, it was very, very clear that the paralyzed man was extremely excited to see the rabbi. He tried to move, as if to stand out of respect, but of course, he was unable to do so.

"Do you want to be healthy?" Rabbi Eliyahu asked him.

"Of course," the man responded.

"So then get up!" Rabbi Eliyahu told him.

The paralyzed man looked at him in disbelief.

But Rabbi Eliyahu said again, "Get up!"

Ben Atar's father-in-law had tremendous respect for rabbis, having immigrated to Israel from Baghdad, where he had been raised to revere the Ben Ish Hai. He saw Rabbi Eliyahu as carrying on the Ben Ish Hai's traditions and path, so he attempted to obey and get up, but failed.

The doctors and nurses in the room didn't understand what was going on. They thought Rabbi Eliyahu was just trying to encourage him. They watched in wonder at this strange spectacle.

"Get up," Rabbi Eliyahu said again. But when he saw that the man wasn't managing to stand, he extended his hands, saying, "I said get up, so get up!"

The bedridden man started to move from his bed. Suddenly he sat up completely and, still grasping the rabbi's hands, stood on his own two feet. The doctors and nurses were dumbfounded.

"Walk!" Rabbi Eliyahu commanded.

And, sure enough, the man began to walk unassisted.

"Go home," Rabbi Eliyahu told him. "Don't go back to that bed." And with that, he wished Ben Atar's father-in-law goodbye. He left the room, giving blessings to all the staff.

Ben Atar accompanied Rabbi Eliyahu to his car and then returned to his father-in-law's room. He was packing up his stuff and buttoning his coat in preparation to leave the hospital. The staff was all still standing there, flabbergasted by the miracle they had just witnessed.

The doctor in charge of the man's treatment was similarly shocked. "According to everything I know," he said, "it's simply beyond the laws of nature that something like this should occur."

Indeed, that formerly paralyzed man went on to live another twelve years, "above the laws of nature," walking on his own two feet and moving around like everyone else.

Caught on Camera

Rabbi Yisrael Gliss, a well-known Orthodox journalist in Israel, was once working on a documentary film about celebrations in Meron on Lag B'Omer. He hired five cinematographers to work with him, instructing them to circulate around Meron and film different things going on there in various locations. Rabbi Gliss accompanied them, of course.

Close to midnight, Rabbi Eliyahu arrived. Hundreds of people gathered around him, in addition to the busloads of people who had followed him from Jerusalem. Some of the camera operators followed Rabbi Eliyahu on his visit, recording him as he studied Torah next to the tomb and as he danced outside in the courtyard. His face was radiant the entire time, and he seemed to be overflowing with happiness. Of course, people were constantly approaching him for blessings throughout.

Rabbi Gliss was among that crowd, and though he was standing right near Rabbi Eliyahu when the following incident took place, he only noticed it afterward, when he reviewed the camera footage.

A man approached Rabbi Eliyahu with a sad expression on his face. He was pushing a wheelchair with a boy around five or six years old sitting inside.

"Please, Rabbi Eliyahu, bless my son. He can't walk."

Rabbi Eliyahu's face was positively glowing at that moment. "Put him on the ground," Rabbi Eliyahu said, "and he will walk."

The boy's father looked so confused and sad. "But he can't stand up on his own," he said.

"Put him on the ground!" Rabbi Eliyahu instructed, still smiling.

The father carefully picked his son up and put him on the ground. Just a moment later, the boy stood up on his own feet.

"Start walking," Rabbi Eliyahu said.

The boy began to walk. His steps were slow and careful at first. And then he gained more and more confidence. In later footage, the boy could even be seen dancing with other people in the circles.

It would be unbelievable. Except it was filmed and documented, preserved for generations to bear witness to the miracle.[9]

Open My Lips

A couple was extremely distraught that their son hadn't uttered a single word and he was already three and a half years old. Although he clearly understood everything that was being said to him, he simply did not speak, not even one word. The couple took their son to one specialist after the next, trying all different kinds of medical treatments and therapies, but everything was to no avail. They worried that their child might never speak at all.

---

9. As heard from Rabbi Yisrael Gliss.

One day, they decided to take their son to Rabbi Eliyahu for a blessing. The rabbi looked at the boy, smiled, and said, "G-d, open my lips, and my mouth will declare Your praises!"[10] Then he said to the parents, "You'll see the blessing quickly."

The boy's parents didn't know what to expect. But before they'd even left the Eliyahus' apartment building, their son began to speak. He was talking and talking so much that he had to stop to take a breath. "It was so amazing," the parents later recalled, "that until this day the story still leaves us breathless."

There's a verse in *Yeshayahu*, *It will be that before they call I will answer; while they yet speak I will hear.*[11] Indeed, there are prayers that are heard before the need ever arises, and there are prayers that are heard as soon as they have been expressed. Rabbi Eliyahu was among those whose prayers and blessings were answered immediately.

"Every time our son opens his mouth to speak, we are reminded of this story," the boy's parents remarked. "We even know of others, whose children had the same problem, and the rabbi uttered the same verse and they were cured. Having gone through so much sorrow and distress, and having poured out so many heartfelt prayers, we give thanks to G-d every day for the miracle Rabbi Eliyahu brought to fruition," they said.

Returning Lost Property

Rabbi Shalom Cohen used to pray every day with Rabbi Eliyahu in his sunrise *minyan*. One night, there was a break-in at the Cohens' home, and all of Mrs. Cohen's jewelry was stolen, as well as the family's expensive video camera. The Cohens were understandably terribly upset about the robbery and all that it entailed, especially

---

10. *Tehillim* 51:15.

11. 65:24.

the loss of the jewelry and the awful mess in the house, which had been turned upside down. Nevertheless, though Rabbi Cohen was very close with Rabbi Eliyahu, he decided not to mention it to the rabbi so as not to cause him distress, too.

About two weeks after the break-in, Rabbi Eliyahu asked Rabbi Cohen, "What happened? Why are you so down? Over the last two weeks I noticed that you're not the same Shalom we know!"

Rabbi Cohen related the story of the break-in, describing how upset his wife was about her jewelry. He didn't mention the video camera that had also been stolen.

"Don't worry," Rabbi Eliyahu assured him. "Blessed is He who returns lost property to its owner."

When Rabbi Cohen returned home, he opened his closet to put away his *tallit* and *tefillin*, and lo and behold, there in the closet was all his wife's jewelry. Even more amazing was that though all the jewelry had been returned, the video camera had not...

The Cohens were so excited and happy; they shared their story with their family and relatives. When Rabbi Cohen's brother heard the story, he mentioned that he had also been robbed about six months ago, and his wife's jewelry had been taken. He asked Rabbi Cohen to get Rabbi Eliyahu's blessing for him.

Rabbi Cohen didn't want to trouble the rabbi but his brother was insistent. So he finally related the story to Rabbi Eliyahu, who simply repeated, "Blessed is He who returns lost property to its owner." No more than a few days passed when all his sister-in-law's jewelry was found in their storeroom.[12]

Blessing in Intensive Care

Rabbi Uzi Barnea, the *gabbai* of Rabbi Eliyahu's synagogue, related that his brother-in-law was hospitalized and lay unconscious

---

12. As heard from Rabbi Shalom Cohen.

for three days. On the third day, the family decided to go to Rabbi Mordechai Eliyahu for a blessing for his recovery. Rabbi Eliyahu was also hospitalized at that time.

"I arrived at the hospital, where the rabbi was lying attached to a respirator and all kinds of tubes, equipment, and IV drip lines," Rabbi Barnea recalled. "When I entered his room he motioned to me to come closer. I drew near and told him about my brother-in-law's situation. I repeated his name a few times and the rabbi clasped my hand tightly. After a while, he opened his eyes and signaled to me with his hand. I repeated the name again, and he signaled to me with his hand that everything would be fine."

A few minutes later, Rabbi Barnea left the room and called his sister to ask how things were. His sister reported that just a few minutes earlier, her husband had regained consciousness.

With a trembling voice and eyes full of tears, he told her that just moments earlier, he had left Rabbi Mordechai Eliyahu and that the rabbi had blessed her husband. She burst into tears, telling her brother that the first words her husband had said when he came to consciousness were, "Rabbi Eliyahu blessed me, Rabbi Eliyahu blessed me!"[13]

A Song of Thanks

A number of years ago, Eldad and Avigayil Cohen of Kochav Hashahar celebrated the birth of their daughter, Shir. But the baby was extremely ill and vomited nonstop. By the time she was one and a half, she weighed only 11.5 pounds (5.2 kg) and had barely achieved any of the milestones a baby normally reaches during that time. The doctors couldn't find a solution and the family was at a total loss about what to do.

---

13. As heard from Uzi Barnea.

In desperation, the couple went to Rabbi Eliyahu, pouring out their hearts over the sad situation and precarious health of their baby. "She's not called Shir at all," Rabbi Eliyahu announced. "Her name is Shira."

The next morning, the baby's father was called up to the Torah, and he got the opportunity to make a special blessing for his daughter, "Shira *bat* Avigayil." Within a few days, the vomiting had stopped entirely, and the baby — Shira — began to develop just like any other child her age.[14]

THE WORLD ABOVE

The Story of Sharon Nahshoni

Rabbi Sharon Nahshoni, today a rabbi in southern Israel, was a soldier in the Shimshon Unit,[15] an undercover brigade in the southern command. One day, Sharon got into his Subaru to head to reserve duty at the Julis base, near the Malachi Junction, between Highways 40 and 3. After just four minutes on the highway, his front left tire burst. The car swerved onto the other side of the road, colliding with a commercial vehicle coming from the other direction. The powerful head-on collision left Sharon unconscious.

He had been driving at around 40 mph (65 kmh), and at the time of the collision, the engine was forced into the back seat. The

---

14. As heard from Eldad and Avigayil Cohen.

15. This unit's mission was focused around undercover operations against Palestinian terrorists in the Gaza Strip. Shimshon was disbanded in 1995, following the Oslo Accords.

front seats were completely crushed, and Sharon had broken his pelvis. The engine had twisted his legs, injuring them both; his left hand was totally crushed; his lungs were punctured; blood was trickling out of his mouth; and the (empty) baby seat, which had been in the back, had flown to the front, giving him a strong blow to the head. Sharon didn't know it, because he was unconscious, but he was completely trapped inside the car.

Emergency rescue services had to break open the car and pull Sharon out from beneath the engine that was pinning him down. By the time the rescuers got to him, he wasn't breathing and had no pulse. The medical team determined he was dead, covering him with a sheet. The police investigator on the scene meanwhile began working on the report, listing Sharon among the dead.

In the massive traffic jam that ensued, a number 212 bus traveling from Ashdod to Yavne was stuck in the standstill. A young man got off the bus and presented himself as a medical assistant or maybe an army doctor — "medical officer" was written on his epaulettes.

"Can I help?" he asked.

The rescue team directed him, "Go help the injured lying over there."

"Wait a minute!" said the man from the bus. "What about this guy who's lying here, covered up?"

"Leave him," the doctors answered. "He's dead."

The army doctor, or whatever he was, checked Sharon thoroughly, took a ballpoint pen out of his pocket, and used it to perform a field operation right there at the scene of the accident. Using the writing implement as a makeshift trocar, a surgical instrument used for withdrawing fluid from a body cavity, he managed to puncture and open Sharon's lungs, releasing the built-up fluids and opening them for breathing.

To their great astonishment, the emergency rescue team watched

Sharon begin to breathe and groan, even though seventeen minutes had elapsed since they had determined his death. They raced over to him, continuing the treatment and loading him into an ambulance.

Afterward, the rescuers searched for the army doctor who had performed the field surgery but they couldn't find him. The bus had continued on its journey in the meantime, but the man had vanished.

Sharon's brother-in-law Shahar Eshbal later related that when Sharon was taken into the operating theater, the family received more distressing news. Their Aunt Miriam had passed away; she had been sick with cancer for a long time. She had been a truly righteous woman, a person who had spent all her life helping others. The news came as a big blow to the family, who were already deeply anguished over the accident.

When Sharon regained consciousness after the surgery, the first thing he asked was, "What's with Aunt Miriam? Where is she? Is she alive or dead?"

On the advice of the doctors, the family lied to him, saying she was alive and well. But Sharon ignored them, repeating his questions over and over again. The matter was clearly weighing heavily on him. The family found it difficult to understand why he was so distraught about Aunt Miriam. Here he had been in an extremely serious accident and had just undergone major surgery. The family didn't know what had happened to him, or what he had undergone out there, but from Sharon's post-surgery mumblings, they realized he had been through a very traumatic and emotional experience.

One day, Sharon asked his brother-in-law if he knew Rabbi Mordechai Eliyahu. Though Shahar did not know him, Sharon went on to say that he had to find Rabbi Eliyahu and meet with him. All this time he persisted in asking what had happened to Aunt Miriam and whether she was alive. No one understood what was burning inside him. Finally, he shared what had happened to him while he was "dead."

He had been in the world above, he related, but he was reticent to share what had occurred there, for fear that his family would think he had truly lost his mind.

He said that during the seventeen minutes he had been classified as clinically dead, he had seen himself in another world, which he described at great length. He depicted the judgment that had been pronounced upon him there, complete with prosecution and defense.

"The prosecutor said to me, 'You or your Aunt Miriam. One of you stays here,'" Sharon related. "At first I didn't understand why they were talking about Aunt Miriam. What did this have to do with her? And suddenly, to my astonishment, I noticed her, standing right beside me on the stand," he recalled.

"'One of you has to stay here in the world of truth,' they told us. Right away I jumped up and said, 'I'm ready to stay.' But then a very warm and pleasant voice began to speak, and said that both of us, Aunt Miriam and I, had responsible souls. We were concerned about others and had passed on to the family, as our grandfather had, the tradition of doing acts of kindness, especially for brides and grooms, orphans and widows," Sharon said.

He continued, "Then the voice said that I must stay in the world below, and a new soul would descend to the world inside a baby that would be born to the family, and that new soul would perpetuate my grandfather's good deeds, as the family line had to continue. And then the judgment began, where they took me through everything I had done all my life."

His experience also included a rabbi he didn't recognize — and who he would only identify with certainty after meeting him.

The rabbi intervened on his behalf, standing up for him and guaranteeing that he would return to the world of the living. This rabbi made Sharon promise that he would fix his actions and complete his atonement in the world, devoting his time to good deeds and acts of kindness.

After Sharon had recovered enough to get out a little, he went to Rabbi Mordechai Eliyahu's office, as he was fairly certain that this was the rabbi he had seen in the Next World. Hobbling into the rabbi's room on crutches, he immediately recognized the face that had saved him in the world above. "It's you! It's you!" he shouted.

The office staff rushed over immediately, concerned about Rabbi Eliyahu's safety. But Rabbi Eliyahu motioned them away. "Are you going to do what you promised?" Rabbi Mordechai asked.

"Yes," Sharon replied.

Rabbi Eliyahu then sent Sharon to see his son in Safed. There, Rabbi Shmuel told him that he must tell his story to strengthen people's faith. But he said that Sharon must also strengthen himself in Torah, so that he could teach people this most important thing. Rabbi Shmuel urged him to share this story, using it as an introduction to open the heart.

And that's what he did. Sharon went to study at a yeshivah in the south, lecturing on the Torah he was learning — and sharing his story at the same time. He was suited to the yeshivah environment and made progress over the years, eventually earning rabbinic ordination. Today he serves as a rabbi in the south of Israel, trying to continue his family's legacy, as he learned in the world above.[16]

Thousands of Lights

Asher Masoud Biton works for the *hevra kaddisha*, the burial society, in Kiryat Shemoneh, a town that has repeatedly suffered

---

16. As heard from Rabbi Sharon Nahshoni.

from the Katyusha rockets that Hezbollah fires over the border from neighboring Lebanon. Kiryat Shemoneh is a town that has frequently seen Israeli soldiers called there to protect it and all of northern Israel. Some of those soldiers paid with their lives, and some returned on stretchers, seriously wounded or missing an arm or a leg.

Asher, who worked in the cemetery, was familiar with such sights and knew the value of the soldiers' devotion. Every time he found a free moment from his holy work, he would recite Tehillim for the IDF soldiers, who were protecting the country — body and soul. Asher's Tehillim for the soldiers became a kind of personal custom and mission.

One day, Asher suffered a heart attack, quickly followed by a stroke. He lost consciousness — and he lost his life; the doctor in the emergency room had already determined his death. But Heaven had other plans...

Asher related with great emotion that when his soul left his body, he was "still there." He saw his brother Mahluf hugging his body and weeping, and it was clear that that body was lifeless. Asher also saw the mayor, who was there, too, as he was a close acquaintance. Everyone was crying, but Asher actually felt happy and content. He was floating above everyone, invisible.

Mahluf didn't give up. He begged the doctor to try again to resuscitate Asher. The doctor agreed, trying repeatedly to shock Asher back to life. But nothing helped. After administering six electric shocks, the doctor saw that it was useless. On realizing that no help would come from the medical team, Mahluf turned to a great kabbalist and righteous rabbi whom he knew, beseeching him to pray for Asher. The rabbi thought for a moment and said, "Tell the doctor to give him one more electric shock, and he will come around."

Mahluf returned to the doctor, asking him to do as the rabbi had advised, but the doctor refused, saying there was no chance. It had been over an hour since Asher had been pronounced dead, and the doctor truly believed it was useless to even try. But Mahluf wouldn't give up, and he continued begging and pleading. Finally, to calm him down, the doctor agreed to give Asher just one more electric shock. And Asher immediately came back to life.

What happened to Asher in the meantime, during that hour and a quarter that he had been lying lifeless, was, in his words, "incredible." He recalled, "All that time I had been in the Heavenly Court above, where I saw an earth-shattering scene. All the words in my vocabulary can't possibly describe how the Heavenly Court looked. At its head was the great kabbalist Rabbi Mordechai Eliyahu.

"At that time he was actually undergoing treatment in the intensive care unit of Shaare Zedek Hospital in Jerusalem, but in the Heavenly Court above, he appeared in his full glory and splendor. There was a great light upon him, a light that is simply impossible to describe in terms from this world."

Asher recognized Rabbi Eliyahu; he had seen the rabbi speak at a few functions, but he had never interacted with Rabbi Eliyahu personally. Although he was aware of what a great scholar Rabbi Eliyahu was, he had no idea of the extent of his holiness.

In the Heavenly Court, Asher said, the rabbi's face was radiant. "The light was so big and intense," he said. "Even if I took four hundred candles and joined them all together, I wouldn't reach a quarter of the light that was radiating from his face. It was simply a huge aura of light. I understood then that the rabbi was a very holy person, one of the righteous on whom the world rests."

Together with him in the court sat the holy Rabbi David Abuhatzera,[17] who Asher said he has never been able to make eye

---

17. Rabbi David Hai Abuhatzera, known as Rabbi David, is the former chief rabbi of

contact with since the Heavenly Court incident. The third was Hacham Bentzion Abba-Shaul. Asher didn't know him beforehand, but he was in Hacham Bentzion's yeshivah in Jerusalem after his rehabilitation. When he saw the Hacham's picture on the wall he nearly fainted. And there was one other person there, but Asher has not revealed his identity.

In the Heavenly Court, they judged Asher for desecrating Shabbat. Now, he was a person who observed Shabbat, but in the Heavenly Court he learned that becoming angry on Shabbat or talking during the prayers in synagogue were viewed in Heaven as desecrations of Shabbat; after all, the holy day was given to the Jewish people for pleasure — and not to get angry or become preoccupied with idle chitchat.

"I was so embarrassed when I realized how serious my actions were," Asher said. "Meanwhile, defending me were people dressed in white. I soon realized that they were the soldiers for whom I had prayed. I had prayed for them in this world, and now they had come to defend me in the world above. And so I was taken up to the High Court, at the head of which Rabbenu Yosef Haim, the Ben Ish Hai, was sitting.

"There, too, I was defended by lines of white-clad soldiers," Asher said. "I even recognized some of them. They were soldiers from Kiryat Shemoneh who had given their lives protecting the Jewish people. I had taken care of them during their burials," he recalled.

He described how the soldiers placed before the court jars of tears he had shed when praying for them and for all the deceased whom he had cared for, or whom he had been with at the moment when their souls left their bodies. "There were entire jugs of tears…

Nahariya, and is a grandson of the Baba Sali. People flock to him from all over the world for blessings and guidance.

And from there, they took me up to an even higher court. There sat Rabbi Shimon bar Yohai, and others. It is totally impossible to describe the size of the light that was radiating from the faces of all these righteous men, seventy lofty souls in all."

Before his eyes, Asher saw the tears he had shed and the prayers he had pronounced for the soldiers, and he watched as they weighed the scales in his favor. He had won the judgment. "From there I was taken to Gan Eden (Paradise). But first I was cleansed and refined by way of troubles; this was something that happened each time I went from one court to the next."

He related that afterward, two people with particularly radiant faces approached him and said, "We don't want you here in the higher world. We want to see you joyous in Meron, dancing like you do every year. Go back down to the world below."

And at that very moment, the doctor gave him the seventh electric shock, as his brother had requested, and he regained life. Although Asher said he had heard descriptions from other people who were in the Heavenly Court, nothing prepared him for what he saw there, especially the tremendous light and holiness. It took him many years to publicly share what had happened to him up there. But after witnessing the Heavenly Court himself, he came to truly understand the nature of the greatness and holiness of the people he had seen.

"Every time I see Rabbi Eliyahu's picture, I cry. He was so, so holy, but his true greatness wasn't known in this

(Credit: Rabbi David Balachsan)

world. He helped save my life. It's such a shame that we didn't really know him during his lifetime..."

A Modest Promise

During a certain period, there was a man who would stand outside of Rabbi Mordechai Eliyahu's synagogue, telling the worshippers that they didn't know how truly great Rabbi Eliyahu was. He himself didn't look like he was accustomed to praying much, but nevertheless, he would repeat a story about his wife and the rabbi's greatness.

She had been in a state of clinical death. When she came back to life, she related how she had seen Rabbi Eliyahu intervening in her case in the Heavenly courtroom. She described how they had judged her harshly because she didn't dress modestly, but Rabbi Eliyahu promised the others that if she came back down to this world she would take it upon herself to dress more modestly and complete her atonement. And she did indeed come back to life after the clinical death she experienced.

One time, one of the regulars at the synagogue suggested that the man bring his wife to see Rabbi Eliyahu. Seeing his hesitation, he pressured the man a little. And lo and behold, the next morning the man arrived with his wife. When Rabbi Eliyahu exited the synagogue, the man approached with his wife, who wasn't dressed exactly modestly.

The rabbi walked to his car. When he was already seated in the car and speaking to her through the window, he asked in a low whisper, "Why aren't you doing what you took upon yourself?" And he immediately signaled to his driver to set off.[18]

---

18. As heard from Uzi Barnea, *gabbai* of the Hechal Yaakov synagogue.

No Regular Table

Uri Barhum,[19] a carpenter by profession, was a student of Rabbi Eliyahu's when he taught in the Magen David school.[20] He was very connected to Rabbi Eliyahu and attended his classes regularly for over twenty years.

When Rabbanit Tzviyah needed to order new cabinets for their kitchen, she felt it was only natural to ask Uri to do the work, and he completed the job to her total satisfaction. When he finished the cabinetry, she asked Uri to build them a new kitchen table out of the same material. Although he said he wasn't an expert in table design, he agreed to take the measurements for the table.

After just a few days had passed, Uri brought a table to the Eliyahus. It was made exactly according to the *rabbanit's* specifications, and he told her that he had found a piece of wood in his storeroom that was exactly the right size and color he needed. He related that he had had that piece of wood for many years, and had brought it along with him, moving it from storeroom to storeroom over the years.

During all that time, he didn't know what to do with it, and he had thought about throwing it away many times. But, for some reason, he felt he just couldn't get rid of it. Then, when he was looking for a piece of wood for the Eliyahus' table, he realized that it fit exactly, and he finally understood why he hadn't thrown it out all those years.

Two days later, the carpenter called the *rabbanit* in total shock, relating that a man had come to him in a dream during the night. He said that he had been reincarnated in that very piece of wood

---

19. Barhum still runs a carpentry business based in Jerusalem.

20. When he was a young man, Rabbi Eliyahu taught at this school, based on David Yellin Street in Jerusalem, for about two hours every day.

that had been sitting in his storeroom for around thirty years. He thanked the carpenter for not throwing the piece of wood away during all those years, and he said he was glad the carpenter had made a table from it that was now furnishing the rabbi's house. Two days later, the same man appeared to him in a dream yet again, and told him that Rabbi Eliyahu had recited the blessing after meals at the table, and in the merit of that, the man's soul had found its complete atonement.

Uri wanted the *rabbanit* to ask Rabbi Eliyahu if the dreams were true. When she heard the story, the *rabbanit* was horrified and scared. She thought to herself, *If I have a kitchen table with a reincarnated soul in it, I'm throwing that table out of the house right now!*

She went to her husband and told him what Uri had related. Rabbi Eliyahu laughed. "It's over! After atonement, the soul went up to its rightful place. Now the table is just a regular table like any other. You don't need to be afraid."[21]

Sketches from Beyond

Once, a woman who did not appear to be mitzvah-observant arrived at the rabbi's house. She related that she had been in a state of clinical death and had seen the world above. It was important to her to describe it, she said. She had written a book, including some colored sketches she had drawn, and she wanted Rabbi Elazar Ben Shlomo,[22] who was visiting the rabbi, to show the book to Rabbi Eliyahu to get his approval. When Rabbi Ben Shlomo looked at the sketches, she explained, "This is what I saw in the world above."

Rabbi Elazar took the book to the rabbi on her behalf. Rabbi Eliyahu looked through it and read it. When he saw a sketch

---

21. This story was heard from Rabbanit Tzviyah Eliyahu.

22. Rabbi Elazar Ben Shlomo is the head of the Orot Yitzhak community in Modiin.

of angels, it was clear that he wasn't happy about it, but he said nothing. But when he arrived at a sketch the woman had drawn of the "light of the Living G-d," which she had seen in the world above, Rabbi Eliyahu snapped the book shut and said, "Tell her that such drawings should not be done!"

Rabbi Ben Shlomo went back to the woman, who was waiting at the entrance to the house, and related what the rabbi had said. He went on to repeat the rabbi's advice not to publish such drawings but to bury them, as is done with holy books. In answer to her question why, he explained that the main problem was with drawings of G-d.

It was clear that the rabbi's instructions weren't to her liking. She had gone through such a meaningful experience and had put so much effort into drawing what she had seen there so that her depictions would leave an impression on the readers. Rabbi Elazar opened the book to show her which drawings weren't acceptable or appropriate, and they immediately saw that the pages of those sketches had somehow become separated from the rest of the book.

Every page that had a sketch on it had become loose. When Rabbi Elazar had finished turning the pages of the book she was holding, every single inappropriate sketch was in one hand, while the rest of the book remained in the other hand.

As soon as she saw and understood what had happened to the book in her hands, she went pale. A perfectly bound book had started losing pages in only a matter of minutes. And only the pages of sketches that the rabbi had forbidden were now loose.[23]

Returned from the Next World

Every Friday Harel Hatzroni would go to visit Rabbi Eliyahu

---

23. As heard from Rabbi Elazar Ben Shlomo.

after the morning prayers — that was the time when he would read the letters of the many people who turned to him for advice. Harel would ask his questions aloud.

One Friday, while he was waiting in line to speak with the rabbi, Harel overheard a story someone else was telling Rabbi Eliyahu. "I've brought a family member here who experienced clinical death this week and saw the rabbi in the Heavenly Court above," said the man.

Rabbi Eliyahu didn't appear to get excited about what he had just heard.

"She wants to ask the rabbi a few things," the man continued.

Rabbi Eliyahu went out of the synagogue to speak with her. Waiting there was a woman in her late thirties, who didn't appear to be religiously observant. The family member who accompanied her introduced her to Rabbi Eliyahu, saying, "She was in the hospital just a few days ago."

Apparently, she had felt unwell, and then her condition suddenly and rapidly deteriorated. Within moments, she was dead. After the doctors had determined her death, and the family had signed all the forms, they noticed that she was waking up. She related that she had experienced clinical death and had been to the Heavenly Court above...

On hearing these things being related, the woman became very emotional and began to tell the story herself. "I began to cry. I told the Heavenly Court, 'Not long ago I gave birth to a daughter, and I also have a son. I want to bring up my children. I don't want my children to be orphans. I ask you to give me another chance.' But the Heavens didn't agree."

She looked at Rabbi Eliyahu and said, "And suddenly you came, and turned to me, and said, 'If you observe the laws of modesty — head covering and everything that a woman needs to do — you can come back down to this world. Do you take it upon yourself to do this?' I told you that yes, I would take it upon myself so that I could return below. And then in Heaven it was announced that if Rabbi Eliyahu said that I could return, so it would be."

The rabbi didn't deny anything. "And now I've come, because I want the rabbi to tell me what to do," she said, finished with her story.

"I already told you there," the rabbi answered. He finished abruptly, "Do what I told you to."

The woman nodded, like someone who was once more taking it all upon herself.

"It's possible that she came just to confirm everything, to make sure she hadn't just imagined it all," Harel said. "It wasn't imagination. With my own eyes and ears, I saw and heard the rabbi's reaction. I was left open-mouthed."[24]

Connecting Worlds

There was a man whose brother was hospitalized in a closed psychiatric ward for around twenty-five years. After the brothers' father passed away, he appeared in a dream to one of the cousins in the family. In the dream, he requested that this cousin move his son, the patient, to a more open psychiatric hospital, instead of a closed one. Later, he reappeared to that same cousin, but this time it was during the day when she was awake. He instructed her to do the same thing.

Apparently, he knew from above whom to turn to, as this cousin was a senior social worker and had the authority to move psychiatric patients from place to place. What was also amazing was that she was an extremely sensible, logical kind of person, making these stories all the more plausible. Nevertheless, the family decided to

---

24. Harel Hatzroni, of OU Israel, related this story.

ask Rabbi Eliyahu about the visions and whether they should heed the deceased father's requests.

Rabbi Eliyahu said that this man had done many good deeds in his lifetime, and so in Heaven they had allowed him the privilege of taking action for his son. Based on this, Rabbi Eliyahu instructed the family to pay regard to the dream and the visitation. Although the family was quite surprised, as Rabbi Eliyahu was a man of law who they thought wouldn't give consideration to such dreams, they did as he advised.

They had the brother moved to a semi-open ward, where he received wonderful attention and care from the warm staff. His condition improved dramatically. He was no longer a danger to other people; he started working, and even showed himself to be a positive, good person.

Rabbi Eliyahu requested that the family publicize the story so that people would understand the power of the Next World.

Decreed in Heaven...

Yael Ben Eliyahu, Hacham Mordechai's granddaughter, recalled that when she was about fourteen years old, in eighth grade, she had a close friend named Michal. Michal's smile could light up a room and her joy was contagious. One day at school, she began to feel unwell, and she fell, spraining her foot. Several days later, she fainted, and her parents took her to the hospital.

After many rounds of testing, the doctors discovered that a vein had burst in Michal's brain, causing a brain hemorrhage. The hemorrhage was caused by a very rare, difficult-to-identify disease that is usually discovered only when the person collapses. Her condition was very serious — and growing worse.

Yael and her father went to see Hacham Mordechai. She was in tears and in a very difficult emotional state. "Saba, tell me she will live," Yael cried to her grandfather. "We're all praying for her around the clock. How can it be that G-d doesn't hear our prayers? I know that you can pray for her. Please, do something. We want her to live!"

Rabbi Eliyahu didn't give a blessing that Michal should live. Rather, he said that G-d should do what He saw fit in His "eyes" and that He should do what was good for Michal. As he said this, he looked at his granddaughter with eyes full of love and tenderness. He explained that G-d always hears our prayers, and that prayers never go to waste or go unfulfilled. "They always help someone," he explained. "But sometimes what we ask for a particular person isn't always good for them, so it doesn't always happen."

Yael began to cry harder. "Tell me she will live, Saba," she begged.

Though he clearly demonstrated his deep love and concern, and Yael felt her grandfather's strong love and support, the rabbi didn't say a word. He would not agree to promise that she would live. "At that moment I felt — and deep inside me I already knew — that Saba, with his Divine inspiration, knew she would not live, that the judgment was already decreed," Yael recalled. The very next day Michal returned her holy soul to its Maker.

Speaking through Dreams

Gila was a religious woman who had returned to Judaism some eighteen years previously. At one point, she decided to go consult with Rabbi Eliyahu, as she had numerous worries about all the changes she'd made in her life. Rabbi Eliyahu told her to read certain chapters of Tehillim and assured her that everything was fine. The main thing, he said, was not to think badly of herself.

Nevertheless, she was still worried, and the rabbi reassured her that she was fine and that everything was fine. She then asked when she would merit to get married, and he said, "Don't worry — it's near!" Sure enough, she did indeed get married shortly thereafter.

About six years later, she was a mother of three and was praying for a son. And then, on the eve of Shabbat, just two days before Rabbi Eliyahu left this world, he appeared to her in a dream. He was overflowing with great joy, sitting at a long table with good people, and he was at the end of the row on the left. Suddenly he stood up and said to Gila, "With the help of G-d, you will have a son, and all will be well, don't worry. But now I have to leave here, and I won't be able to help you any longer. You'll have to manage on your own and think only good about yourself."[25]

BRINGING DOWN THE BLESSINGS

A Stadium Full of Rabbi Eliyahu's "Children"

The power of Rabbi Eliyahu's prayers was well known, and thousands of people were delivered from their suffering and pain in the merit of those prayers. Rabbi Yosef Elnakwa, one of Rabbi Eliyahu's students, served in the rabbinate in the Gush Katif settlement of Neve Dekalim.[26] At that time, there were a number of women in the area who hadn't yet been blessed with children.

Many years ago, after Sukkot ended, Rabbi Elnakwa came to the Eliyahus to write down the rabbi's Torah thoughts. While he was there, he asked Hacham Mordechai for the *etrog* over which he had uttered a blessing.

---

25. As heard from Gila.

26. The largest Jewish settlement in the Gaza Strip, Neve Dekalim was founded in 1993, following the Israeli withdrawal from the Sinai Peninsula. Home to around 2,600 people, the settlement was evacuated as part of Israel's unilateral disengagement plan in August 2005.

"What do you want to do with it?" he asked.

Rabbi Elnakwa replied that he would make *etrog* jam with it as a *segulah*, a spiritual remedy, for barren women to conceive. The rabbi smiled and said, "Go for it!"

Rabbi Elnakwa took the *etrog* that the rabbi had so lovingly used and made blessings over during Sukkot. He made it into a jam and distributed it to many of the childless women in his community. All who merited

receiving a small sample of the rabbi's *etrog* jam (of course accompanied with heartfelt prayers) conceived that year. Thirty-nine previously barren women conceived in Neve Dekalim, thanks to the blessing of the rabbi.

Rabbi Mordechai Eliyahu with the Four Species

That story spread like wildfire. For many years, Rabbi Elnakwa continued taking the rabbi's *etrog* and making it into jam, which he distributed to childless couples. The salvation continued year after year. When the *rabbanit* saw how many requests there were for the jam, she began to make great quantities of it herself.

A couple from Kiryat Malachi heard that the rabbi blessed women to conceive, so they traveled to Jerusalem. Just as they arrived at the Eliyahus' home, they heard that the rabbi was in the middle of giving a class. The husband thought they should go back home, but his wife insisted on staying and waiting for him. "I've come all the way here, to Jerusalem," she said, "and I'm not leaving until the rabbi blesses us!"

They waited for a while and the husband again urged his wife to return home, but she refused. Eventually she began sobbing. "We have no children!" she cried to her husband. "I just want to get a blessing from the rabbi…"

The rabbi heard the disturbance out on the stairwell and asked his *rabbanit* to go see what was happening there. She heard their story, and she related it to her husband. Rabbi Eliyahu gave them three pieces of the *etrog* over which he had uttered the blessing. The wife ate the three pieces, uttering fervent prayers, and she conceived triplets.

Her doctor advised them to "reduce" the pregnancy and leave

just one fetus, but when they asked the rabbi what to do, he answered, "Don't touch them." Three healthy babies were born.

It is thought that thousands conceived from eating just a small piece of Hacham Mordechai's *etrog*. In fact, people sometimes said to the rabbi, "We could fill a stadium with all of the rabbi's 'children'!"[27]

Boy or Girl?

When Rabbi Eliyahu was nearing the end of his first hospitalization, a couple came to the entrance of the intensive care unit, begging the nurse to admit them to see him. The nurse refused, as no one was allowed in to see him, due to his condition. One of Rabbi Eliyahu's assistants, Yosef Aharoni, was with the rabbi at the time, and the nurse asked him to step outside to speak to them.

When he came out, the couple told him that they had been married for six years and still hadn't been blessed with children. They begged him to get a blessing on their behalf. Rabbi Aharoni nodded and went back to Rabbi Eliyahu.

He told Rabbi Eliyahu the couple's story.

"What do they want?" Hacham Mordechai asked.

Rabbi Aharoni thought that Rabbi Eliyahu hadn't understood the story, so he repeated it. But Rabbi Eliyahu soon clarified his question: "So what do they want? A boy or a girl?"

Rabbi Aharoni answered that although he hadn't asked them, he was sure they would be happy with either.

"Well," Rabbi Eliyahu responded, "just so there won't be any doubt, let's bless them with twins — a boy and a girl."

---

27. Rabbi Mordechai Nagari of Maaleh Adumim and Rabbi Yosef Elnakwa related these stories.

Rabbi Aharoni went out to the couple to share the good news: the rabbi had blessed them with twins.

Ten months later, Rabbi Aharoni got a phone call from abroad. The woman on the line asked if he remembered the details of their story and their case. When he answered in the affirmative, the woman announced that the rabbi's blessing had been fulfilled completely: They had just celebrated the birth of twins, a boy and a girl. Now they wanted to thank the rabbi and get his advice on their names.

Rabbi Aharoni related all this to Rabbi Eliyahu.

"Tell them not to thank me," he said. "They should thank the Creator of the Universe!"

I Know It's a Boy

There was a couple who had waited many years for a child, and though the wife did get pregnant several times, there were always complications, and she never merited completing a pregnancy. They were deeply saddened by the difficult situation.

One day, Rabbi Mordechai Eliyahu called the husband and said, "Do you want me to be *sandak* (the person honored with holding the baby at a *brit milah*) at the circumcision of your son in a year's time?"

"Of course I do!" he replied.

"Rabbi Moshe Deutsch of Hasdei Yosef[8] is sitting with me," Rabbi Eliyahu said over the phone. "He's collecting money for food cartons that will be distributed before Pesah to hundreds of needy families across Israel. He has most of the items, but he doesn't have enough money left for oil for all the cartons."

---

28. Hasdei Yosef is a Jerusalem-based organization dedicated to assisting the poor in a variety of ways, including a soup kitchen, food distribution, activities for children, vocational training and more. It is headed by Rabbi Moshe Deutsch.

Rabbi Mordechai Eliyahu as *sandak* at a *brit milah*

The childless man asked how much money the organization needed, and he immediately took it upon himself to make that donation. Shortly thereafter, his wife conceived. During one of the ultrasounds, the technician asked the woman if she would like to find out the gender of the baby. "There's no need," she replied. "I already know."

She delivered a healthy baby boy.

Chapter Thirteen

Greater in Death

There have been many stories related about the power of the rabbi's prayers. The *admor*[1] of Belz would always say that whoever was *a ladder rooted in the ground with his head in Heaven*,[2] that is, who was connected to both this world and the world above, was also connected to Heaven and earth after his passing, existing in Heaven but spreading his good influence down here on earth.

Since the rabbi's passing, many people have gone — and continue to go — to visit Rabbi Eliyahu's grave on Har Hamenuhot in Jerusalem, next to the tomb of the Hida. And stories continue to emerge about the power of the rabbi's prayers, proving that although Hacham Mordechai is no longer here in body, his influence, inspiration, and even his blessings are still as powerful as they were in his lifetime.

---

1. A rebbe or spiritual leader in the hassidic movement.
2. This is ostensibly a reference to Jacob's ladder, as described in *Bereshit* 28:10–19.

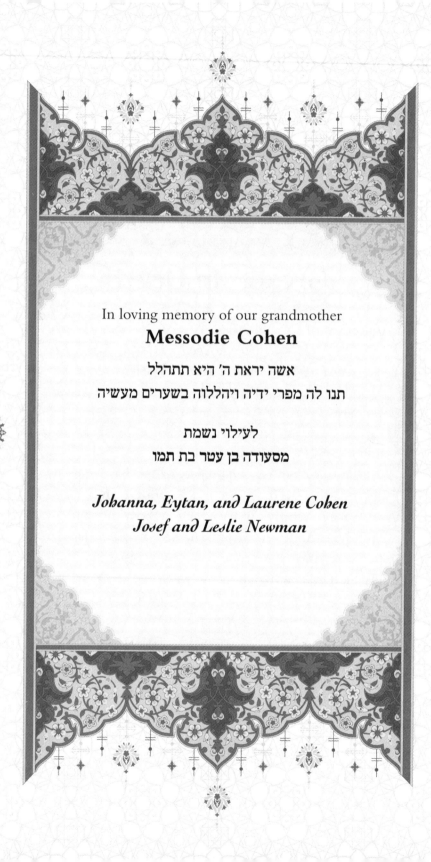

In loving memory of our grandmother

Messodie Cohen

אשה יראת ה' היא תתהלל
תנו לה מפרי ידיה ויהללוה בשערים מעשיה

לעילוי נשמת
מסעודה בן עטר בת תמו

Johanna, Eytan, and Laurene Cohen
Josef and Leslie Newman

DEPARTURES

Go in Peace

Mrs. Naomi Knobel recalled the last time Rabbi Eliyahu was in the office. "It was just two days before Pesah, the same year that the rabbi fell ill," she remembered. "We were extremely busy with the *kimha d'pis'ha* (food for Pesah) project, in which, in the merit of the rabbi and *rabbanit's* great efforts, we were able to distribute food cartons or coupons to thousands of needy families across the country."

She was sitting at her desk, telephone receiver perched on her shoulder, totally engrossed in the phone conversation so she could type the details as the speaker relayed them. "I noticed something going on around me," she said, "but I just carried on with my work. After a few minutes, though, something grabbed my attention and I turned around to see what was going on."

She continued, "I was shocked to see the great rabbi himself standing next to my desk, waiting patiently. I was so surprised that I jumped, and Rabbi Eliyahu immediately said, 'Forgive me for disturbing you. I just wanted to wish you a happy Pesah.' He lifted his hand to say goodbye and left."

She saw his assistants waiting for him behind the glass door, and one of them shook his head at her in wonder and disapproval. After they returned from escorting Rabbi Eliyahu to his home, one of the assistants came into the office and asked Mrs. Knobel, "What happened? Do you have any idea how long the rabbi was standing there waiting for you?"

Mrs. Knobel was stunned. She really hadn't known he was there. "Why didn't you tell me?" she asked.

"I don't really know," he said. "We thought that maybe Rabbi Eliyahu wanted to tell you something private, so we waited outside."

Mrs. Knobel said she realized later that it wasn't anything private. He just wanted to say goodbye before he parted from this world. And, in his usual way, he was careful not to disturb her work, always sensitive and respectful of every person — even the office secretary.

"For the rabbi," Mrs. Knobel recalled, "there was nobody who was 'just' the secretary or 'just' someone else. In my eyes, this is one of the most moving stories about Rabbi Eliyahu — his attitude toward every person was an attitude of true respect."

In Operation at His Own Funeral

A *rosh kollel* from Safed was disseminating hours of Torah classes to his students, but his own son was meanwhile growing distant from the faith. His son was extremely bright, but he went through a crisis, after which he could no longer see the point in learning Torah, praying, or even observing the commandments. He began to look outside the walls of the yeshivah, and found himself in a terrible, dark emotional place, full of worry and doubt.

Although his parents and teachers had had many conversations with the boy and had shed countless tears in prayer over him and his state, the situation looked bleak. He was no longer attending yeshivah, was barely making blessings or praying, and seemed to have a murky future ahead of him.

The day the family heard the terrible news of Rabbi Eliyahu's passing from this world, they were on their way to central Israel for a wedding. They immediately changed their plans and drove into Jerusalem before the huge — and inevitable — traffic jams took hold. They arrived at the yeshivah and, lost in the crowds, this *rosh kollel* found himself being pushed in the direction of the hearse that was carrying Rabbi Eliyahu. Knowing the power of Rabbi Eliyahu's prayers, this man continued trying to get as close as he possibly could to the moving car.

Walking alongside the car, he found himself crying like a baby, asking Rabbi Eliyahu to pray for his son. He remembered how Rabbi Eliyahu had cared so much for the young, and had worried about their Torah learning. Like a son begs for something from his father, this man cried and cried, standing among the crush of people crowded around the car.

The tremendous crowds pressing in around the car caused the tires to burst from pressure. The axles soon broke as well. Yet, the car kept moving — somehow. The driver began shouting from the window to a nearby police officer, yelling that he couldn't go on, that the car was broken. And the police officer responded that he must continue to drive no matter what. He was worried that stopping the car would put numerous lives in danger, as hundreds of people were pushing in toward the car from all sides.

"You can't stop!" the officer shouted.

"But I can't continue. The car is broken!" the driver shouted back. "No tires, no axles. How can I drive?" he asked.

"Just drive," the police officer urged. "It's too dangerous to stop."

Miraculously, the car kept going, ever so slowly progressing, until it reached the burial site. Although thousands of people witnessed that miracle, the other miracle that happened that day had only one witness: the *rosh kollel* from Safed. He had poured out his heart at that funeral, begging Hacham Mordechai to help his son.

That confused boy turned around right after the funeral. Within two days, he had already returned to yeshivah and was studying with great diligence. No one really understood what happened — except his father.[3]

Holy Men's Help

When Rabbi Eliyahu returned his soul to his Maker, Rabbi

---

3. As heard from the *rosh kollel* in Safed.

Eliyahu's assistants immediately consulted with the family regarding where they would like him to be buried. The family explained that Rabbi Eliyahu had purchased a burial plot, but the burial society had accidentally laid someone else to rest there.

During the conversation, someone remembered that the rabbi had, on numerous occasions, mentioned the burial plot that Rabbi Yitzhak Nissim had purchased for himself next to the grave of the Hida. In the end, Rabbi Nissim had not been buried there. Now it seemed that Hacham Mordechai had been hinting that he should be laid to rest there...

Outside the tomb of Rabbi Mordechai Eliyahu

Rabbi Nissim had bought the plot next to the Hida because he had been the one involved with bringing the Hida's bones to Israel for burial. Rabbi Nissim had appointed Dr. Della Pergola[4] and Dr. Shlomo Umberto Nachon, of Livorno, Italy, where the Hida was originally buried, to safeguard the coffin until it was sent to Israel.

When the Hida's remains arrived in Israel in 1960, Rabbi Eliyahu,

---

4. His first name is unknown.

who was then in his early thirties, was appointed to supervise their reinterment. Rabbi Eliyahu, along with a team of other rabbis, arranged for the Hida's reburial on Har Hamenuhot. Rabbi Nissim bought the plot next to him. But within seven years, Israel had recaptured the Mount of Olives, and Rabbi Nissim decided he would prefer to be buried there. And that's how the plot next to the Hida remained empty and available — and Rabbi Eliyahu came to be buried beside him.

After the *shivah*, the family and Rabbi Eliyahu's close assistants sought an architect to help plan and design the tombstone and burial site. They were looking for a professional with a strong sense of spirituality. One thing led to another, and someone recommended a woman named Michal, an architect who was supposed to be an expert in masonry.

As it turned out, Michal's wedding had actually been performed by Rabbi Eliyahu, and her family had been connected to him. Not only that, she was actually the granddaughter of Rabbi Nissim. It seemed unreal. As Rabbi Eliyahu's assistant was jotting down the information, he realized he didn't even know the architect's last name. "It's Della Pergola," she said. Hearing that name made him go pale.

New edifice of the tomb of Hacham Yosef David Azoulay (Hida) and Rabbi Mordechai Eliyahu

She was married to the grandson of Dr. Della Pergola — the same one who had brought the Hida's bones to Israel, as per Rabbi Yitzhak Nissim's instructions. And that plot had been purchased because of that story of the Hida's remains. And it had led to the match between her and her husband. And now it was again coming into play with Rabbi Eliyahu's grave…

CONTINUED BLESSINGS

Saba Wakes the Sleeping

Hacham Mordechai's granddaughter Yael recalled one Erev Rosh Hashanah,[5] just a few months after her grandfather passed away. The yearning for him had not decreased. Yael said, "Someone once told me that even though the deceased are not with us in body, their souls nevertheless continue to accompany us from above. I never felt how true it was until that Rosh Hashanah."

Usually, Yael and her family traveled to their uncle in Safed, Rabbi Shmuel Eliyahu, for Rosh Hashanah. In the evening, as everyone was on their way to bed, Rabbi Shmuel asked — to continue the tradition of his father, Rabbi Mordechai — who among the children and guests wanted to get up for the sunrise prayers. The men, some of the women, and most of the teenagers, including Yael, expressed their desire to rise in time for the early morning prayers.

As Rabbi Shmuel was the cantor and the *ba'al toke'a*, the shofar blower, at the sunrise *minyan*, he had to arrive for the beginning of

---

5. In 2010.

the prayers, which began at 5:45 a.m. That necessitated him leaving the house at 5:30 a.m. So the family arranged for everyone to wake up at around 5:15 a.m., and they relied on the inner "clock" of Rabbi Shmuel and Yael's father, who were known for their early, accurate rising.

It was nighttime, and everyone was sleeping. In the middle of the night (or at least that's how it felt to Yael), she sensed a hand on her shoulder. A familiar, beloved voice was trying to wake her. "Get up, Yael, good morning. It's time to get up for the sunrise prayers. You have to wake the rest of the family!"

She opened her eyes, and saw the image of Hacham Mordechai right in front of her. And again she heard his soft, loving voice calling her to get up for prayers, just as he used to do when she was a child and wanted to accompany him to the early morning prayers.

Sure she was dreaming, Yael curled back up in her blankets. But she kept on hearing his voice. To make sure she wasn't dreaming, she went to the doorway, to the narrow ray of light peeping through it, and looked at the hall clock to see what time it was. The clock read exactly 5:15 a.m.

"I was in shock," Yael recalled. "I had never had a natural inner clock, and never, as much as I tried, had I managed to wake up at the time that I wanted. I looked again, but Saba's image had vanished, and only the memory of his warm voice continued to accompany me throughout that cold, dawning morning."

Yael went out into the hall, wondering why the house was so quiet and nobody was up or waking anyone else up. "It was a strange feeling," she said. "Was it possible that I was the only person who had woken up? The only person awake? I went upstairs and woke my father, and then roused the rest of the family who had wanted to get up for prayers."

She described the surprise on their faces when they realized Yael had woken up and had woken everyone else, something that had never happened before. Usually she was the last one to wake up at such an early hour. "Just me, Saba, and G-d knew the truth. Saba had helped us so we wouldn't be late and wouldn't delay all the congregants," Yael said.

She continued, "At the time I was so emotional that I didn't say a word to the family. Only after I calmed down was I able to tell the story. Why did I merit it? I have no idea. If only we could all merit seeing the glow of his face again, together with the rest of the deceased of Israel, with the resurrection of the dead, speedily, in our days!"[6]

A Dream of Prayers

Rabbi Mordechai Valnov, a senior lecturer at Elon Moreh yeshivah, gives guidance to grooms in the yeshivah before their weddings — and continues to advise them after their weddings, if necessary. One of the grooms he had taught had not yet merited having children. The couple experienced many years of heartbreak and still hadn't been privileged to hold a child of their own in their arms. They were living in a reality of ongoing pain.

Rabbi Valnov tried to support and assist the couple through their trial, advising them, and attempting to decrease their pain in whatever way he could, but he had no real solution. One morning the husband called Rabbi Valnov, saying he had had a dream about Rabbi Mordechai Eliyahu, who appeared to him and said, "Be careful about the evening prayers and, please G-d, you will have your own children."

The man mentioned that he had never been in touch with Rabbi Eliyahu in his lifetime, and in fact, hadn't had contact with any

---

6. Yael Ben Eliyahu shared this recollection.

other rabbis outside the yeshivah. He wanted to know what he should do and if he should take heed of the dream. Rabbi Valnov told him to do what the rabbi had said. The childless man took it upon himself to be stricter about attending the evening prayers, to be careful to pray with a *minyan*, and to try especially hard to pray with concentration during that prayer.

After about a month, the husband called Rabbi Valnov, very excited. The miracle had happened — his wife had conceived without any treatment. He asked how it could possibly have happened, and Rabbi Valnov explained that even after their passing, the righteous continue to carry out the acts they performed during their lifetime. Every day of Rabbi Eliyahu's life, he was involved with people's problems and challenges, and especially the troubles of barren women still waiting for children. He would say many prayers for them, and numerous miracles and wonders came about through him while he was alive.

And so he is continuing now, from the Next World, praying for those who haven't yet merited having children. May it be G-d's will that Hacham Mordechai continue to pray for the barren, for the Divine Presence to rise from the dust, and for the complete redemption to occur speedily in our days, just as he prayed for so much in his lifetime.[7]

Pictures Calling from the Wall

Sderot is a town threatened by Qassam rockets. Sometimes there's a lull, and sometimes there's an escalation. But the threat is always there. During one of the periods when the town was under attack, the IDF's response wasn't forceful enough, and the terrorists in Gaza continued firing.

---

7. As heard from Rabbi Mordechai Valnov.

One of Sderot's residents, Netanel Sarussi, recalled an open miracle that occurred during that time. "It was a really wonderful, happy day in Sderot. The Dahan family, well-known in Sderot, was celebrating the dedication of a new Torah scroll, and many residents joined in the celebrations."

Although that day saw some thirty missiles pelt the town, hundreds of residents nevertheless showed up to celebrate the new Torah scroll, which was being taken to the Ohel Yitzhak synagogue. There was a festive meal, many speeches were given, and words of Torah were shared. Sarussi continues, "Everything had been peaceful and smooth until then. And then everyone began to head home. After the last of the celebrants left the synagogue, the red alert siren[8] sounded. Everyone tried to run back to the hall where they had just eaten, hoping to take cover, but the synagogue was locked. Left with no choice, everyone took cover wherever they were, with some feeling angry and upset at whoever had locked the synagogue."

The missile fell very close to them. Although they heard it and felt the impact, the celebrants didn't know where exactly it had landed. All the electricity in the city went down. As everyone slowly stood up and came out from where they had hidden, they began to turn on flashlights and investigate what had happened. "It was only then that we beheld the great miracle that had taken place," Sarussi recalled. "The missile had fallen exactly where we had eaten the festive meal just moments before." Not only that, they had all wanted to take cover there — but they hadn't, because the hall was locked.

When they opened the hall that had been hit, they quickly saw

---

8. The IDF installed this early-warning radar system in several towns surrounding the Gaza Strip to warn civilians of imminent rocket attacks. Standard air-raid sirens are used outside the Gaza-belt area to warn of rocket attacks.

the extent of the damage. Everything was broken and lying in complete ruin and devastation. There were just two pictures left on the wall, both hanging on tiny nails: one of the Baba Sali and one of Rabbi Mordechai Eliyahu. According to all logic, they should have fallen off the wall and been lying there among the rubble. But they remained in their places. "It was as if the two righteous men were protecting us from Heaven," Sarussi said.

A Match at the Rabbi's Tomb

Rabbanit Tzviyah Eliyahu once went to visit her husband's grave. While she was there, a young, single girl approached her. "Two years ago, I came to see the rabbi. He blessed me to find my life's partner, but I'm still not married," she said through tears.

"If that's the case," the *rabbanit* said, "then tell the rabbi. Cry out that he should pray for you there, in the Next World, before the Creator!"

A short time after, that girl came to see the *rabbanit*. This time she was glowing and radiant. She said that she had done as the *rabbanit* had advised, and as she left the graveside, a young man emerged from the other side. Something clicked between them, and in a very short time, they got engaged. Now they were preparing for their wedding.[9]

A Blessing, Doubled and Tripled

Yoram and his wife lived in Rabbi Eliyahu's neighborhood. Many years had passed since they had married, but they had not been blessed with children. Yoram went to the rabbi to ask for advice and a blessing, and the rabbi told him, "I promise that you will have children."

---

9. As heard from the *rabbanit*.

But the promise didn't materialize. And so Yoram and his wife waited for the fulfillment of the rabbi's promise for many long years. Every time they went to Rabbi Eliyahu, they heard the same words: "I promise you, you *will* have children."

Their hopes were not in vain. After seventeen long and painful years they were blessed with twins — two beautiful girls. They saw how the rabbi's promise had indeed been fulfilled.

After some time, the rabbi passed away, and during the year of mourning, Yoram's wife dreamt that Rabbi Eliyahu came to her and said, "You're expecting again — this time with triplets. Don't think about 'reducing' the fetuses — you will deliver them early, but the circumcision will be on time."

Yoram and his wife had been hoping for a boy to complete their joy, but despite that, his wife just couldn't believe she was carrying triplets. She was no longer young — she was over forty already, and now a triple blessing like this?

But, just as the rabbi had told her in her dream, it came to pass: When the doctors examined her, they discovered three fetuses alive and healthy in her womb. As expected, the doctors pressured her to "reduce" the fetuses so that one would be born healthy, but Yoram's wife held firmly to her dream and the rabbi's promise in it. She gave birth to all three exactly as the rabbi had said, before their time but whole and healthy. The circumcision was indeed celebrated on time.[10]

Blessed Oil

Before Shavuot, about a year after Rabbi Eliyahu passed away, a couple from Avne Hefetz, a settlement in Samaria, called Rabbanit Eliyahu. Their daughter had gotten a terrible head injury in a road

---

10. Name withheld upon request.

accident and had been paralyzed for some time, unable to move any of her limbs.

They asked for a piece of the *etrog* that the rabbi had blessed on Sukkot, but the *rabbanit* told them she was saving that *etrog* for women who hadn't succeeded in conceiving. She felt bad saying it, but the *rabbanit* really didn't know what would help them. Immediately after hanging up, she remembered an incident of a paralyzed child. The girl's parents had come to Rabbi Eliyahu, who told them to smear her with the leftover oil from Hanukah. Indeed, she had gotten up on her own two feet after that.

The *rabbanit* took some of the oil that was left over from the Shabbat flames she had kindled and from the memorial candles the family had lit for the rabbi during the first year after his passing. She gave this oil to the parents, advising them to rub it on their daughter in hopes that perhaps the merit of the mitzvot would help.

It was truly a miracle. Just a few hours later, the girl came back to life. The rumor about the "wonder oil" grew wings, so to speak, and many other people came to see the *rabbanit* with cases of paralysis. It didn't help everyone — and the *rabbanit* wasn't always privy to the conclusion of these incidents. But she did know at least three people who said it helped.[11]

More Precious than Diamonds

Rabbi Avi Berman, head of OU Israel, told a story about his brother and sister-in-law. They had been married for five years and still had no children — and fertility treatments hadn't helped. They began to consider adoption.

After Rabbi Mordechai Eliyahu passed away, they heard the

---

11. As heard from Rabbanit Tzviyah Eliyahu.

many stories that were publicized about couples who had conceived thanks to the rabbi's blessing and, like many others, they asked why they hadn't known about it before, while the rabbi was still alive.

Rabbi Shmuel Eliyahu suggested that Rabbi Berman ask the *rabbanit* for a piece of the *etrog* that the rabbi had blessed on Sukkot. It had helped many times before, and perhaps it would still help. Rabbi Berman went to Rabbanit Tzviyah and she gave Rabbi Berman a few slices of the *etrog* to give to his brother and sister-in-law, warning him, "Guard the slices more than diamonds — they are slices from the *etrog* that the rabbi used to do *hakafot* (circuits) on Sukkot. Tell the couple to make a blessing on the slices and eat them at the appropriate time."

It's hard to believe how the blessing worked. Not long after, Rabbi Berman's sister-in-law shared the news that she was expecting, and it soon became clear that she was carrying twins. She gave birth safely and at the right time, and those twins were also more precious than diamonds...[12]

A Joyous Dream

A couple had been married for three and a half years and hadn't yet merited having children. But shortly thereafter, they got the good news that the wife was expecting.

One night, at the beginning of the wife's pregnancy, the husband had a dream. In the dream, he saw Rabbi Mordechai Eliyahu sitting in the Heavenly Court, full of joy. During the entire dream, he was bursting with a great happiness, the likes of which the father-to-be had never seen. Sitting beside the rabbi were other Heavenly judges.

Rabbi Eliyahu looked at the young man and said, "Be happy!"

"I agree!" the father-to-be said.

---

12. As heard from Rabbi Avi Berman, head of OU Israel.

"Be happy and you will have a son with a great soul," he said.

In the dream, the man said, "I'll call him by your name, Eliyahu." But Rabbi Eliyahu wouldn't consent to it. "Not Eliyahu," he said.

The other Heavenly judges asked Hacham Mordechai, "Why not call him by your name?"

But Rabbi Eliyahu didn't reply. Instead, he insisted, "Call him Yaakov or Yisrael as a second name."

Then the rabbi fixed the date of the baby's birth as Tishah B'Av, and he was very insistent about it, not resting in the Heavenly Court until they agreed that the birth would be exactly on that date. Finally, a *bat kol*, voice from Heaven, announced that the baby would indeed be born on the ninth of Av.

The next morning, the father-to-be awoke with a clear memory of the extraordinary dream. He felt so inspired and moved, and believed it was a true dream, something totally real. Three months before the birth, his sister-in-law gave birth to a boy and named him Eliyahu. Now he understood why the rabbi didn't want them to call their son Eliyahu.

During the entire period of the pregnancy, the young couple was full of happiness, pouring out their hearts in prayers of hope and thanksgiving. They prayed at the rabbi's grave and many other places, asking for G-d's help that the pregnancy would pass successfully, and that they would merit raising their son in holiness and purity.

Tishah B'Av arrived, and with it, the labor pains. The new mother gave birth on the same day, exactly as the rabbi had told the young father in his dream. Eight days later, they made the circumcision of their firstborn son in Hechal Yaakov, the rabbi's synagogue. They named him Menahem and added a second name, Yisrael, according to the rabbi's request in the dream. It was indeed a dream come true, down to the last detail.

A Speedy Recovery

A well-known lawyer was very close to Rabbi Eliyahu. He had a son who was born with many health problems. He had to be fed via a tube through his nose and faced many other complications. Even though he was already two years old, he was still suffering and not improving. It had all started with a severe infection in the baby's blood.

The poor baby had received so many medications and infusions that his tiny body was covered with marks from all the various treatments. But, despite all this, there was still no improvement. The boy's father couldn't bear to see the suffering of his little son, and he went to the tomb of Rabbi Eliyahu to pray there. Pouring out his heart — and his tears — he asked the rabbi, who loved every Jew so much, to help from Heaven. He begged Rabbi Eliyahu to pray on behalf of his child, begging him to beseech the Heavens for the little boy's health.

That night, the father had a dream in which Rabbi Eliyahu said to him, "A speedy recovery! A speedy recovery! A speedy recovery!" After saying that three times, Rabbi Eliyahu told the father not to worry, moving his hand in his signature gesture of dismissal.

The next morning, the father rose from bed with the memory of the dream fresh and firm in his mind. He went to the hospital to visit his son, and his heart was full of hope. When he arrived, the doctors and nurses informed him that his son's condition had miraculously turned around. For the first time, his blood tests showed great improvement, and the medical team was even considering removing the feeding tube, to see if the toddler could eat by himself.

The doctors' experiment was even more successful than expected. For the first time since the little boy was born, he was able to consume regular food. The doctors began to think about discharging him.

Indeed, the righteous are greater in death...

Repaying a Good Deed

During the week of the *shivah*, one of Rabbi Eliyahu's students attended the lecture of his rabbi and teacher, a great and famous kabbalist. This rabbi told his students that it would be a good idea to go and learn Torah beside the fresh grave of Rabbi Mordechai Eliyahu, as this would bring great pleasure to his soul.

The rabbi added that a righteous man does not remain in debt and will always return the favor to whoever brings him pleasure. (Of course, this should not be the reason for going to pray, the teacher said, but rather to repay the rabbi for all the help he had given everyone, and also to perform the mitzvah of *hesed shel emet*, a good deed done for the deceased who cannot return it.)

On Thursday evening, this man visited the fresh grave of Rabbi Eliyahu, learning the *Zohar* and all the *Ohr Hahaim*[13] on the Torah portion of the week. He also prayed there for the Jewish people and for the redemption. The next morning, his brother-in-law called, telling him that a community in a certain Israeli town was looking for a rabbi. They wanted to know if this man was interested in filling that role. He said he would ask his rabbi.

When he went to discuss the position with his rabbi, the rabbi thought for a few moments and then asked if he had been to visit the grave of Rabbi Eliyahu. When he answered in the affirmative, the rabbi advised him to accept the proposition.

He agreed, and things worked out well. He feels he is carrying

---

13. A popular commentary on the Tanach, written by the Moroccan-born scholar and kabbalist Haim ben Moshe ibn Attar (1696–1743), and first published in 1742.

on the path of Rabbi Eliyahu, trying to help the Jewish people to return to their Father in Heaven. And interestingly, the community in which he serves bases their Torah learning and approach to Jewish law on the blessings and guidance of Rabbi Eliyahu.

Blessings Don't Expire

A number of years ago, Shalom Konaniyan Cohen, the rabbi's early morning driver, was experiencing terrible stomach pains. His doctor sent him to get an ultrasound at Hadassah Hospital. When the doctor began the test, he immediately cried out, "You have a tumor!"

Shalom fell into a deep depression, not knowing what to do. The next morning, just as he did every day, he arrived to take Rabbi Eliyahu to the synagogue. The rabbi asked him what was wrong, to which Shalom replied, "Nothing!"

When they were driving, the rabbi again asked, saying, "*Nu*, now tell me what's wrong."

Shalom said he would tell the rabbi after prayers. But Rabbi Eliyahu wouldn't give up, saying, "No. Tell me now."

He finally relented and told the rabbi that they had found a tumor in his stomach and that he had to undergo a complicated test.

The rabbi replied, "You don't have anything; nothing at all!"

On Shabbat night, a group would get together at Rabbi Eliyahu's house, where they would study together. Shalom would sit next to the rabbi there. In the middle of the learning that Friday night, the rabbi said to him, "Shalom, you're worrying for nothing. I told you, you don't have anything wrong with you!"

Suddenly, the rabbi got up and came back with a drink bottle. Hacham Mordechai held the cap in one hand and the bottle in the other. He poured some of the liquid into the bottle cap and ordered Shalom to drink, which he did. Then the rabbi repeated, "You don't have anything wrong with you!"

On the Sunday morning that he went for the test, Shalom went alone, which astonished the doctor, as it was a complicated test that involved cutting open the stomach. Just to be sure exactly where to cut, the doctor performed another ultrasound. He put the transducer probe on Shalom's stomach, and Shalom immediately saw the doctor's face light up in wonder.

"What's going on?" Shalom asked.

"I don't see anything. It's gone!" the doctor exclaimed. He repeated the test again and again, but nothing changed — he didn't find a thing. In the end, he said, "I can't find anything wrong with you — you can go home!"

Thirteen years later, Shalom again ended up in the emergency room with severe stomach pains. The doctors checked him and then informed him that he had a tumor growing between his liver and kidney. They measured the growth, estimating it to be 1.5–4.7 inches (4–12 cm) in size. The doctors scheduled a surgery for Erev Shavuot, almost exactly a year after the rabbi had passed away.

Shalom went to speak to the rabbi's sons, Rabbi Shmuel and Rabbi Yosef, about what was happening. They quickly reassured him, saying, "Don't worry, our father's blessing still rests upon you."

On the appointed day, Shalom arrived at the hospital and dressed in a hospital gown. They intended to perform laparoscopic surgery to remove the tumor. Before the doctor began, he did an x-ray to verify the exact location of the growth. He stared at the results, standing as still as a stone. He didn't see anything. He repeated the test, performing additional procedures to verify the results — and found nothing. Finally, he stuttered, "I don't know what to tell you. There is no growth. Everything is totally fine!"

Right then and there, the doctor and his medical team began to dance with joy. Shalom went home, and since then, everything has been fine. It seems that the rabbi's blessing continues today...[14]

The Eye of G-d

The very same day that Rabbi Eliyahu passed away, Reb Ezra Brunner, one of the regular attendees at Hechal Yaakov, had to receive an injection in his eye. He had an extremely rare, severe, and painful eye condition. Although a specialist was brought to examine him, it seemed there was no one in Israel with the experience, expertise, or capability to treat this rare condition. He was advised to travel abroad for surgery.

The attending doctors and specialists set up an appointment for Ezra to return in a month's time. At that appointment, they would determine which surgeon would perform the operation and where and when that would take place.

Ezra felt lost and confused, and though he desperately wished to consult with Rabbi Eliyahu, he could not, as the rabbi had passed away that very same day. As he considered what to do, he remembered that the rabbi had once advised him to go pray at the Hida's tomb on Fridays. So he went to the Hida's grave, which was next to the rabbi's grave, and prayed at both. There, Ezra poured out his heart, telling the rabbi about his serious eye problem, and asking him to pray and advocate for him from Heaven.

After a month had gone by, Ezra returned to the hospital for his appointment, where they scanned his eye with a CT machine. The specialist was looking at Ezra in wonder. "There's no need for surgery," he announced. "The tear that was here has almost

---

14. As heard from Shalom Konaniyan Cohen.

healed. I just don't understand; this is not the same eye I saw just a month ago!"

The astonished doctor sent him home without any treatment, instructing him to return every six months for a follow-up visit. Ever since then, Ezra has been going every six months for his regular check-ups, and he's been told everything is fine. "I truly believe that this sudden change in my condition and the healing of my eye are thanks to the rabbi and my prayers at his tomb," he said. "I really believe he is still praying for me — and all of us — even now, even after so many years have passed."[15]

THOUGHTS AND MEMORIES

Until Eliyahu Comes...

Adi Aharon, the editor of the five-volume Hebrew series on Hacham Mordechai, *Avihem Shel Yisrael*, said, "I have not parted from Rabbi Mordechai Eliyahu, and I never will. His image, the light of his face, his smile, and his noble character traits accompany me every moment."

Aharon shared that less than two weeks after the passing of the rabbi who had changed his life forever, he was asked to join the editorial team that was working on the first volume of *Avihem Shel Yisrael*. It was printed just in time for the rabbi's *sheloshim*.

"I still remember our feeling of utter bewilderment and astonishment," Aharon said, "and this was later true of everyone who read that first volume. We were all thinking, *Such a great,*

---

15. As heard from Reb Ezra Brunner.

righteous man was in our generation and we didn't know. Or, *We never realized just how great he was.*"

The book positively influenced Jews of every shade and stripe — religious and non-religious, *haredi,* and more. *Avihem Shel Yisrael* was, quite simply, the rabbi. The editors got so much positive feedback from people who had been encouraged by reading the book.

"I especially remember the story of a girl who had come back to the faith, but her parents had not yet done so," Aharon recalled. "Her mother read the book, story after story, unable to stop. What any number of conversations with her daughter hadn't done, one book did. She began to wash her hands in the morning, and gradually drew closer."

The image of the rabbi, which rose up out of the pages, touched everyone in such a gentle, tender, and revitalizing way. People just couldn't ignore or remain immune to the words of truth they were hearing. That one volume led to more and more volumes as people came forward with their own stories, or they remembered incidents from long ago.

"My inbox was flooded with stories about Rabbi Mordechai Eliyahu," Aharon said. "And my emotion upon reading the first story and thousandth story was just the same. There's no being accustomed to the rabbi, be it with regard to his tremendous humility, his prowess in Torah learning, or the mindboggling miracles that came about through his merit." He continued, "I never became 'familiar,' as one can never grow habituated to such things."

As time went by, the editors continued to receive stories. But many of them were "new" stories, stories that had happened after the rabbi's passing: hair-raising stories about dreams coming true, barren women conceiving, and hearts drawing closer to G-d. The rabbi's grave became a pilgrimage site for all those who didn't manage to reach him during his lifetime — or for those who did but wanted to remain connected. People needing advice, blessings, salvations — or just to feel close to a truly righteous man who was on this earth not so long ago — they're all still flocking to the grave.

"My feeling is that the rabbi is with us now," Aharon said, "accompanying us on the difficult journey to the much awaited redemption, a journey that looks like it's going to come to an end soon, please G-d, with mercy and good. So I haven't parted from the rabbi, and I believe that none of us have. Until Eliyahu comes..."

Reflections from Jonathan Pollard

In response to the painful news about Rabbi Eliyahu's passing, Jonathan Pollard shared his thoughts and memories with his wife, Esther. Jonathan was very close to Rabbi Eliyahu, considering him a beacon of light during the darkest years of his incarceration, and he wrote that the loss of the rabbi was too great to bear, and too hard to grasp, leaving him and his wife bereft as "broken-hearted orphans."[16] These reflections are recorded here:

Baruch Dayan Ha'Emet, Blessed is the True Judge. We haven't experienced such a profound and unbearable loss since we both lost our mothers. We are heartbroken. We are bereft. We are orphaned in the deepest sense of the word. The rabbi left us a wonderful legacy, and that's what we have to focus on. For all the years that we had the blessing to be part of his life, he gave us strength; he gave us direction; and he gave us hope. In terms of all of *Am*

---

16. Some of these thoughts were published on Pollard's website, jonathanpollard.org.

Yisrael, the rabbi provided all the People of Israel with a model of what a true Jew should be.

The rabbi was unafraid, he was strong, he was wise, he was sure, and he was dedicated. He was unwavering in his devotion to the Land and the People of Israel. He was a true servant of Hashem. He feared no man — only G-d. That's the model he gave us, and that's the model that will continue to inspire us. That's the model we hope to live up to.

Baruch Hashem, we have so many rich memories of the time we spent in the rabbi's company, and of the humor, warmth, wisdom, and absolute kindness with which he continually blessed us.

How very fortunate we are to have had the enormous *zechut* of being his children and coming under his influence. May the memory of our beloved rabbi be a blessing for all of *Am Yisrael*.

Unveiling the Headstone

The headstone on Rabbi Eliyahu's grave on Jerusalem's Har Hamenuhot[17] was erected and custom-built by Jewish artisans from the Givot Olam Farm, near the town of Itamar in Samaria. Asaf Kadron, who designed the headstone, explained, "The tombstone was crafted from stones from the four holy cities — Jerusalem, Safed, Tiberius, and Hevron. Stones from the yeshivah building at the Tomb of Joseph in Shechem were also included, after the building was destroyed by rioters."[18]

In addition, hundreds of people of all ages came — from all over Israel and abroad — to symbolically take part in the creation of the tombstone. At the end of the project, the completed headstone was

---

17. Har Hamenuhot is the largest cemetery in Jerusalem. This burial ground is situated in the western part of the city, on a hilltop adjacent to the Givat Shaul neighborhood.

18. Joseph's Tomb has been the scene of repeated Palestinian attacks and damage since even before the Oslo Accords in 1995.

Interior of the tomb of Rabbi Mordechai Eliyahu

brought to Jerusalem and installed on the grave. The inscription was composed by Rabbi Shabtai Sabato, *rosh yeshivah* of the Mitzpe Yeriho yeshivah,[19] and his brother, Rabbi Haim Hasofer Sabato, one of the founders of the Maale Adumim yeshivah.[20]

The Sabatos devoted a great deal of time to composing the text of the inscription, working to ensure that every word was carefully chosen and precise. The site of the grave, the rabbi's eternal resting place, is a place where people continue to connect to Rabbi Eliyahu, his holiness, his life's mission, and his love of the land of Israel.

---

19. Rabbi Shabtai Hacohen Sabato, who resides in Bet El, is the *rosh yeshivah* of Netivot Yosef High School and the president of Yeshivat Maor Tuvia in Mitzpe Yeriho. He is also the rabbi of the Hechal Gabriel synagogue in Bet El.

20. Rabbi Haim Hasofer Sabato is one of the founders and *rosh yeshivah* of the Birkat Moshe *hesder* yeshivah in Maale Adumim. He is also an internationally acclaimed author.

Photos

Thank you to the entire staff of

Israel Bookshop Publications

especially

Rabbi Moshe Kaufman
and **Mrs. Liron Delmar**

for their unwavering support to the
Sephardic Legacy Series "Institute for
Preserving Sephardic Heritage"

May Hashem bless you all for your
continued special work that you do
in honor of the organization

Sincerely,

Yehuda Azoulay

Rabbi Eliyahu at *Birkat Ha'ilanot* in Kiryat Moshe, Jerusalem

Rabbi Eliyahu checking the Four Species

Rabbi Eliyahu
on Sukkot

Rabbi Eliyahu
on Sukkot

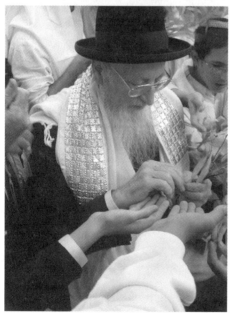

Rabbi Eliyahu
distributing his *aravot*

Rabbi Eliyahu entering the *bet midrash* to
give a *Kol Tzofecha* Torah class

Rabbi Eliyahu giving a Torah class

Crowding around Rabbi Eliyahu after a lecture

The table from which Rabbi Eliyahu gave over his weekly classes for many years

Rabbi Eliyahu
at *hakafot shniyot*
in Jerusalem

At a reception for Rabbi Eliyahu in the Jewish quarter of Jerusalem

Selihot at Me'arat Hamachpelah

At a *siyum masechet* on Erev Pesah in Jerusalem

Rabbi Eliyahu in his office surrounded by *rabbanim*
(credit: Rabbi Shmuel Zafrani)

Rabbi Eliyahu learning Halachah with his *chavruta*
(credit: Eliyahu Family)

On Tishah B'Av in the Hechal Yaakov *bet knesset*